Walter Arties, founder, Breath of Life Minis
Elder Charles D. Brooks is often referred to ... :h,
he has long been fascinated with words and ... .ng
them strategically. Thus he will prepare and ... left
grateful for what we have heard as we anticipate his next pισσσ...

Delbert Baker, vice president, General Conference
C. D. Brooks is a mentor, exemplary leader, and personal friend. His legacy as a generational role model and spiritual changemaker is globally recognized and appreciated among all ethnic and cultural groups in the Adventist Church. Therefore his pioneering legacy as a preacher, evangelist, and media personality will always be a part of the proud history of Seventh-day Adventists in general and African Americans in particular.

Rosa Banks, associate secretary, General Conference
Beyond a doubt, Charles D. Brooks is one of the greatest preachers the Seventh-day Adventist Church has ever produced. His preaching style is natural, simple, life-related, clear, personal, educational, emphatic, animated, moral, biblical, direct, and urgent. His humility shines through most when he stops his busy schedule and sits down with neophyte preachers like me to help us arrange the best of topics for a two-week meeting. He has done this for me, and the results were productive ones. Many others have also come to him, and I don't believe he has ever turned anyone away.

George Brown, former president, Inter-American Division
C. D. Brooks is unquestionably one of the most distinguished preachers of the Seventh-day Adventist Church, a model preacher whose messages are always relevant to the times, persuasive, Bible-based, Christ-centered, and Spirit-empowered. His contribution to Adventist preaching and evangelism has been monumental. He will go down in Adventist history as a true servant leader, an esteemed colleague, and a Spirit-empowered preacher whose ministry has transformed the lives of thousands of people in the U.S.A. and abroad.

G. Alexander Bryant, executive secretary, North American Division, and associate secretary, General Conference
Elder Brooks's ministry has made a very profound impact on the life of the Seventh-day Adventist Church and its mission to the world. It is a blessing to this church to capture and chronicle some of the many contributions of this stalwart man of God!

Randy Roberts, pastor, Loma Linda University church
The oratorical excellence of C. D. Brooks helped to form and challenge several generations of young adults. His legacy will live on.

Calvin B. Rock, retired vice president, General Conference
Charles Brooks has had a prophetic impact within and upon the people of God. We needed him, and God uniquely equipped him to do a special work. As a schoolmate, friend, and comrade in arms I salute him and the love of his life, Walterene, for allowing God to use them in such a wonderfully productive ministry.

Danny Shelton, founder, 3ABN
I thank God for allowing my life to cross paths with Pastor C. D. Brooks. I have learned so much from this man of God. . . . I've learned about integrity, Christian commitment, perseverance, faith, and trust in God!

Ella Simmons, vice president, General Conference
There are many ways to describe Elder C. D. Brooks, of which few could be adequate. When I hear his name, there is one description that comes to mind: It is that man of God of whom Ellen White spoke who will not be bought or sold, who in his inmost soul is true and honest, who does not fear to call sin by its right name, whose conscience is as true to duty as the needle to the pole, that man who will stand for the right though the heavens fall.

Mervyn A. Warren, dean, School of Religion, Oakwood University
When listening for a pulpit voice that carries a "certain sound" amid curious decibels in uncertain times, a voice of gospel resonance bringing unease to disturbing dissonance, look no further. That gospel voice is here. That voice has been here for more than half a century. That voice is C. D. Brooks! Now let us be further blessed by this look into his life.

Derek Morris, editor, *Ministry*
As a young pastor in Pennsylvania I reached out to Elder Brooks, asking him to mentor me as an evangelist. His words of encouragement and counsel not only impacted my life and ministry but have blessed the lives of thousands of pastors and evangelists around the world. Thank you, Elder Brooks, for giving us an example to follow, in word and also in life (1 Cor. 11:1).

Carlton P. Byrd, speaker/director, Breath of Life
"Christlike," "spiritual," "refined," and "full of integrity" are just a few of the words that come to mind when I think of Pastor C. D. Brooks, a great evangelist, preacher, teacher, pastor, mentor, and friend. Elder Brooks's impact is felt positively both nationally and internationally. I am privileged, honored, and humbled to stand on his shoulders in the Breath of Life ministry.

John Carter, president, The Carter Report
Elder C. D. Brooks is a burning and a shining light, and we rejoice in his light. His monumental, prophetic sermon on Methuselah, preached with passion so many years ago, moved a worldwide audience who sensed that God was profoundly speaking through His servant. I was stirred by his oratory, and, like so many other young pastors of that day, took courage and lighted a candle from his blazing torch. He was indeed a man sent from God.

William Fagal, associate director, Ellen G. White Estate
I have long respected and admired C. D. Brooks for his powerful preaching and for his decisive, fearless affirmations of biblical truth and of the writings and ministry of Ellen G. White. Like Paul who said, "Follow my example, as I follow the example of Christ"

(1 Cor. 11:1, NIV), Pastor Brooks has given us an example worthy of following.

Mark Finley, former speaker/director, It Is Written
Some people's ministries leave a mark, others leave a legacy. C. D. Brooks has left a legacy on the lives of thousands of preachers and tens of thousands of church members and hundreds of thousands of viewers of the Breath of Life telecast. His unique blend of humility, brilliance, and deep spirituality has impacted countless lives. His ministry has been a positive influence on my own. In 1996, when I was conducting a satellite evangelistic series from Orlando, Florida, Elder Brooks graciously accepted our invitation to answer written questions from the audience during the series. I listened in amazement to his short, concise answers. They hit the mark every time. He had the ability of taking deep biblical truths and making them simple. During the time that we were together during this satellite series, I saw another side of Elder Brooks. Although I had always been impressed with his enthusiastic proclamation of the Word of God, I now saw him as willing to accept whatever role the Lord assigned. I pay tribute to a preacher par excellence, a brilliant scholar, a spiritual mentor, and a godly man of faith. It is a joy to know him as a friend and fellow colleague. I am confident that the book you hold in your hands will lift your spirits, encourage your heart, and draw you closer to the Savior.

Denyce Follette, personal assistant to C. D. Brooks
I've had the privilege of working as Elder Brooks's secretary since 1986. As with others on the Breath of Life staff, I affectionately call him Chief. Throughout the years I have found Elder Brooks to be all that people think he is: genuine, noble, kind, and a Christian gentleman through and through. My time with him has been a real blessing, and we are at 27 years and counting . . .

Clifford Goldstein, editor, *Adult Sabbath School Bible Study Guide*
From the day I first got to the General Conference about 30 years ago, C. D. Brooks loomed large, a legendary figure in his own time. I was awed by him then and still am now. He was, and remains, a revered figure in the Seventh-day Adventist Church. And rightly so.

Daniel R. Jackson, president, North American Division
I have had the great privilege of working with Elder C. D. Brooks for the past three years. He moves through our building with the grace of a prince. The depth of his spirit, the kindness of his words, and his warmth always make you feel like engaging with him. He is a warrior prince who has now turned his focus on shepherding younger leaders and warriors. We love having him here.

Connie Vandeman Jeffery, associate manager, Adventist Media Center
Consummate Christian gentleman; pioneer Adventist broadcaster; powerful preacher. If there were ever candidates for sainthood, C. D. Brooks and my father, George Vandeman, would top the list! Elder Brooks's sermons move me and inspire me. I am humbly grateful for the privilege of calling him my friend.

William Johnsson, former editor, *Adventist Review*

My friend Pastor C. D. Brooks, whom I have known for many years, is a person of integrity. All that he has done in a long life of service has been marked by dignity and excellence. We serve together as life trustees of the Ellen G. White Estate, and I know firsthand his unwavering devotion to the messenger of the Lord.

Leslie Pollard, president, Oakwood University

The ministry of C. D. Brooks is synonymous with excellence, discipline, passion, and perspective. While the first three descriptors might be self-explanatory, perspective refers to Elder Brooks's unwavering devotion to end-time proclamation. As a preacher, Elder Brooks will be forever seen as a sentinel of the imminent second advent of Jesus Christ. This book provides readers insight and instruction into the influences that made the man so fiercely prophetic in his preaching ministry.

Jan Paulsen, former president, General Conference of Seventh-day Adventists

When God called Elder C. D. Brooks into His service more than 60 years ago, He gave the church a powerful, eloquent voice for truth. As a pastor, evangelist, administrator, and television evangelist, Elder Brooks has had an extraordinary impact on the life and witness of our church in North America and around the world. Yet his "public persona" fails to tell the whole story. For all his many accomplishments, Elder Brooks is, first and foremost, an unfailingly gracious, faithful, and gentle man of God—and for this, I honor him.

C.D.

The Man
Behind the
Message

To order call **1-800-765-6955**

Visit us at **www.reviewandherald.com** for information
on other Review and Herald® products.

C.D.

The Man Behind the Message

HAROLD L. LEE **WITH** BENJAMIN BAKER

REVIEW AND HERALD® PUBLISHING ASSOCIATION

Since 1861 | www.reviewandherald.com

Published by Review and Herald® Publishing Association, Hagerstown, MD 21741-1119

The Review and Herald® Publishing Association publishes biblically based materials for spiritual, physical, and mental growth and Christian discipleship.

Scripture quotations credited to NIV are from the *Holy Bible, New International Version.* Copyright © 1973, 1978, 1984, 2011 by Biblica, Inc. Used by permission. All rights reserved worldwide.

Cover design by Bryan Gray, Review and Herald® Design Center
Cover photo by Tyrone McMillan Photography
Interior design by Derek Knecht, Review and Herald® Design Center

PRINTED IN U.S.A.

17 16 15 14 13   5 4 3 2 1

Library of Congress Control Number: 2013954536

ISBN 978-0-8280-2787-8

DEDICATION

To Walterene, whom the Lord chose

ACKNOWLEDGMENTS

Many helped make this book a reality. First, our appreciation goes to the Brooks family for their willingness to assist in whatever way they could. C.D. and his wife, Walterene, interviewed extensively with us and read the manuscript, providing necessary feedback. Walter Arties did the same. History could not have been made nor the story told without these three individuals.

The staff of the Bradford-Cleveland-Brooks Leadership Center were vital to this effort, most notably Saylene Hitchcock and JoAnn Bushner. Also, the Office of Archives, Statistics, and Research at the General Conference, including the director, David Trim, and associate director, Peter Chiomenti, provided strategic assistance. The institutions of Oakwood University and the General Conference supported this endeavor fully. The Review and Herald team was essential to the production of the volume you hold in your hand.

Finally, our families gave much-needed support in the long hours required to complete this project. To Barbara Lee and Delbert and Susan Baker we are indebted.

—Harold Lee and Benjamin Baker

TABLE OF CONTENTS

FOREWORD

A s with many people, I stand in awe of Elder C. D. Brooks and the abilities conferred on him by the Lord. He and his wife, Walterene, are some of the most gracious people alive and reflect characters refined by their connection with Jesus.

I first became acquainted with Elder and Mrs. Brooks when they joined the Columbia Union Conference office staff in the 1960s. At the time my father was the president of the Columbia Union, and I was a teenager. The way in which Elder and Mrs. Brooks treated me as a young person and all those connected with the union office endeared them to us. From that time to now, we have had a wonderful rapport with the Brooks family, and Elder Brooks has been a hero in my eyes. He and my father remained very close friends and colleagues until my father's death. It was a privilege to have Elder Brooks give a homily at his memorial service.

Elder Brooks epitomizes the Christian who knows what he believes and is willing to say it with directness and grace. His fidelity to the Bible as the Word of God is fundamental to his perspective on how the church can best proclaim the message of salvation in Christ. He has shown all of us what it means to preach the Word in season and out of season, through the power of the Holy Spirit, giving thousands of people a new lease on life—a "breath of life"! He pioneered the media ministry of Breath of Life, bringing to television and the Internet the powerful three angels' messages pointing to Christ's soon coming. Indeed, the great objective of Elder Brooks's life has been to point people to the promise of eternal life through the life, death, resurrection, and high-priestly ministry of the One whom Elder Brooks loves supremely, our Lord and Savior, Jesus Christ. Truly the Lord has used him mightily for the building up of His last-day remnant church.

The book you hold in your hands is a tribute to one of the greatest evangelists and soul-winners of the Seventh-day Adventist Church. You will read in its pages the amazing way in which God spoke to Elder Brooks's mother, helping to set her son on a pathway of lifelong service to God. When he was a young man, Elder Brooks's goal to become a dentist—and he would have been a good one—but God had other plans. Instead of repairing other people's mouths, God has used Elder Brooks's mouth to proclaim the eternal truths of the Word of God and thus repair people's entire minds and bodies in preparation for the new earth. This spiritual journey and ministry begun early in life has taken Elder Brooks to the farthest corners of the globe and into some of the most intriguing settings.

In this special book you will find thrilling stories of God using this powerful preacher to blaze new trails in evangelism, church organization, and human relations. You will also learn how to lean on God in various circumstances, bringing encouragement to your life and walk with Jesus. Ultimately, as you read about Elder Brooks's life and ministry, you will be inspired to rededicate your life to Jesus and to tell others of His saving power.

—Ted N. C. Wilson, president of the General Conference of Seventh-day Adventists

HOME

"The grace of God overshadowed me as a child."

On a boiling Thursday afternoon on July 24, 1930, Charles Decatur Brooks was born in a big house in the country outside of Greensboro, North Carolina, the tenth child of Marvin and Mattie Brooks. On that day, Mattie, renowned for her saintliness, dedicated her gigantic newborn son to God. Neither she nor her midwife could know that the oversized infant in her arms would become one of the greatest evangelists of the twentieth century.

Mattie Brooks's Vision

A half year later at St. Leo's Hospital the matriarch of the Brooks brood lay on a cot in critical condition, her family braced for the worst. After an unsuccessful surgical procedure, the doctors soberly admitted to the large family that they could do nothing to save Mattie. She would die soon. After the physicians had pronounced their grim prognosis, they disappeared down the corridor, and the Brookses huddled in numb shock, gripping one another for support.

Later that night a dazzling light brightened Mattie Brooks's hospital room, and a voice called her by name.

"Mattie."

Like Samuel of old, the suddenly invigorated woman was wide awake and listening.

"Keep My commandments."

A faithful Methodist her entire life, she was perplexed, venturing, "Lord, which one? I thought I was a commandment keeper."

Only silence met her.

Mattie waited, then the fourth commandment flashed into her mind: "Remember the Sabbath day to keep it holy." Inexplicably, she instantly grasped that the Sabbath in question—the seventh day—was Saturday, not Sunday, as she had observed since childhood.

Suddenly the thought plunged the mother of 10 into despair. Who knew this? Her family certainly didn't. Neither did her friends and fellow Methodists. She cried out to God in the tradition of Southern Christians that He grant her deathbed request: "Before I die, let me tell others about this truth."

Then the voice, which had been silent for a spell, whispered, "Mattie, I want living sacrifices."

"Lord, if no one else keeps Your Sabbath, my children and I will," she vowed.

Marvin Brooks

In an isolated forest cabin with mud-daubed walls heated only by a small fireplace, Marvin Bishop Brooks was prematurely born on a freezing night in 1886 in Chatham County, North Carolina. Some nights his mother would lay the infant in a shoe box to sleep. Yet throughout the length of his life Marvin was a man of phenomenal strength, both mentally and physically.

When he was 9 years old, his father, Jackson Brooks, left for the local railroad headquarters to try to find work in order to earn some money to alleviate the desperate poverty that dogged his family. After kissing his wife, Pattie, and the baby girl cradled in her arms, Jackson walked with his two sons, Marvin and Arthur, until he had to tell them that they had accompanied him far enough and now they must return home to take care of their mother. The two boys would never see their father again. Jackson Brooks died of pneumonia at a railroad stop far away, and it was too expensive to send his body home.

For a while young Marvin Brooks was de facto the man of the house, earning money to feed his family by doing chores for White people and hunting fish and rabbits. Then his mother, Pattie Brooks, married a man named John Williams, who, Marvin soon discovered (to his consternation), was an abusive, short-tempered alcoholic. In no time the stepfather exploited him and Arthur like slaves, forcing them to drop out of school, leave home, and work full-time on a plantation. To make matters worse, Williams instructed the already merciless employers to whip the Brooks boys if necessary, and to be sure to inform him of it so he could administer his own punishment after work. Also, as in the days of slavery, the boys received as food the undesirable parts of animals—chicken heads and hog feet—and had to make do on freezing winter nights with insufficient bed-covers. But rather than weaken him, such experiences only made Marvin Brooks tougher.

As the years passed, John Williams' explosive behavior grew increasingly out of control. On one occasion he hit Marvin in a plowed field so hard that the youngster fell and fractured his arm. Because the family was poor and Williams was unsympathetic, the injury never received medical treatment, so the arm grew back crooked. But one time later as his enraged stepfather thrashed him, Marvin fell and broke his arm again, miraculously setting it right.

Unbearable to the teenage Marvin Brooks, however, was the abuse Williams visited upon his mother. As the years went by the son's tolerance lessened as his physical strength increased. The tipping point occurred when one day Williams teetered into the house drunk, ready to pummel Pattie. It was then that Marvin and Arthur, both teenagers and weighing more than 400 pounds combined, emerged from their room, blocking Williams from carrying out his intent.

"You've hit Mother for the last time," Marvin announced.

John Williams sputtered and fumed, making as if to lunge at the brothers. Neither of the boys flinched. Their stepfather's bluff was all bluster, and everyone knew it.

"Get out of my house," Williams boomed as a last resort, expletives punctuating his words. "Nobody is going to live under my roof and disrespect me!"

"I will go," Marvin replied, "but never so far that I cannot come back and kill you if you touch my mother again."

John Williams never hit Pattie Brooks again.

Mattie Brooks

Ninety-one delegates from across the United States converged on the Seventh-day Adventist Church in Minneapolis, Minnesota, on October 17, 1888. What followed were three weeks of the most contentious debates in the history of the church. But interspersed in the wrangling were talks by two young men who had journeyed from California named A. T. Jones and E. J. Waggoner. The message of righteousness by faith in Christ alone was their focus, Ellen White describing it as "a most precious message" and "bread that cometh down from heaven," and that disregard for it was the "rejection of Christ" and His message. The session was a watershed for the Adventist Church and an important event in salvation history.

That year Charles Brooks's mother, Mattie, was born.

Near Death

While Mattie Brooks hovered near death, the newborn Charles came down with a case of pneumonia that threatened to terminate his life just after it had begun. As the infant struggled to breathe, the only adult to care for him and his siblings, their father, Marvin Brooks, prepared for the bleak six-mile walk to the hospital to check on his dying wife.

As Brooks trudged through the forest and into the city he prayed. He didn't know if his wife would live, nor if his newest child would also die. But a durable faith steadied him. At the hospital he discovered that his wife was still alive, and after sitting and talking to her motionless, unresponsive body, he kissed her and headed back into the night.

By faith Marvin Brooks entered a store and purchased Vicks salve, mutton tallow, and snuff. Relieved to hear his son's cries when he opened the door to his house, he immediately built a fire. Brooks poured the items from the store into a pot and set it to heat over the fire. In no time the concoction coagulated into a lump of goo. Heating a half dozen gallons of water, he gave Charles a warm bath. After bathing the baby, he toweled him off and began rubbing the glowing slime all over his body. Finally, the still-prayerful Brooks swaddled Charles in a woolen blanket and held him on his lap in front of the fire, the light of its flames dancing on the faces of father and son.

The fire warmed the young one to his core, the father's care fought the infection, and the prayers to God made Charles whole. The baby began to breathe normally as the darkness outside fled and light spilled over the eastern horizon. Miles away, Mattie also mended. The crisis had passed.

Making It

But previous crises still hung like a specter over the Brooks family. Marvin and Mattie Brooks actually had 16 children in all, 10 girls and six boys. Four had died before Charles's birth. Two boys, Clifton and Clevis, perished in infancy. A girl, Odessa, died young of sudden disease. And a third son, George, was laid to rest while a teenager as a result of a heart condition. Brilliant and handsome, before he died he cradled his infant sister Virginia in his arms and reminded his brothers and sisters to love God and each other. Mattie Brooks would later tell Charles again and again that

God graced her with him to take George's place and to comfort her after the devastating loss. Thus Charles's upbringing was generally happy, but at the back of it was a sobering awareness of the deep, deep sadness that life's tragedies could yield.

Another reminder of the harshness of reality was the nation's economic situation throughout Charles's early years. The Brooks family was poor, but always had food, unlike some of their neighbors. Indeed, in the midst of the Great Depression the family was self-sustaining, growing a variety of produce and raising livestock and poultry on a small farm outside of Greensboro. They lived in a modest house purchased by the sweat of Marvin Brooks's brow, who eked out a living by a variety of trades.

On the Brookses' 40-acre farm, dozens of rows of corn stood like soldiers at attention in straight lines, prepared, when ripe, to fuel the growing children in various ways. Apples and peaches weighed down the branches of trees, calling to be canned or dried. Wheat waved in the air like golden wands, later baked into bread whose aroma wafted through the house. Yams matured below ground, eager to yield their crimson treasures. When the family strung scores of onions from sills over the basement and red and green peppers overflowed from wooden buckets, the produce resembled Christmas tree decorations.

Cows provided milk and butter. The family slaughtered pigs for meat. Often it took five whole chickens to feed the Brookses at a given meal. The boys in the family, taught how by their father, would fish. Often the Brooks children went on hikes in search of edible wild nuts and berries.

The Brooks Brand
Occasionally the Brookses needed items they did not grow on their farm. One particular day, when he was 9 years old, his parents sent Charles to fetch sundries, and upon arriving in the grocery store he found the owner engaged in a lively conversation with a friend. Neither noticed the youngster among the aisles.

"I know people are suffering and I want to help," the grocer said to his friend. "But folk never seem to do what they say."

Charles could hear the other person's monosyllabic notes of agreement.

"If people would do half of what they promise, I could help them, and they could help themselves."

Charles knew that the grocer sold goods on credit and had a drawerful of debt logs. By that time it was said that the Great Depression was over, but rural residents in North Carolina still seemed to be in the thick of it. A dollar for a 10-hour workday was the norm.

The boy's head snapped up from locating the sugar when the owner proclaimed in a loud voice, "About two and a half miles down yonder is a Colored man named Marvin Brooks."

Charles stood still.

"If Brooks tells you he is coming in on Friday to bring you $3, you can count on having $3 in your palm on Friday! If everybody was like him, I would be doing very well."

The statement made such a profound impression on him that right then and there, Charles Brooks decided to be a man of his word like his father.

Doing Good

Although the Brookses needed the farm's output to feed their 13-member family, Mattie Brooks was generous almost to a fault, searching out those who needed food in the tough times and giving bounty away freely. One day, while in her large garden cutting vegetables, she called for Charles to bring the wheelbarrow. After weighting it with a colorful array of cabbage, tomatoes, beets, and lettuce, she directed him to take it to a neighbor.

With houses being spaced considerably apart from each other in the country, Charles determinedly set out over the uneven dirt road. No sooner had he returned from his errand than his mother began heaping more vegetables in the empty wheelbarrow. Filling it again, this time she instructed him to go to a different neighbor farther away. It happened several more times. Finally Charles spoke up.

"Mom, I just don't understand you."

"What do you mean, son?"

"Well, here you are sending me to hand-deliver all of this food to people who talk about you behind your back."

Mattie Brooks smiled, the cutting knife in her right hand glinting in the sunlight.

"Son, the Lord says to love your enemies and to pray for those who despitefully use you."

With that, she placed the next load in the wheelbarrow.

Keeping the Sabbath

What the neighbors were saying about Mattie Brooks behind her back had to do with her bizarre habit of worshipping on Saturday instead of Sunday. After her deathbed experience and her vow, she began to observe the Sabbath the best way she knew how. Often in the late hours before the clock struck 12:00 on Friday night, Mattie would be frantically baking and scrubbing. She didn't realize that according to the Bible, Sabbath extended from sundown to sundown.

On Saturday morning the matriarch gathered her children and sat them in a circle. After she read them a Bible passage, they then sang a hymn or two, recited the Ten Commandments, and offered a prayer for family and neighbors, the sick and needy, and church members. Because Marvin Brooks had not accepted Saturday as the Sabbath and still required his children to perform their chores to keep the farm running, Mattie explained, "Children, the commandments say 'Remember the Sabbath day, to keep it holy,' but they also say 'Honor your father.' Now, I don't know how to handle this, but if you will go prayerfully about your chores with Jesus in your thoughts, I'm sure He will understand, for He knows your heart." She continued in this way for 10 years with no minister, books, or church to encourage and instruct her.

In fact, the Methodist congregation the Brookses belonged to, once warm and friendly, turned cold and antagonistic after Mattie's discovery of the seventh-day Sabbath. Despite the family being unobtrusive and gentle with their convictions, church members began mocking them, claiming their presence was "quenching the Spirit" in the church.

During his Sunday morning sermon the minister began to take potshots at Mattie Brooks by intoning, "The sun is shining like the Sabbath this morning. Those trying to bring back the 'law of bondage' ought to know that Jesus took that away. How could folks be so foolish?" His prayers contained similar thinly veiled attacks. Patiently and cheerfully the large family sat through it until Mattie stopped attending, because she felt she was a source of distraction to the members. Yet she still faithfully sent her children to Sunday school bright and early. And tellingly, although shunned by her fellow members because of her beliefs about the Sabbath, whenever any of them fell seriously sick, Mattie Brooks received a knock at her door, often in the middle of the night, begging for her prayers.

The Little Preacher
Meanwhile, Charles, although mischievous, playful, and rough like most boys his age, had an unusual proclivity toward spiritual things. At the age

of 6 he taught a Sunday school class at his church, instructing his peers and the older kids in the Scriptures. In time he developed a reputation as the most religious youth in the area.

One night during a packed citywide revival held at the Brookses' church, the speaker, a legendary Methodist minister by the name of Leadbetter, grew upset with the audience when no one knew the answers to his questions on a subject he had spoken on the previous night. After a litany of interrogatives that only elicited blank looks, the preacher whirled around to his host—the pastor of the Brookses' church—and demanded, "Where is that little boy you were telling me about?" With a wide smile, the man responded by simply pointing to the front row where Charles sat.

"Stand up, son," the speaker said, "and tell these folks the answers to my questions!"

Charles obeyed, rattling off the correct replies.

The speaker then spent an inordinate amount of time complimenting the lad, and everyone seemed to be in awe of him. Such incidents caused the older members of Charles's church to remark, "That boy is going to be a preacher someday!" But the lad had no desire to be a preacher—in fact, he resisted it.

Increasingly, though, the youngster found himself called upon to deliver devotionals and lead in church programs. At 6 years of age he even received charge of his Sunday school class. However, all of this came to a halt when Charles responded to the query, "Why does your family keep Saturday for Sunday?" from one of his young students. His forthright answer got him summarily relieved of his responsibilities.

The Committee

The tipping point for the Brooks family occurred when their church's pastor organized a committee to "exorcise" Mattie Brooks of her Saturday-keeping spirit and coax her and her children back into the fold and the accepted orthodoxy. They set a date for a meeting at the Brooks home. That the congregation even went to such trouble testified to the essential place Mattie held in the congregation despite the slander.

On a cool spring Sunday the church committee arrived at the Brooks home, headed by the first deacon and composed of members who had been friends of the family for years. After exchanging pleasantries, the committee then presented their mission. On one side of the room sat the Brooks brood; on the other, the church committee.

In a patronizing manner the deacon explained that his group was there to save Mattie Brooks from error and bring her back into the fold of fellowship. He urged her to give up her Old Testament legalistic beliefs and thus stop binding the saints in the Spirit. God had nailed the law to the cross, he said, and Christians were no longer under its bondage.

When the deacon had finished pontificating, Mattie Brooks responded. Although she was not one to argue, she had diligently studied the Bible on the matter and would not keep silent at what she considered to be an assault on truth.

"My brother, if what you say is true, that God's law is destroyed, then please explain these texts," said Mattie Brooks, quoting three New Testament scriptures upholding the commandments.

The deacon sputtered an incoherent reply, now off-balance.

"According to Paul," she continued, " 'where there is no law, there is no sin.' If the law is destroyed, then so is sin, and the devil can go to heaven."

Once again the deacon and the members of the committee became speechless, suddenly finding something on their shoes or the floor that captured their interest.

But Mattie Brooks was not done yet. "If the law is done away with, then it is all right for me to steal that beautiful lamp in your home that I always compliment your wife on, brother deacon."

At that the chairman stood up, bringing the meeting to an abrupt halt. "Well, Sister Brooks," he said, "we didn't really think we could change you. Since you believe as you do, I've brought you a present I think you will appreciate." He then handed her a rectangular package wrapped in brown paper and tied with khaki twine.

After thanking the deacon, Mattie walked the church group to the end of her long driveway, as was the manner of country people in those days. As she bade them farewell, there was an unspoken acknowledgment that their fellowship had come to an end.

The Church

It was a crisp Thursday afternoon in 1940 when Charles came home from school and couldn't find his mother in the usual places in the house. Knowing she had a "prayer room" and often went there, he hurried to it. Sure enough, Mattie Brooks was on her knees, both hands held up to the sky. Sensing someone else in the room, she turned her head and opened her eyes, which lit up when they took in her son.

"We have found a church!" she exclaimed, happiness dancing on the features of her face. "We found *our* church!"

It all started with the little gift the deacon had handed to Mattie Brooks that momentous day. After returning from seeing the entourage out, the Brooks matriarch had fetched a pair of scissors and handed them to Charles to open the package.

Curious, he snipped the twine and tore the paper from around it. It was a book with the title *The Great Controversy* by an author named E. G. White. Later there would be much speculation among the Brookses as to whether the "E" stood for Edward or Edith or Ernest or Elizabeth. But whoever the author was, the gripping words and potent truths contained in the volume captivated the family, leading them like a guide with a lantern on a dark night to the crest of a mountain.

The Great Controversy especially made a deep impression upon Pattie Black, Charles's older sister. Although she had married an upstanding Methodist minister, she continued to observe the seventh-day Sabbath in her marriage, the couple enjoying an amicable unity in their shared love for Christ. Busy when a door-to-door book salesperson knocked at her home one Thursday, Pattie was nevertheless a Southern woman to the core like her mother, so she invited the stranger into her home anyway. The man turned out to be long winded, rambling on and on about religion. As kindly as possible, the harried Pattie cut him short.

"Sir, I'm really not interested in what you are saying. Instead of doing all this talking you need to obey the Lord and keep the Sabbath." She simply wasn't going to tolerate someone who might be a hypocrite, and besides, she was increasingly having questions about those who claimed to follow the Lord but worshipped on the wrong day.

Instead of being rebuffed, the man smiled, and jettisoning his rehearsed spiel, replied, "What day is the Sabbath?"

Nonplussed by his smile, Pattie answered, "Saturday—the seventh day of the week."

"Ma'am, how would you like to be a part of a church where everyone believes that?"

In no time Pattie had told her mother and siblings about her discovery. That was the day that Charles happened upon his mother in her prayer room. The very next evening—on a Friday—the pastor of the Seventh-day Adventist church of Greensboro visited the Brooks home. What he had to say to the rapt family was like inserting the final missing piece into a puzzle.

Bright and early the next morning the pastor returned and escorted the family to the Seventh-day Adventist church in town. Up the steps and into the church building walked the dozen new visitors. The congregation of 70 adults and choir of 15 youth turned to look when the Brookses entered. In the sanctuary the floor was uncarpeted, the seats unpadded, the windows hand-painted, and a potbellied stove sat in the middle of the room. Yet the Brookses had never felt more at home.

When the 10-year-old Charles first laid eyes on the banner suspended from the ceiling behind the pulpit on which the Ten Commandments were emblazoned, he thought, *This is it!*

The Revival

Because the Brooks family owned no automobile, the dozen had to trudge a mile and a half through forest and across streams to reach the bus stop. From there, they changed into dress shoes and paid a 10-cent bus fare to the center of town. Next a trolley waited to transport them three more miles to the Seventh-day Adventist church. After the service the family ate sandwiches packed before the Sabbath and returned home the same way but in reverse. When it was cold or rainy, a man from the church named Shoffner would pick them up, refusing to accept a dime for his troubles.

It wasn't long before the church's pastor, Napoleon Smith, held a revival. Smith was not a big man by any means, but he was tough and athletic. Dressed impeccably every night, he wore tailored suits that included cloth-covered buttons and double-breasted vests. Young Charles grew to admire immensely Smith's blend of personal style and preaching prowess.

The Brooks family thrilled at the powerful Bible teachings exposited night after night. They had never heard anything like that before. For Smith, the Bible was not just a book to read a passage from—it was a textbook. From a single sermon Mattie Brooks could write down 20 or 30 texts, all lending power and harmony to a single subject or doctrine. And amazing to the Brookses, every night he presented a different topic. They had no idea that there were so many things in the Bible!

Another aspect to the services that impressed the Brookses were the illustrations that brought the sermon to life. Smith used a "stereopticon lantern" that projected a vivid slide show. He had hundreds of 3"x 5" Preiger slides. The Brooks family would excitedly discuss the meeting on the way home at night and all throughout the next day.

They couldn't wait to get baptized. However, when Mattie told the pastor that she wished to be baptized, he said, "Sister Brooks, I think it best you wait awhile."

Incredulous, she replied, "Wait? Awhile? I've been waiting for 10 years!"

Patiently Smith explained that there were things the Brookses hadn't learned yet, things they would have to be instructed on before taking the big step.

For example, the Brookses ate pork every day, raising prizewinning Hampshire and Poland China hogs. On the occasions the pastor had visited the Brooks's farm, Marvin Brooks proudly showed the minister the beautiful corn-fed pigs, for which Smith genuinely complimented him. But the pastor did not support the family dining on the meat three or four times a day. There was also the matter of jewelry and makeup.

And so the pastor visited the farm to prepare the Brookses for baptism. When confronted with the radical lifestyle changes, Mattie Brooks's only response was "Show me from the Bible." As did most Adventist ministers of the day, the pastor knew the Bible like the back of his hand, and when he flipped to the appropriate passages, she shook her head in agreement and asked, "All right, what else?" By the time Smith had left, the pork, jewelry, and makeup had departed with him.

On a Sabbath in 1940 Charles Brooks went down into the watery grave along with six of his sisters and his mother.

CALLING

"I will help you make truth clear."

Although Charles had been baptized, he had not yet consented to God's calling for his life, and, like any teenager, struggled with the world's temptations. Attending James B. Dudley, a public high school in Greensboro, he found himself constantly bombarded with allurements that undermined his new faith. Yet as God had steadily but surely guided the Brooks family into His truth, so He imperceptibly led Charles into the great purpose He had designed for him.

The young man's first hurdle on the road of faithfulness was sports. Hitting a growth spurt at 15, he shot past most of his peers in height. His outgoing personality and quick thinking made him a natural leader. Add to that his natural athleticism, and Charles was a shoo-in for a high school football career. Indeed, for as long as he could remember he had loved football, cherishing the dream of being a star on the gridiron. However, his family's new understanding that the Sabbath started Friday at sunset instead of Friday at midnight doused his plans, for the big football games almost always fell on Friday night. Although it frustrated him, he did not dare attend a game during the holy hours and never even tried out for the football squad.

He did, however, compromise in another of his favorite pastimes, and sorely regretted it. Charles played the snare drums in the Dudley High School band, but because of his size, one year the school called upon him to play the big bass drum in the annual tristate band competition in Winston-Salem. No one else could do it: the girls were not strong enough, and the other boys were too small. The bass was the most important instrument, setting the cadence and keeping the whole band in step. And, of course, the big event was smack-dab in the middle of a Saturday.

His teachers and bandmates constantly impressed upon him that everything was riding on his performance—first place in the competition, the school's reputation and legacy, and the pride of the city of Greensboro. Participating in the practices leading up to the competition, Charles unwittingly gave in little by little to the major compromise demanded of him. He had unwittingly made his decision before he actually decided.

James B. Dudley High's band uniforms were resplendent. The jackets were a rich dark blue with shiny brass buttons and bright gold braiding that cascaded off the left shoulder and snaked under the arm. The pants were a lighter shade of blue with a thick gold stripe running down the outside of the leg. The hats were expertly trimmed to perfection. The majorettes who flanked the band wore variations on the uniform but with bleached white bottoms, the contrast stunning in the sun.

On the Saturday of the competition, Charles Brooks cut a handsome figure in his blue-and-gold uniform but was in turmoil inside. The weather matched his mood. Instead of the sunny, cloudless day predicted in the forecast, the sky was threatening, the air chilly. The high school band from Greensboro soon discovered that the parade route meandered seven miles across the hilly terrain of Winston-Salem. After that first phase of the competition the bands would perform at halftime at the football game.

As Charles hefted the bass drum that Saturday morning, the harness strapping the instrument to his arms and back effectively made him and the drum as one. In order to negotiate the inclines and declines of the course, he had to lean back in an unnatural stance, keeping his arms bent at the same angle the entire route, striking the center of the drum to get the deepest boom. Applause rewarded the band members along the human corridors formed by the onlookers, but Charles felt only recrimination in his mind.

When the band stopped to rest after a couple of miles, someone unsnapped Charles's harness. As he started to place the big drum on the ground he realized in terror that his arms would not unbend. The muscles had frozen in place! He now imagined the judgment of God on him for defiling the Sabbath, while the bandmaster saw their chances for winning the competition on the football field in jeopardy if their drummer was paralyzed. Frantically the members gathered around Charles. After someone brought a first-aid kit, others peeled off his jacket and shirt and liberally splashed rubbing alcohol on his arms. The majorettes knew how to do massage, and in a few minutes his arms began to relax and return to normal.

Charles and his band arrived at the football stadium at 2:00 p.m. By that time the sky had made good on its threat, and rain poured steadily. The rain soaked the teenage band competitors as they huddled in the uncovered stadium. Charles worried that the rain would ruin his instrument, but Dudley High made it through the day and placed second in the tristate competition. Knowing that he had lost in the most important battle, Charles vowed never to violate his conscience again.

The very next week he found his vow tested. The bandmaster, electrified with excitement, announced that the band had done so well at the tricity competition that they were being asked to perform for homecoming at the Agricultural and Technical College of North Carolina on Saturday. The band burst into cheers, but when they learned that Charles would not participate for "reasons of conscience," the mood immediately soured. Although Brooks was excoriated in front of his bandmates and even threatened with expulsion, he wouldn't budge this time.

Best Friends

Charles's stands on principle molded his teenage years, and once perhaps even saved his life. His best friend during most of his high school years was a person that we will call Max. He and Brooks were so close that if you saw one, you'd see the other. The two were the same age, had similar tastes, and just naturally gravitated toward each other. Max's mother called Charles "her other son," and his grandmother adored him. It was the same with the Brooks family toward Max. But at the close of their junior year things changed.

Max had begun to hang out with two guys named Joe and Ed, normal teenagers in those days other than the fact that they were a little too "sophisticated" in Charles's view. No one told him this, or forbade him from fraternizing with them, but he thought it best to keep his distance. Although all the Blacks in the area were poor back then, Ed drove a long, shiny Cadillac to school. Both he and Joe gravitated to different, more adult things than their classmates, having no interest in the simple pastimes that engrossed others their age. And so the duo of Charles and Max became the trio of Max, Joe, and Ed.

In time Max's mother noticed a change coming over her son. One night Charles went to visit her and she fell on his shoulder, weeping.

"Why don't you and Max go around together like before?" she asked tearfully.

Hugging the distraught woman who was like a second mother, Charles explained that Max was still his friend but he could not be close to him the way he used to because of the company he kept.

A couple years later during a Week of Prayer at Oakwood College Charles received a stunning telegram. It informed him that Max and Joe had been arrested for murdering a White merchant in Greensboro during a robbery.

The Ghost

But perhaps one experience more than any other strikingly illustrated the depth of the teenage Charles's religious beliefs. Later, throughout his ministry he always stressed "the truth, the truth, the truth," but it's a whole different thing to confront whatever challenges your belief, facing it head-on.

The Brooks family lived in the country, but every day Charles and his brothers and sisters attended school in the city. A yellow bus stopped in front of their house and collected them, then dropped them back home after school.

In the winters when the sun went down early many recreational activities occurred at night. Whether it was hanging out at the local diner, sports events, strolling with a girl, or just chatting with friends in the park—it all happened at night. If you wanted to have any fun in those days, you couldn't be scared of the dark.

That would not be a problem for those who had a car, or someone to pick them up. But when Charles or his siblings skipped the school bus to attend nighttime activities, getting home could be daunting. The last city bus of the day disembarked at a wealthy subdivision called Fairfield. From there, Charles and others had to walk a mile and a half through dark country streets and pitch-black woods to get home.

After a mile along the highway the path snaked among trees that blocked out the sky. Nocturnal creatures rustled about, and the sound of crunching leaves and snapping twigs kept one's nerves on edge. Owls hooted, and often in the slivers where the moon penetrated the octopus-tentacled tree branches one could see bats flittering in the air.

To get to the Brooks home required fording two creeks. Then you had to pass the infamous Hatcher Plantation. Hatcher was a bizarre man, a tobacco farmer who frightened everyone in the county. He had five vicious dogs that roamed his plot, and if you wanted to cross the property without them detecting you, you had to tiptoe across a patch of sand, being sure to not make a sound, for any one of these canines could hear a pinecone hit the ground a mountain away. One time an unlucky boy was crossing the plantation at night and made a sound. The dogs instantly lunged toward him. Frightened to the point of wetting his pants, the terrified youth ran up a tree, where he cowered in terror. The snarling hounds at first leaped at the tree, trying to reach the boy. When they couldn't, they lay around the trunk's base, waiting their prey out. In the morning a search party found the kid clinging to a limb, wide-eyed, traumatized, but unharmed.

Charles knew that he was nearing home when he glimpsed the porch light that his mother left on at night. There remained just one more obstacle when the light was visible: the Schloser pasture. Schloser was a beef butcher who was only a little less eccentric than Hatcher. Throughout the day and part of the night the old man would sit on his porch rocking trancelike in his chair. A glimpse of Schloser in the moonlight could inspire one to reach home in half the time it usually took.

One night Charles stayed late in the city, talking with friends over a soda. When it came time to say good night, it so happened that he was the only one among the group who lived in the country, so he'd have to make the walk home alone. Stepping off the bus at Fairfield, Brooks entered the forest, which seemed even darker than normal. Hearing movement all around him, he hurried his pace.

Charles maneuvered through the Hatcher Plantation without incident, running across the sand so as not to rile up the dogs. In minutes he was approaching Schloser's pasture. As he came into the clearing that afforded a full view of the forsaken land, he stopped dead in his tracks. On a hill about 100 yards away in Schloser's pasture was a sight that made his blood run cold. Silhouetted by the moonlight was a tall man wearing a white shirt, both arms stretched out. But he had no head.

Staring at the sight for a moment, Charles then squinted, rubbed his eyes, and squinted again. Was he seeing things? It looked like a ghost, wandering the countryside on a full moon.

But Charles didn't believe in ghosts. He believed that the dead were dead, awaiting the second coming of Jesus. The Bible stated that "the dead know nothing." But here was a headless apparition in plain sight, apparently contradicting his belief.

At that moment Charles sank to his knees. He prayed that God would help him understand what was happening. During his prayer he couldn't help stealing glances at the sinister figure up on the rise. Eerily, it hadn't moved an inch since he first saw it.

Finally Charles rose to his feet and started forward. After a couple steps he felt stones under his feet, so he picked up several and threw them toward the being on the hill. The white shirt rippled slightly when a soft wind wafted past, but it made no other movement.

Next Charles called to it. He knew it didn't make sense to speak to a headless corpse, but what else could he do after the being didn't even budge despite rocks thrown in its direction? The figure still didn't respond, but as Charles got closer the white shirt gleamed brighter in the moonlight.

When he was about 70 feet from the summit of the hill on which the man stood, Charles had to stoop and crawl beneath the barbed wire that snaked around Schloser's pasture. Once through he approached the hill. When he was within 50 feet of the figure he stopped, then broke into a relieved laugh.

The "headless man" was a tree stripped bare of its leaves, branches on either side halfway up the trunk looking like outstretched limbs. The "white shirt" was an elaborate spiderweb circling the tree many times over. The silk of the web gleamed bright in the moonlight, appearing bleached white.

Influences

Although becoming a minister was the furthest idea from Charles's mind in all but his final year at James B. Dudley, several people provided a foundation for the preaching for which he would later be renowned. Angeline Bailey, Dudley's English teacher, aimed him toward his lifework in an indirect way by assigning her students compositions that recognized and developed their gifts. Bailey sponsored the school's newspaper, *The Panther's Claw,* and after reading Charles's assignments, she recruited Charles to write for it.

The teenager's first published piece was a descriptive essay on his impressions while walking in the moonlight. Even at that young age he showed traces of his later descriptive prowess, his adjectives like brushes painting the scene on the canvas of the reader's mind. He even included a touch of history, referring to the ancient pagan practice of moon worship. Bailey's kind encouragement and belief in him, as well as seeing his words in print, increased his interest in writing and literature. During his senior year he was the editor of *The Panther's Claw.*

Margaret Simmons was Charles's homeroom teacher and counselor during his senior year. She possessed a mother's interest in her students—

especially for Charles. On the night of his commencement service, her green eyes filled with tears when he received his diploma. Afterward she grabbed him by the arm and dragged him to a remote corner of the cavernous gym where the graduation ceremony took place. Large tears rolled down her cheeks as she looked at him with such love and concern that he never forgot the experience.

"Brooks, you've got a good mind," she said. "You go on to college and make something of yourself!"

Charles was too embarrassed to reply. Later when he remembered the incident, not only would it inspire him when his courage flagged, but he wished that he had the opportunity to express his appreciation to her.

Charles never saw Margaret Simmons again after that night in June 1947.

The Firebrand

The year of 1947 was tough for African Americans in the South. The majority of educated people of color were teachers, ministers, or small-time entrepreneurs. The powerful unions controlled such specialized trades as masonry, plumbing, electrical engineering, carpentry, and mechanics but largely excluded Blacks from such occupations. Domestic and manual labor employment was readily available, however, and most Blacks resigned themselves to a lifetime of servile monotony. The privileged became physicians or dentists, though they were rare because the cost of medical school was simply beyond the means of most.

Thus for all the talk of bright futures showered on seniors, the James B. Dudley graduating class of 1947 had few doors open to them. Nevertheless, the ambitious 16-year-old Charles Brooks had aspirations to become a dentist, seeing in the profession an occupation that would challenge his fertile and nimble mind while affording him a good living. His three closest friends were leaning the same way, so each applied for the predentistry program at the North Carolina Agricultural and Technology College. Throughout the summer they awaited their acceptance letters.

Charles spent the weeks working in his brother Elliott's business, clearing lots for construction. Elliott was nicknamed "Rock" by his father because he was just plain tough. Laboring alongside Charles was his good friend Ernest Gray, one of his classmates of good character and uncommon strength.

Ernest, however, was not successful with girls. One Sunday their group of friends got together in a popular spot on Market Street in downtown

Greensboro for some refreshments. After a spell, it was time for them to break away and spend time with their girlfriends. One of the guys in the group motioned Charles aside.

"Hey, everybody has a girlfriend except Ernest. He can't go with me. He can't go with you, either. So we've decided to just quietly ease out one by one and leave him here."

Charles didn't want to be encumbered either, but he couldn't abandon his friend that way.

"Let's just explain it to him. He'll understand."

"Nah. He's been with us all afternoon, and we've had a great time. He'll be hurt if we tell him we've got to leave him and go see our girls when he doesn't have one."

Charles was in a minor dilemma because he had hitched a ride with the friend talking to him, and they were planning a double date in his car. But if he stayed with Ernest he'd have to skip his date and make the long walk to his home in the country at night. Ditching Ernest, however, would mean a pleasant date with a young woman and a ride to his front door. Ever loyal, Charles decided to stay with his friend. He did not know at the time that his decision would alter the course of his life.

Charles and Ernest remained behind, the rest leaving for their dates. Charles didn't know what to do with an evening that had once seemed so promising—he couldn't take Ernest on his date with him, he wasn't going to go home early, and he had seen all the movies showing at the theater. Then he had an idea. Soon he and Ernest made their way to Ashe Street, where a fiery young preacher was running an evangelistic campaign.

The firebrand's name was E. E. Cleveland. Never had they heard a man speak as Cleveland did that night in the canvas tent. In a no-holds-barred manner the tall, wiry preacher laid biblical truth out fearlessly and directly. Riveted by what he heard, Charles did not miss a single service of the two-and-a-half-month campaign after that. The power of the Lord began to rest on Charles Brooks that first night, and things would never be the same. Years earlier he had been baptized, but now he was being converted.

On a Saturday night not long after hearing Cleveland preach, Charles and Ernest went to the Carolina Theater to see the movie *The Yearling*, starring Gregory Peck, Charles's favorite actor. As they walked along, the friends discussed what the meetings meant to them and how they wanted to do right from that day on. Stopping at the red light diagonally across the street from the "Colored Entrance" to the theater, Ernest stepped off the curb when the light turned green. Charles did not move. Ernest wheeled around when he realized he was in the intersection alone.

"What's the matter?" he asked.

"We're talking about doing right," Charles said.

"Yeah."

"From now on?"

"Yeah."

"Well, then, why are we going to the theater?"

Ernest returned to the sidewalk where Charles still stood. "If you don't go, I don't go," he announced.

The Impression

That summer E. E. Cleveland took Greensboro, North Carolina, by storm. Preparing his way, a fleet of Bible instructors saturated the community with literature and flyers for the campaign. By the time Cleveland arrived, the massive tent on Ashe Street was bursting at the seams, with an overflow 14 people deep, all of them curious to see for themselves what the buzz was about. They weren't disappointed.

When he wasn't preaching his soul out, you could find Cleveland at the YMCA, challenging any comers to a round of table tennis. His only condition for playing was that whomever he beat had to attend his tent meetings. Cleveland was a gospel version of the con artist who wanders into the saloon acting inept at billiards and then, once the betting commences, takes everyone's money. He thoroughly whipped all comers at table tennis, and many a defeated foe sat under his preaching and was baptized.

Meanwhile Celia Cleveland, E.E.'s spunky and determined wife, formed a choir made up entirely of community residents. Nearly 60 voices sang at the meetings, and they were so good that they were featured on Sunday morning radio programs across the state.

In no time the Adventist tent meetings were a staple in the community, and when held in the evenings it seemed as if all of Black Greensboro showed up. One night as the gathering sang "I Shall Not Be Moved" a flash storm swooshed in and felled the tent. But even as the canvas collapsed, everyone stayed in their seats.

Perhaps the Greensboro campaign of 1947 had the most profound effect on the men of the Brooks home. One Sabbath after a service under the tent, Charles Brooks sat alone, everyone else gone to dinner. Because his house was out in the country, he had decided to remain for the afternoon meeting instead of footing it home and having to turn right back around.

It was a lovely summer day, a cool breeze wafting through the air, not too hot or humid. The brightness of the sun transformed even the most mundane of objects into a shining marvel. The young man's future was as bright as the day, since he had just received his acceptance letter to the dentistry program at North Carolina A&T. With only two weeks before preregistration, Charles looked forward to matriculating at college with his three friends, who had also been accepted.

Staring at the pulpit, Charles reflected on his life. He had done some smoking and drinking and had gone to movies and other questionable events. While those thoughts swirled in his head, out of nowhere he had an overmastering impression: "Charles, this is what I want you to do. I will help you make truth clear."

The teenager had never felt the presence of God so powerfully. Glancing around, he saw that he was still all alone. He shook his head to clear it.

"Make truth clear."

Suddenly Charles Brooks saw himself behind a pulpit, explaining with power and clarity God's last warning message to the world. Then, as people began filing into the seats around him, the vision faded.

During the service that evening Charles shrugged off his surreal experience, chalking it up to a flight of fancy. "Oh, I was just carried away by the inspiration of the day," he told himself. "After all, my acceptance letter just arrived from A&T. My buddies and I will be dentists. We can open up a joint practice."

But as soon as Brooks was alone, walking home, again the words came: "Make truth clear."

Sunday morning, as soon as he opened his eyes, he heard in his mind, *Make truth clear.*

The young man wondered why the impression didn't fade away like other childhood reveries. He went to his mother, whose knowledge about matters of the heart and conscience had never failed her children yet.

"Son," Mattie Brooks responded when he told her about his private struggle, "when you were born, I gave you to the Lord. Now He is calling you to His service." She wasn't surprised or taken off guard at all—it was as though she knew that day would come.

Charles had thought that in his career as a dentist he was going to fight tooth decay. Now, a higher power had determined that he would fight truth decay. After talking with his mother, he abandoned all plans to pursue dentistry. He would become a minister. And he would go to the Seventh-day Adventist school down in Huntsville, Alabama, called Oakwood.

Determined

E. E. Cleveland's Greensboro campaign revolutionized the life of another Brooks man that summer of 1947. When Charles, his mother, and six sisters had been baptized years earlier, Marvin Brooks did not participate and resented the new religion. At times he kept Charles from going to church with his mother and sisters. In fact, during Cleveland's campaign he had grown so angry with the denomination that he had exploded, "I'll never step foot inside a Seventh-day Adventist church!" To be fair, Marvin was indeed gracious toward the Brooks women about their faith. But Charles was his last son, and he perceived the Adventist Church as taking his boy away from him; so he declared that it would not happen if he had anything to do about it.

When Charles had accepted his calling and decided to go to Oakwood instead of A&T, his father flatly opposed the plan.

"You're our last son at home, Charles," Marvin Brooks said, raking leaves into a large pile on the center of the lawn. "Your mother and I are getting on in age now, and it will be such a comfort to us to have a son at home for a while longer." He paused, wiping his brow with his shirt sleeve before finishing, "You can go to school here."

"God called me to the ministry, Dad," Charles said. Greatly respecting his father, it pained him to go against his wishes, but he was dealing with a higher authority than even his father.

"I have no objection to your being a preacher," Marvin Brooks replied. "But can't you study ministry here?" He then named several preachers in the area who had all studied at A&T.

Charles explained that he had respect for each of the men mentioned, but that since he was training to be a Seventh-day Adventist minister he couldn't do that in a state school.

Suddenly Marvin stopped, standing up straight with rake in hand. "Son, if you stay here, I'll buy you a car."

In the 1940s that was quite an offer. A Black teenager owning a car was unheard-of. The thought tugged at Charles's heart.

"Sir, I can't do it," he finally said quietly.

"All right! Go ahead and leave! But you understand this—I will not give you a dime! Not one dime!" Marvin Brooks's face tightened as he angrily began to work again, the scratching of the rake against the ground ripping into the warm day.

"All right, Dad. I guess I'll be forced to stay here," Charles said, intimidated and crestfallen. Then, strengthening, "But I am going to prepare to go to Oakwood next year."

By faith Charles sent his application to Oakwood the next day, even though he knew that for financial reasons he wouldn't be able to attend the autumn session. Shortly after he had mailed the papers, the total of confirmed cases of polio in the South had grown so high that medical authorities proclaimed it an epidemic. As a result, Oakwood postponed the opening of classes for 10 days.

Five young people from Greensboro were going to Oakwood on the Tuesday after Charles had the conversation with his father on the lawn. The Adventist church scheduled for Saturday night a big social to honor them and give them a grand send-off. Hurt that he was not among the fortunate number heading to Alabama, Charles tried to keep his spirits up. As the Sabbath sun dawned beautifully over the hills of North Carolina, the young man awoke and had worship. He didn't know what the future held, but he knew that he wanted to be faithful no matter what.

After he had dressed for church, Charles went looking for his mother to ask her about some small matter. When he didn't find her in her usual places, he knew that she was in the prayer room. Sure enough, there she was. Charles hurried to her when he noticed her tear-filled eyes, but soon realized she was not crying tears of pain, but joy. A glow rested on her countenance that had nothing to do with the late summer sun.

"What is it?" her son asked.

"Have you seen your father?" she replied. "Go find him."

Charles rushed to his father's room. He couldn't believe what he saw as he stopped in the doorway. Marvin Brooks sat in his best blue suit, a Bible and baptismal bundle in his lap. That Sabbath day E. E. Cleveland baptized Marvin Brooks into the Seventh-day Adventist Church.

When Charles witnessed his father plunge into the watery grave he felt that the day could not possibly get any better. But then that evening his father, who now had a glow on his face not unlike his mother's, approached the young man.

"Son, are you going to the social tonight?"

Charles had forgotten the send-off event for the Oakwood students all day, so entranced had he been by what God had done in his father's life.

"I haven't thought about it, Dad."

Marvin Brooks smiled. "Well, you are going to Oakwood, aren't you?"

The Storm

On Sunday as Charles arose he looked out the window and saw his father coming up the path from his neighbor Buddy Reynolds' place carrying a large trunk on his strong back. It turned out that Marvin Brooks had seen the trunk in Buddy's shed and had bought it just minutes before Charles awoke. That morning his father went to work, painting the trunk and repairing its lock. As he was busy doing that, Charles's older sisters brought socks, underwear, towels, sheets and toiletries, setting them beside the trunk. Once their father had finished, they expertly packed it for their younger brother.

The Tuesday that the young people were to depart for Oakwood was both terrible and wonderful for Charles. It began with a torrential downpour that in the evening brought on the worst flooding in recent memory in the region. Then the family discovered that Mattie Brooks had fallen ill the night previous. Midmorning Charles received a letter from Oakwood that contained the line "Do not come to Oakwood. Seek to continue your education elsewhere." Because of his previous conversation in the yard, Charles had left the financial arrangements section blank on his Oakwood application, and the school had assumed that he could not afford to enroll. Upset but knowing that the Almighty was extremely active in his life and his family's, Charles cast about for a way to attend Oakwood. His older brother, Rock, suggested that he go see E. E. Cleveland about it.

When Charles and his brother arrived at the place where the Clevelands were temporarily lodging on the far side of Greensboro, E.E. was not home. But his wife, Celia, was. She invited them in and asked how she could help them. As Charles told her about the rejection letter she shook her head, the beginnings of a wry smile tugging at her lips.

"Forget that letter," she pronounced. "You go on to Oakwood. If there is any problem, you tell them to call us!"

Knowing that the Clevelands never told anybody to do anything that didn't end up working out, the two brothers headed back to their home to fetch Charles's trunk. By this time the streams had swollen and begun lapping over into the road. The Brooks brothers dashed through forest and city at a breakneck pace.

Upon arriving home, Charles gathered the rest of his belongings, amazed at the rapid pace of developments. His ill mother had whispered words of encouragement to her son. Marvin Brooks, who had vowed to Charles just days earlier, "I will not give you a dime!" now opened his snap-latch pocketbook and took out every dime he had and handed it to Charles. It was $310, a princely sum in 1947.

"I wish I had more to give you, son," the father looked Charles in the eye, "but I am giving you a good name."

Fighting back tears, Charles took the gift, knowing that for his elderly father it had been an especially tremendous sacrifice.

After kissing everyone goodbye, Charles and Rock loaded the trunk into Rock's 1943 Buick Century amid the pouring rain, which was now like being under a shower head on full blast, and climbed in soaked. In order to reach the Greensboro train station where the Oakwood students were to depart, Rock would have to maneuver the vehicle through flooded streets. From back roads to highways, Greater Greensboro was like a great, muddy, swirling lake. Cars sat backed up for miles, dozens partially float-ing. Charles despaired. After all that he had come through to get to this moment, now this!

Desperately Rock tried alternate routes, only to be met with red water rushing down the streets. When it seemed at every turn they were faced with either unmoving traffic jams or swirling rapids, Rock hit his hand on the steering wheel in frustration. Charles looked at his watch and was ready to acknowledge that it was all over.

"Irving Park!"

Charles glanced at his brother.

"Irving Park," Rock repeated, louder this time. "We'll try that way!"

Irving Park had been developed three decades earlier around the golf course of the Greensboro Country Club, and was the richest area in the re-gion, a neighborhood in which Black people could enter only when wear-ing servants' uniforms. Black youth wouldn't be caught dead in Irving Park unless they wanted to be caught dead in Irving Park.

The storm had hit Irving Park hard. The great mansions were flooded, geysers spouted up through the manhole covers on the streets, and the wa-ter was above the tires of parked cars. Rock set his face as his Buick plunged into pools where the roads proved uneven. Soon water had gathered on the floor of the car, the level getting higher each time the floodwater rose above the bottom of the doors. But as the Buick gained higher ground, it slowly seeped out. At last the Brookses reached the Southern Railway Depot to the relief of the five Oakwood students who had been nervously awaiting them.

Hurriedly Charles purchased a ticket as his brother barreled the Buick to the freight area. By the time he rushed around to meet him, Rock had already loaded his trunk into the train's baggage car. As brother embraced brother, the train began moving. A cheer rose as Charles entered the "Colored Car," joining his friends. There he fell into his seat exhausted, bound for Oakwood.

OAKWOOD

"My years at Oakwood were a delight."

The General Conference of Seventh-day Adventists had founded Oakwood Industrial School in 1896 as a place of higher education for the increasing number of African American converts to Adventism, then mainly concentrated in the southern region of the United States. The church chose the city of Huntsville, Alabama, as the site for the school because of its proximity to Nashville and Graysville, Tennessee, important Adventist centers in the South. Huntsville was also comparatively tolerant in racial matters in the turbulent Jim Crow era, and the low cost of land was an attractive option for Adventist leadership in the North.

The site for the industrial school itself, however, was not so promising. First suggested by veteran Black minister Charles Kinney, the 360-acre plot had been a slave plantation called the Beasley Estate, whose owner was reported to have brutally abused his Black captives. To make matters worse, the Alabama landscape was sloping and uneven. The red clay was hard as granite from being overworked, and dense brush covered the property.

Although pressed for money—and loath to funnel funds into a questionable enterprise in Alabama—the top three church administrators nevertheless surveyed the plot and decided to make the investment. Known unofficially as the "Huntsville School Farm," or just "Huntsville," the school was officially called "Oakwood" for the 65 oak trees that stood on the property.

Oakwood Industrial School was slow out of the gate after its doors opened on November 16, 1896, with a charter to train Black students to serve humanity through their respective areas of expertise and to spread the good news of Adventism to the world. Challenges with funding, staff, and students—not uncommon during the beginnings of any college—almost extinguished the fledgling school. But through the persistent efforts of Ellen G. White after her return from Australia in 1900, and solid leadership at the school from staff and students, Oakwood survived and even prospered.

In 1909 Oakwood graduated its first class, and the next few years witnessed the establishment of a sanitarium and orphanage, as well as the construction of numerous buildings. The first ministerial student finished his course in 1912, and in 1917 the school officially became Oakwood Junior College. In 1931 Oakwood students engaged in a peaceful revolt, demanding that the church address racial inequities, update the curriculum, improve student living conditions, and hire more Black staff, including a president, a position heretofore occupied by White men. Each of their demands was eventually met, including the installment of a Black president, James L. Moran, the next year. Four years before Charles Brooks matriculated to Oakwood as a freshman, the church renamed the school Oakwood College.

Change in the Church

The years leading up to Charles's enrollment in Oakwood were unprecedented in the history of the Seventh-day Adventist denomination as well. In 1947 the world was still recovering from the devastation of World War II, with various nations jockeying for position in the new balances of power. In the United States African Americans increasingly demanded equal rights as citizens, thereby laying the foundation for the civil rights movement. Race relations were also troubled in the Adventist Church, but the civil rights movement of Adventism, as it were, would result in a kind of resolution before the peak of its counterpart in 1963 with the March on Washington.

As early as 1889 the first ordained Black Adventist minister, Charles Kinney, proposed separate Black conferences, because of the persistent race-based discrimination African Americans experienced in the church. Kinney had crisscrossed the United States, trying to interest Blacks in the Adventist message in any way he could. He met with modest success in the Midwest. In St. Louis he baptized a number of African Americans and brought them to the only Seventh-day Adventist congregation in the city, one predominately White. The new converts experienced such mistreatment from the White members that Kinney, in despair, made his suggestion for separate conferences. Besides being discriminated against on the local congregational level, Kinney also foresaw that because of White prejudice Blacks would continue to be underevangelized and underrepresented in church ministry and leadership. When Ellen White visited the St. Louis congregation a year later, the racism there so saddened and shocked her that God gave her a vision to correct the situation.

The start of the twentieth century promised more of the same upheavals characterizing the 1800s until a satisfying solution to the unequal status and ill-treatment of African Americans could be found, both in the nation and the Adventist Church. Lewis Sheafe, the most influential and successful Black minister in the denomination in the early 1900s, was outspoken in his calls for racially integrated congregations. While his highly effective evangelistic methods in Washington, D.C., resulted in several new interracial churches, church administrators viewed them as problematic. Ideological clashes led to a declaration of independence by one of Sheafe's Washington, D.C., churches in 1907, and that same year for all intents and purposes Sheafe himself left the denomination. Still, plans began to develop for ways to address the persistent and stubborn question of the "color line." The Negro Department was church leadership's answer. In order to meet the needs of a growing Black constituency as well as facilitate mission among African Americans, the General Conference established it in 1909. Incidentally, it was the same year that volume 9 of Ellen G. White's *Testimonies* appeared with its controversial section "Among the Colored People."

The Negro Department was ultimately unable to fulfill its purpose, especially as Black membership increased and racial dynamics grew more complex. Charismatic Black minister James Humphrey brought the unresolved issues to the fore. Like Sheafe, Humphrey was among the denomination's most successful evangelists, baptizing hundreds in New York City in the 1910s and 1920s and establishing several churches. In the late 1920s Humphrey devised the Utopia Park Benevolent Association, a retreat facility where Blacks could learn the Adventist message and adopt more healthful lifestyle practices. His ideas clashed with church leadership, however, and ultimately the denomination disfellowshipped Humphrey and his congregation.

The final straw, as it were, was the Lucy Byard incident. Byard was a light-skinned Adventist senior citizen from New York City who in 1943 sought treatment for severe pneumonia at the Washington Adventist Sanitarium in Takoma Park, Maryland. Initially admitted by the White staff, the hospital discharged her when it discovered that she was African American. Her husband and friends rushed her to the Freedmen's Hospital (now

Howard University Hospital) across town, but Byard died a few days later.

The reaction from Black Adventists was one of unbelief, outrage, and then action. A group of mostly laypeople formed "The Committee for the Advancement of World-Wide Work Among Colored Seventh-day Adventists," in April 1944, distributing a document titled "Shall the Four Freedoms Function Among Seventh-day Adventists?" It outlined the discrimination and outright racism against Blacks practiced in the church and made specific recommendations for redressing them in the educational, medical, administrative, supervisory, occupational, and spiritual realms of the denomination.

This grassroots movement and other similar constituencies did much to spur Adventist leadership to address racial inequity in the church. Among other things, the 1944 Spring Council of the General Conference, after extended discussion, voted to establish regional, or Black, conferences. In 1945 the church inaugurated three conferences: Allegheny (divided into Allegheny East and Allegheny West in 1967), Lake Region, and Northeastern. The next year it organized South Atlantic (divided into South Atlantic and Southeastern in 1981) and South Central, and in 1947 introduced Central States and Southwest Region.

Charles Brooks was converted and called to the ministry the year that the final regional conferences were organized. Addison Pinkney, cochairman of "The Committee for the Advancement of World-Wide Work Among Colored Seventh-day Adventists," conducted the baptisms in Brooks's first campaign in Chester, Pennsylvania. Frank Peterson, an influential voice in favor of Black conferences at the 1944 Spring Meeting, was Charles's college president at Oakwood, and one with whom he would have a close relationship. John Wagner, Brooks's father-in-law, was the first president of Allegheny Conference. Finally the minister with whom Charles would first intern, J. G. Dasent, was the initial president of Lake Region Conference. Providentially, Charles Brooks accepted his call to the ministry at just the time when new administrative structures could enable and facilitate him in leading thousands to Christ. Ultimately, he would be one of the main individuals responsible for the success of regional conferences.

Getting There
Charles Brooks and his five friends from Greensboro started out on the train to Huntsville, electrified about the future, knowing that God's plans for them were bound to brim with adventure and fulfillment. At a stop in

Atlanta a bevy of Oakwood students joined them, at Asheville more, and at Chattanooga, still more. In those days railroad regulations confined Blacks to the front of the train in hard high-backed chairs. Their coaches lacked air conditioning so that fine dust and soot particles blew in through the open windows. When the train finally arrived in Huntsville at midnight, the young people were exhausted.

The tiny train station was long closed, the ticket booths unstaffed. Charles and his new friends almost despaired as they left the train and stepped into darkness. But then, like on the first day of Creation, lights flashed on from the dark. Cars and trucks belonging to Oakwood staff roared to life as kindhearted individuals came forward to assist with the baggage. Greeting the new faces, then hefting their luggage into the vehicles, Charles and the others crowded into the vehicles. The nighttime ride to the fabled campus where they had been told angels resided enchanted the young people.

The campus was long asleep by the time the caravan arrived. The unbending rule was lights off at 10:00. After checking in at Henderson Hall, staff members directed Charles and the other men to Moran Hall, where they would temporarily bunk barracks-style in the auditorium. The men ended up staying there for three months. Charles occupied a bunk under a window with the heating system and water pipes directly above it. Hanging his only suit on the ledge of the windowsill, he put his trunk at the head of the bed. He was now an Oakwoodite.

Work

Upon registering for a full load of classes, Charles realized that the money his father gave him would not last long. He was not a World War II veteran either, so GI severance pay was not available for him. The only option was to finance his education by the sweat of his brow. And so he applied for one of the only jobs on campus available at the time: dairy worker.

On his first day of classes Charles reported to the dairy at 3:00 a.m. and began his task of caring for Oakwood's Holstein cows. His duties included feeding and bathing the cattle; regularly deworming and delousing them; keeping their living areas clean and intact; overseeing grazing; facilitating births; and of course milking. Charles worked from 3:00 a.m. to 6:00 a.m. and 3:00 p.m. to 7:00 p.m. every day, even on Sabbaths, for the cows had to eat and be cared for on the rest day also. Deciding that Sabbath work should be nonremunerative, Charles donated his earnings to one of Eva B.

Dykes' charities that fed the hungry. The young man earned 32 cents an hour.

When finished at the dairy, he would eagerly head for the classroom, one of a cadre of promising theology majors in the class of 1951. Oakwood's professors of theology in those days were pillars of Adventism, names that still conjure awe: C. E. Moseley, C. T. Richards, O. B. Edwards, and E. E. Rogers. Each class period would impress their students that they had accepted one of the highest of all callings.

After months of a grueling work schedule and deeply spiritual experiences in his theology courses, one morning long before the sun rose Charles knelt by the side of his bunk and prayed, "Lord, You called me, and here I am. Thank You ever so greatly for bringing me to Oakwood. But please don't let me go through all of this with no substance to preach, just namby-pamby Pollyanna sermons. If You want me to preach, give me something worth saying." Later that day E. E. Rogers taught the prophecy of Daniel 2 with such detail and historical accuracy that Charles thought his head would burst. His prayer had been answered—he would preach prophecy and doctrine.

Changed

Going to Oakwood inevitably changes a person, and Charles was no exception. That first Christmas he returned to Greensboro the "Center" in the Black section of town had a teen night. On a Thursday night all the people would gather for music, dancing, and what they considered harmless socializing. Charles decided to go, because he wanted to see his old friends. His ever-generous brother Rock gave him the keys to his car, and Charles dressed up in his best shirt and dungarees, splashed on some cologne, and was off to the gathering.

When the Oakwoodite stepped into the Center, he encountered hundreds of young people dancing on the expansive floor, festive red, blue, and green lights casting a dimly surreal light. When the number ended and the bright overhead lights flashed on, friends mobbed him. He was of course glad to see them, but he felt a little strange and out of place. It just wasn't the same—no, *he* just wasn't the same. When the music started again, his old acquaintances drifted back onto the dance floor. That's when Charles decided to slip out. The woman in charge of the event spotted him leaving, and, being a friend with his sisters, gently grabbed Charles's arm, begging him not to go. Making up some excuse, he managed to pry himself from the woman's grasp and escape into the night.

As he approached his car he could make out a figure sprawled across the front seat, which back then was a bench seat as opposed to the bucket seats more common today. Opening the door, he saw it was a young man his own age. Charles attempted to rouse him but couldn't. The individual was groggy and, Charles deduced, inebriated. So he slid the sleeping man out of the car and to the entrance of the Center, propped his head upright against the glass, and left. Driving through the night, scenes from the party raced through his mind. Ending up in his high school parking lot, he spent two hours talking to the Lord. He was a different person, a changed man, and he'd never be the same again.

As often happens, Charles's old friends didn't change along with him. One night back at Oakwood during a Week of Prayer given by Walter Starks, Charles received a telegram from the campus bulletin board service. The telegram indicated that Leonard "Max" Broadnax, one of Charles's closest buddies from high school, and an accomplice who was also Black and young, had been charged with murdering a White man. Stunned, after the shock wore off, Charles gathered 20 fellow students from the dormitory and told them of the case. Together the group ascended Oakwood Mountain and prayed for Max in the moonlight. A short time later Charles received word that his old friend had confessed to the murder.

The trial took place months later when Charles was back home in North Carolina for the summer. From his seat in the balcony in the cramped Southern courtroom, Brooks heard the judge advise the all-White jury of their two options right at the outset: since Max had admitted to the murder, they could render a "guilty" verdict, which meant instant death, or a "guilty with recommendation for mercy" verdict that included some leniency.

Charles searched the faces of the jurors for any kind of indication as to which way the verdict would sway. Finding nothing, he scanned the courtroom and settled his gaze on a White woman and a Black woman, side by side, comforting each other. He recognized them—the White woman was the mother of the slain man, and the Black woman the mother of Max, the killer. The image of the two women riveted in his memory, never to be forgotten.

On the day that all the evidence had been presented, the judge again advised the jury: "I want you to forget the color of their skin," he said, referring to Max and the other young man. "Remember they are 18 years old and have their whole lives ahead of them. I urge you to consider their potential." Then the judge dismissed the court for a recess while the jury deliberated.

Sensing that his prayers had been answered, Charles was filled with hope as he exited the courtroom with the others. However, although he and his Oakwood friends had been fasting for the past few days, he still had some trepidation, as his old friend's life hung in the balance. Fidgety, Charles lingered near the door of the courtroom, waiting for the jury to return.

"The jury's back! The jury's back!" a voice boomed from the corridor.

Entering the courtroom, Charles sprinted up the stairs to the balcony. Without any fanfare the judge called for the verdict, and the jury foreman stood up and stated, "Your Honor, we have reached a decision. We, the members of the jury, find the defendants guilty." Then after a pause that seemed to last an eternity, he added, "But we are going to ask for mercy."

The Oakwoodite

Oakwood changed the student, but the students were what made Oakwood the school. Because of their Christian conduct, the community surrounding the school greatly respected the small Black college. When he returned for the fall semester, Charles's sister had given him a $3 check to help with expenses. On that first Friday back he thumbed a ride to town to cash it at the bank the students patronized. Taking longer than expected and sensing the coming Sabbath on the horizon as only a Seventh-day Adventist can, Charles thanked his ride, then dashed into the bank, only to be stopped at the door by a line that was a couple people short of overflowing onto the sidewalk. Between him and the teller were dozens of people, and knowing he couldn't wait, he turned to go.

"Young man, come here!" a voice called.

Charles wheeled around to see an older White man beckoning to him.

"Yes, sir?" Charles answered, the word "Oakwood" emblazoned on his shirt.

"Son, you can get in front of me. The sun is going to set in a few minutes."

Surprised, he accepted the man's offer and cashed his check promptly. Oakwood had a sterling reputation in the community, and strangers even knew the particulars of their faith from the witness of the staff and students!

Another time Charles was ingathering for the college church in a small town in Alabama that resembled the set from a Wild West movie. Charles approached one building, peering through the windows. Inside, three servers in blue-and-white-striped uniforms were lounging, and a bear of a man sat at the bar reading a newspaper. As Charles opened the door and entered, the big fellow looked up from his paper and scowled.

" 'Round back," he commanded.

"I didn't come here for your service," Charles replied with just as much authority. "I came to talk to you."

Glowering, the man went back to his paper while the Oakwoodite proceeded to give him his canvas. When he finished, to Brooks's surprise the man pulled out $3, handed it to him, and said, "I'm always willing to help."

***

As the students dispersed to their homes in all parts of the nation for semester breaks, so the reputation of Oakwood spread with them. One summer Charles searched and searched but couldn't find a job, so he and a friend went to the employment office in Greensboro. Two ditch-digging openings at Christopher and Dixon Plumbing were available, so the friends signed on. No sooner had they arrived at the work site than they were put to work with a pick and shovel. As the two washed their hands in the restroom after a hard day of work on a Friday, a fellow worker sidled up to Charles and asked him if he was coming in tomorrow, because it would be overtime pay.

"I understand, but I won't be in, because I'm a Sabbathkeeper," the young theology student replied, launching into a Bible study.

The toughened construction worker was unreceptive to Charles's mini-sermon, and proceeded to mock him. All of a sudden a toilet flushed and out of the stall emerged the owner of the company, Mr. Christopher. He walked to the sink, stood between Charles and his antagonist, then looked Charles straight in the eye.

"Who are you, young man, and what do you do?"

"I'm Charles Brooks, sir. I am studying for the ministry at Oakwood College in Alabama."

"Why don't I call you preacher?" Mr. Christopher offered.
"Sure."

"Can you work on Sunday, son? I can pay you double time."

"Yes, I can," Charles said, amazed at the turn of events.

"Good. I'll pick you up at 9:00 Sunday morning."

Sure enough, on Sunday a little before 9:00 Mr. Christopher pulled up to the Brooks home. Charles hurried out to the truck, and the two were off to the site, today an emergency hospital for polio patients. When they arrived, 20 or so men in work clothes milled about, talking, sipping from cups, and kicking at the dirt absentmindedly. The owner gave Charles a brief tour of the site, detailing what he wanted done.

"Son, you are to hire five men, and if they don't work, fire them!"

Charles did a double take at the owner, but then quickly regained his composure and nodded. "Yes, sir."

"I've got a golf game. You're in charge. I'll be back at 6:00." And with that he left.

The following Monday Charles and his friend lined up at the door of the company as usual for work. The day before had gone well for Charles— he had completed the job before the owner arrived from his golf game. That morning a fleet of 10 trucks pulled into the employment lot like an army convoy, and Mr. Christopher hopped out of the lead truck, quickly scanned the lined-up workers, and called names out, directing each man where to go. Charles's buddy was assigned to a mud truck, but Charles's name was not called. As the trucks began pulling out one by one, kicking up dust and gravel, he wondered if there had been some sort of mistake.

But then, as if in response to his unasked question, Mr. Christopher drove up next to Charles and called out the window, "Preacher, hop in."

The two rode to the Army base, were admitted upon Christopher's flashing of a badge, and proceeded to the cafeteria. Inside, there was a mountain of fittings obviously in need of repair. The owner marched around the pile for several moments, apparently calculating the time of the task, then turned to Charles. "Son, the Army is closing this camp soon. These fittings here require repairing, and I need a trustworthy person to do it. I'll send someone to check on you once a day, but basically you are on your own."

Off to a fast start that first morning, Charles noticed two things by lunchtime: one, he had made only a small dent in the big mountain of parts. Second, he was all alone. Days into the project, the Oakwood student worked up the nerve to ask his boss if he would consider hiring another man.

"Is he like you?" Mr. Christopher inquired.

"Yes," Charles piped up, "he's a member of my church."

"Then bring him in tomorrow!"

The next day in the lineup of worker prospects, Ernest Gray stood by

Charles's side. Mr. Christopher hired him on the spot, and the two worked in tandem on the cafeteria job. In fact, Ernest worked with that plumbing business for the next decade.

A couple years later when Charles graduated from Oakwood, the first thing he did was buy his mother an electric stove, paying it off at $10 a month. Although Mattie Brooks had mastered the art of cooking with the woodstove, she was delighted with her new electric one. Next Charles went to see Mr. Christopher about installing a new bathroom and plumbing in the family house. When the recent college graduate arrived at the offices of Christopher and Dixon Plumbing and informed the receptionist that he wished to see the owner, she asked if Mr. Christopher was expecting him. Before Charles could explain the reason for his visit a loud voice came thundering from the large office behind the receptionist's desk: "Preacher, is that you? Come back here, and let's talk."

Mr. Christopher and Brooks talked a good long while about their lives, and finally Brooks got around to telling him the reason for his visit. Although Christopher and Dixon was an industrial plumbing company, the owner agreed to take on Charles's project, promising to have someone out to his house the first thing Monday. Then Brooks asked how he wanted him to pay for it.

"Any way you want—but with no interest," came the big man's reply.

On Monday, good to his word, one of Christopher's lead plumbers knocked on the door of the Brookses' home. Charles directed the man to the bathroom, and by sunset Marvin and Mattie Brooks had a new bathroom with hot and cold running water.

***

Another of Charles Brooks's summer jobs was with an outfit called Swift and Company, an international meat packer and marketer. Every day the factory killed, prepared, and packaged 23,000 chickens and 19,000 turkeys. Charles was fortunate to have one of the better jobs located in the cooling room where the temperature was kept chilled. Next to where he worked, in the dust and heat, was the slaughtering area. On the other side was a massive room where hundreds of women removed the entrails of the unfortunate chickens and turkeys. Charles and his fellow workers had the comparatively pleasant task of packing the cleaned-up birds in ice.

All the workers officially finished at 5:30 p.m., but no one could leave until all traces of the meat were stowed away. During Monday, Tuesday, and Wednesday of his first week, Charles grew increasingly aware that he and the workers were not getting off until well after sunset. Friday loomed before him. On Thursday he asked his boss if he could leave early on Friday. The answer was a definitive no—the company would make no special accommodations for anyone. He had to work like everyone else. When Charles approached the manager of the entire operation, the answer was the same: no.

And so Friday afternoon Charles decided to sneak out of the back door of the factory. But as he worked packing the chickens in ice, he concluded that to do so would not be a good witness. An hour before sunset the Oakwoodite was Mr. Outgoing, waving here to coworkers, stopping there to wish him and her a good weekend, smiling at this person and that person. After he had said goodbye to just about everyone, he exited through the front door, his conscience unburdened.

The following Monday Charles walked into work expecting to be fired. But when the boss came in he never said a word. In fact, in September, when Charles informed his boss that it was time for him to go back to college, he replied, "Young man, if you want to work here next summer, just come on back!"

In magisterial language Charles would sum up both Oakwood's influence on the young people who came to the school from far and near, and their impact on the world once they departed, in an article he wrote in the *North American Informant* of July 1951:

"Presently Oakwood boasts a mighty posterity. Her illustrious sons and daughters have gone forth from these portals, and under God have shaken this evil world with the gospel truth. They have made enviable records in all phases of human activity.

"The name of this haven of Christian learning is a memorial in the hearts of her children and friends, whoever determines that Oakwood shall grow only in that purpose for which she was founded, and that she shall continue to be a sweeping finger of light in this shadowy age, pointing the hearts and souls of Negro youth to the stars."

Legends

Charles was blessed to attend Oakwood while legends graced its grounds. One of the most memorable and with whom he had the most contact was Eva B. Dykes. Dykes was born in Washington, D.C., in 1893, and graduated from Howard University summa cum laude with a B.A. in English in 1914. Already a rarity for a Black woman to have a college degree in that era, Dykes went on to attend Radcliffe College (the woman's Harvard) and earn another B.A. in 1917, this time magna cum laude, as well as an M.A. degree the next year. Dykes made history in 1921 when she received a Ph.D. degree from Radcliffe in English, Latin, German, and Greek language studies, becoming the first African American woman to complete the requirements for a doctoral degree in the United States.

Always one to give back, Dykes continued teaching at her high school alma mater, Dunbar High School—she had begun while a Ph.D. student in 1920—until 1929. Next Dykes taught English at her college alma mater, Howard University, for a decade and a half, until joining the staff at Oakwood College as the chair of the English Department in 1944. She was immediately a tremendous asset to the institution, greatly helping it to receive accreditation because of her academic stature, and founding the world-renowned choir Aeolians in 1946, the year Charles Brooks arrived as a freshman.

When the great Mordecai Johnson, the first Black president of Howard University, came to Oakwood to speak, Charles was the student assigned to give him a tour of the campus. Johnson started his speech by paying tribute to Eva Dykes. After praising her as being a first-rate scholar and a superb educator, Johnson related how certain faculty members at one point began to complain a bit that Dykes was giving too much attention to her religion. (She later told Charles that she witnessed a lot, gave Bible studies, and was a leader of an Ingathering band, playing the foot organ while her charges did the soliciting. Apparently it would embarrass some of her peers.) "I told them, you leave Eva Dykes alone," Johnson declared. "Anytime a teacher is that loyal to her God she will be loyal to Howard University."

Later when Mordecai Johnson addressed the students and staff of the Seventh-day Adventist Theological Seminary at Sligo church in Takoma Park, Maryland, he told of Dykes' hiring at Howard:

"I feel especially near to you in this church, too, because one of the finest teachers I have ever known came from your church. Her name is Eva B. Dykes. When I first came to Howard University, her name was brought to my attention in a peculiar way. She had received her doctor's degree some time earlier from Radcliffe, and we were about to engage her as a teacher.

"Prior to taking the job, she had a conference with the dean, saying, 'Before you conclude this contract there is one thing you should know about me. I do not know if after you hear this you will wish to employ me or not, but I feel I must tell you I am a member of the Seventh-day Adventist Church, and beginning at sundown on Friday until sundown Saturday I will be unable to do any work for the university, for in that period my church is foremost in my allegiance, and I shall feel under obligation to do whatever they wish me to do and will be able to give no service to the university.'

"The dean brought her letter to me and said, 'Mr. President, this is a very sad matter. I suppose this finishes it. We cannot employ this young woman. What a tragedy!'

" 'But,' I said to the dean, 'this does settle it. This makes certain we are going to employ this young woman.'

" 'What do you mean, Mr. President? We cannot hire someone who has reservations about service.'

"I replied, 'This is not a reservation but an affirmation. And I would further suggest that any woman who has the center of her life so dedicated is worth keeping, and we should not run the risk of losing a young person of that type. She will be just as loyal to the university the other six days as she is to her church on the Sabbath.' "

Charles had admired Dykes from the start, for she was already a luminary on campus and among Adventists, even though she was only in her early 50s. With a minor in English, Charles had the privilege of taking several classes from the gifted academician, and he noted firsthand her dignified bearing and Christian graciousness, qualities that he incorporated into his own character. During his final year at Oakwood the kindness of Eva Dykes saved him considerable time and money.

Set to graduate in the spring, Charles learned from the registrar that he had to take an American Literature class to fulfill the requirements for his minor in English. However, she added in the same breath, the class was already over the limit, so he would have to enroll in the fall semester. After attempting to persuade the woman into letting him into the class with no success, Charles considered the havoc another semester—a fifth year—would wreak on his nonexistent finances. It would be another semester of waking up at 3:00 in the morning, endlessly milking cows, all to pay the bills.

"Mr. Brooks, Mr. Brooks," Charles was interrupted from his thoughts by a pleasant voice. "Come with me."

It was Dykes, and she was beckoning him to follow her.

Once in her office, she informed him that he was to come to it at 10:30 a.m. on class days and she would give him the course one on one. She never mentioned payment. And so every day at the appointed time it was just the two of them, reviewing literature and even singing the great American folk songs together. Because of her special tutoring, Charles grew to admire his English professor more than anyone he had ever met. The bond was so strong that after he graduated he would visit Dykes at her residence on campus. One year, by then a conference evangelist, he went to her office in the English Department, but she was nowhere to be found. He asked a student where he could find Eva Dykes, to which the young woman replied, "Who is Eva Dykes?"

Instantly angered, Brooks said, "What did you say? Look at that building over there to my left." He motioned to the library. "What's the name of it?"

She was truly confused now.

Brooks walked purposefully to the administration building. He relayed his recent encounter to an administrator. When Charles was finished, the individual explained that Dykes now suffered from senility and couldn't even talk anymore.

"A question such as 'Who is Eva Dykes?' should never even form in the mind of a student, even after the doctor is gone," Brooks responded. "She doesn't have to talk—you talk! Bring her out onstage at freshman orientation. Give her a throne! Present her with a dozen roses, and then you talk!"

To Brooks's knowledge such a thing never happened, and Eva Dykes died in 1986 at the age of 93.

***

The first person Charles Brooks heard about when he joined the Seventh-day Adventist Church was Anna Knight. Born in 1874 in southern Mississippi to a Black woman who was formerly a slave and her White master, Knight early developed an iron will and steel resolve that would characterize her almost 100 years. Teaching herself to read, Knight learned of the Seventh-day Adventist message through literature she obtained by mail, and was baptized just shy of her twentieth birthday. After receiving death threats from the Ku Klux Klan, she was known to carry a pistol with her when walking to worship in the forest on Sabbath. Fortunately, she never had to use it.

In her early 20s Anna Knight studied nursing under the tutelage of John Harvey Kellogg at Battle Creek College. The illustrious physician was so impressed with the young Southerner that he arranged for her to be a representative at the General Conference session of 1901 held in Battle

Creek. Moved by the call from church leaders to go to the mission field during the historic session, Knight made the necessary arrangements to serve as a medical missionary in Calcutta, India, and left for the country a couple months later. In so doing she became the second Black sent by the church on foreign missions, the first Black Adventist woman, and the first Black to do missionary work in India.

The 27-year-old Knight did the job of 10 men while in India, teaching, healing, and spearheading the establishment of a hospital, medical school, church, and publishing house all in just six years. Planning to return to India after a brief furlough in the States, Knight changed her mind after observing the condition of Blacks in her native Mississippi, where the substandard conditions rivaled those in India. Deciding to stay in America, she founded a school and gained minor fame as a lecturer on education. Throughout her productive career she held numerous positions in which she did much to improve the standards of Adventist education and education for Blacks in the South. Knight retired to Oakwood in 1947.

For a time after he was baptized, Charles Brooks believed the elderly Anna Knight to be Ellen White. Because of her very light complexion he also mistakenly thought she was Caucasian. At Oakwood he developed tremendous respect for her—as did all of the students—and sat at the edge of his seat every time she spoke on her life in chapel and other public meetings. His first personal encounter with Knight occurred when he passed her working in her garden on his way to class.

"Good afternoon, ma'am," Charles greeted.

"Come here, boy," Knight said, motioning with her hand. He obeyed.

"Pull up that weed and throw it in the bag." Charles did so.

At his wedding Anna Knight gifted the Brookses with a copy of her autobiography *Mississippi Girl* and a $20 bill.

***

Frank Loris Peterson was the president of Oakwood College when Charles arrived in 1947. Born in Pensacola, Florida, in 1893, he was a Methodist until age 14 when he heard the preaching of legendary evangelist J. H. Laurence, who baptized him shortly afterward. Peterson began studying for the ministry at Oakwood before transferring to Pacific Union College, where he finished in 1916, the school's first Black graduate.

A year later he accepted a teaching position at Oakwood, becoming the first full-time Black on the college faculty. In 1919 he became the first chair of the college's new Music Department. While at Oakwood Peterson married Bessie Jean Elston, and the couple had two sons and three daughters. In 1926 the family moved north to Nashville, Tennessee, where Frank Peterson held three posts simultaneously at the Southern Union Conference.

In 1930 Peterson accepted the position of secretary of the North American Negro Department at the General Conference of Seventh-day Adventists. His book *The Hope of the Race,* virtually a classic soon after its publication, came out in 1936. Peterson became the first director of the office of Regional Affairs in the Pacific Union Conference in 1942, and held several pastorates and other responsibilities until elected the fourth president of Oakwood College in 1945.

Charles Brooks first encountered the president at an early-morning prayer meeting (6:30) on Sabbath morning. Later he would learn that Peterson arose the same time he did—3:00—each morning. Brooks quickly saw that the administrator's schedule was an indication of his character. Peterson was no-nonsense. If he witnessed students kissing he would send them home. When Charles was the editor of the yearbook Peterson would settle for nothing but excellence. Yet he was a fair man, one who mixed compassion with adherence to standards.

As a theology student Brooks admired the president most as a stellar preacher, one who enthralled crowds with majesty of language and rich spiritual insights. Students on campus would quote Peterson's sermons years afterward. They were must-attend events.

One day Charles and a group of Oakwood students were sitting in the barbershop, not so much getting their hair cut as socializing. President Peterson came in the shop and immediately became the focus of attention. They peppered him with questions. One young man asked, "Elder, how do you prepare a sermon?"

"Have an experience and tell it!" Peterson replied, without thinking about it even one second.

After Oakwood Frank Peterson went on to attain yet more firsts. In 1954 he was elected the first Black associate secretary of the General Conference, and the first Black vice president of the world church at the General Conference session in San Francisco in 1962. Although Peterson died in 1969 at 76 years of age, he would continue to live in the hearts and minds of men such as Brooks.

Charles had an opportunity to work closely with the great president as yearbook editor. But the partnership started off on difficult footing when Peterson announced that there would be no *Acorn* (Oakwood's yearbook) for 1951, the year Charles was to graduate. The 1951 class instituted the first-ever student union, with outstanding officers such as Harold Cleveland, Leonard Newton, Russell Bates, Minneola Dixon, and Lovey Davis.

So when the class heard about the president's pronouncement that there would be no yearbook for 1951, they immediately went into action. All the student officers assembled to devise a plan. Brooks was present as the yearbook editor, and his future wife was secretary of the student movement. They decided to request a meeting with the president to air their feelings and hopefully produce a yearbook.

Peterson agreed to meet with them. At the meeting they calmly and reasonably presented their case, knowing that the president would respect such an approach. After they finished, Peterson explained that the previous year the annual had not been properly distributed. People were still getting their copies a year later. The other issue was an outstanding debt of $800 on the 1950 *Acorn*. "There will be no yearbook this year," he stated with finality.

But Charles and his peers kept insisting, tactfully and carefully pressing their point. Finally Peterson relented. "All right, you can have a yearbook if you meet certain criteria. First, you have to get it published before school closes and distributed to all the students before summer break. Number two, you have to assume that $800 debt from last year."

The second contingency was more than a notion. Eight hundred dollars was a lot of money in those days. But the class of 1951 was nothing if not confident achievers. They set up an office and created a voluntary staff. Ruth Margery, who could get a superhuman amount of things done, was on board. Professor Gaines Partridge assisted with artistic consultation.

As yearbook editor Charles probably put the most time into the project. He worked endless hours, made contacts, took trips. Searching high and low for the best price, he discovered a little print shop that quoted a bargain price in a tiny country town 35 miles from the school. Always ambitious, Charles told the proprietor that they wanted a good price for a full-color yearbook. He realized that it would be double the price of black and white. He also knew that it would be the first four-color yearbook at Oakwood.

The 1951 yearbook was a daunting project, but Charles and his staff managed to meet Peterson's criteria: finishing and distributing it on time, and paying off the debt from the previous year. They did the latter with numerous clever fund-raising schemes. The end product was an attractive volume that set a precedent: the *Acorn* would be in full color from that year on.

***

Russell W. Bates couldn't believe he was at Oakwood studying for theology. He had barely survived the whizzing bullets and exploding grenades of World War II half a world away from serene Alabama. Shortly after that gruesome global struggle Bates had found Jesus in the form of the Adventist message. He had been on a search for truth his entire life, and it didn't take any prodding for him to embrace it and be baptized once he heard it. And now at Oakwood it was as if he were in a second Eden.

One day after Charles stepped into the barracks that served as a dorm for the men he happened upon several of them enjoying a lively conversation. One of them was of medium height and brown skin tone, immediately distinguished by his bonhomie and goodwill. It was clear that he was an individual of maturity and deep spirituality. Russell Bates and Charles Brooks immediately hit it off, becoming fast friends.

The two theology majors were roommates for their remaining years at Oakwood. Throughout that time Bates had a profound effect on Brooks, the former soldier molding and maturing this preacher in the making. Charles found Russell to be an exemplar of spirituality, dependability, integrity, and hard work. The two would maintain a lifelong friendship, later working at the church's headquarters together.

But Bates will be forever indebted to Brooks for one particular reason. On a breezy spring day on campus Charles introduced Russell to a lovely and elegant young woman named Marian. Russell married Marian, and has been in love with her for more than six decades.

***

A final vital figure in Charles Brooks's years at Oakwood College was C. E. Moseley. Calvin Edwin Moseley, Jr., was born in 1906 in Demopolis, Alabama, to Calvin, Sr., and Littlelie Belle Moseley, working-class Baptists who early instilled in their son the importance of hard work and integrity. Moseley enrolled in Tuskegee at age 15, majoring in electrical engineering but with plans to ultimately study law at Howard University. It was at the historic Black school founded by Booker T. Washington that Moseley converted to Christianity through the Bible teaching of renowned scientist George Washington Carver. A year later Moseley was baptized into the Seventh-day Adventist Church after attending a tent meeting in Jackson, Mississippi, conducted by J. H. Laurence and F. S. Kitts. The teenager decided to become a preacher when he had a vision of the second coming of Jesus while doing construction atop a scaffold.

Moseley matriculated at Oakwood Junior College in 1925 after Anna Knight urged him to attend the school in his home state. Graduating two years later, he earned an additional bachelor's degree from Emmanuel Missionary College (now Andrews University) in history and religion. He would later obtain his master's degree from the Seventh-day Adventist Theological Seminary at Andrews. Entering the pastoral ministry the year Charles Brooks was born, Moseley married Harriet Frances Slater three years later in Chicago in 1933.

C. E. Moseley was invited to Oakwood in 1934 and became the first Black chair of the Theology and Religion Department and the first Black pastor of the college church. He taught at Oakwood for 17 years, during that time preparing 98 percent of Black Adventist pastors for the ministry. In 1954 the Oakwood College board invited Moseley to serve as president, but he declined. The C. E. Moseley Complex, the building housing the Theology and Religion Department at Oakwood, was named in his honor in 1978.

Charles Brooks took numerous courses from Moseley throughout his four years at Oakwood, soaking up all he could from the gifted professor. Brooks realized in the first class he took with him that Moseley deeply and genuinely believed what he taught, never expressing a hint of doubt or skepticism. He was tough on Brooks, however, rebuking him for participating in drama and warning him and his classmates not to get too involved with the young women until they were upperclassmen and ready to think seriously about marriage. But as with Peterson, Brooks was most moved by Moseley in the realm of preaching, which was fitting, for Moseley was dubbed "The Father of Preachers." To his students he was known affectionately as "The Rabbi."

While a freshman, Brooks witnessed an episode he would never forget as long as he lived, and one he used as the litmus test for powerful, Spirit-filled preaching. It was on a Sabbath, and Moseley was delivering the sermon at the college church. He was in the middle of his sermon when a man arose from the congregation, tears streaming down his face, and walked to the pulpit, where he stood with his head bowed. Moseley had not yet made any appeal. But three more people soon joined the man up front. Then the pews began emptying as more than 40 individuals crowded up front. Moseley kept on preaching as if the group standing in front were totally normal. Marveling in his heart, Brooks knew that this was the effect that he desired his sermons to have. It was the ultimate signature of the Holy Spirit on one's ministry.

Four years later Moseley helped Charles Brooks get hired to his first pastorate when he told the conference president that the young man would be a "safe bet."

The Bell Tower

One of Oakwood's greatest monuments from students to a teacher was occasioned by the departure of C. E. Moseley in 1951 after his 17 years of service at the school. In the early spring of that year Brooks and 34 fellow ministerial students huddled together upon hearing of the teacher's acceptance of the call to the General Conference with one main concern: "What can we do to honor 'The Rabbi' after all he has done for us?"

A talent of Brooks was that of design, one he had honed in an art class taken from Turner Battle. Seeing that the antique bell in the center of campus—once summoning oppressed slaves to the cotton fields in a bygone era, more recently calling Christian students to worship—now lay abandoned in shrubbery after the heavy object had crashed to the ground, Brooks had taken it upon himself to draw up three designs for its rescue. He had forgotten about them, but now it was those sketches that came to the group's collective mind as a way to honor their beloved mentor. They would choose the best of the three and erect a bell tower in Moseley's honor.

And so Brooks and his fellow theologs got to work. Ascending Oakwood Mountain in a farm wagon literally horse-powered by two gray geldings and a World War II vintage jeep, the young men carefully selected several boulders cut long ago from the outcrops atop the plateau-peak. Their teamwork brought seven trips' worth of stones heaved in and out of the wagon bed during a week's time. As a result they created a miniature Stonehenge in the middle of the Oakwood campus. As his students labored, C. E. Moseley often silently observed them from his classroom window in Moran Hall, no doubt wondering what they were up to, once even gently scolding them for "consuming too much time on whatever you are doing."

But Charles and his classmates worked feverishly on the project. Hiring professional contractors to guide the undertaking, the plan was to lay a foundation identical to Moran Hall's, at that time the administration building overlooking the campus center marked by a tall flagpole. Converting Charles's designs to blueprints, they took measurements, removed grass and rocks, and prepared a subbase. They cut and shaped stones. At the completion of each phase of the still-secret project, staff and students alike marveled at the progress.

Finally, on a Friday morning everything was in place to lay the foundation—and just in time, because the students were at their wits' end to finish the task. But the head foreman stated matter-of-factly, "Fellows, you won't have time to finish this today. Cement must have a certain consistency in order to be molded. This is a Friday job. Your Sabbath is coming. You won't have time to wait on the cement. Just plow the joints, and it will look fine considering the distance between the two structures."

The joints—spots where the concreting process halted and then resumed later—could make for a flawed gift to Elder Moseley. Nevertheless, determined to finish before sundown, the crew set to work, readying the base, arranging the forms, mixing the concrete, and finally pouring it. Once the concrete was laid, the contractors received their pay and departed.

The joints couldn't be plowed until the concrete reached a certain degree of hardness. To the Sabbathkeeping collegians, the concrete seemed to remain soft forever. But, unable to wait any longer, they began plowing the joints on the Cunningham Hall side, since the concrete was first laid there. As they worked desperately, part of the sun was obscured by the earth in the west, casting the landscape in a fiery orange hue. Sabbath was almost upon them!

Frustrated, they questioned: "Should we keep working?" "Is this analogous to the ox in the ditch?" "Isn't it lawful to do well on the Sabbath?" "Won't God understand?" The entire sky was a rich magenta now, long shadows reaching for the east. The Sabbath peace was in the air. Soon it would be time for vespers. Then other, stronger considerations arose in the brief but intense discussion. They were theology majors. Soon each would lead churches around the nation, preaching faithfulness to God. People would look to them for a spiritual example. To a man, they decided just to leave it as it was, certain that their efforts would be ruined by not finishing, but valuing faithfulness above that.

Yet when the sun arose the next morning—a friend now rather than a foe—the light revealed that there was not one flaw in the unplowed joints or the unfinished concrete. The foundation was as perfect as possible. To this day Charles Brooks and his surviving classmates believe that an angel finished the job.

On Sunday the theologians completed the bench that was to circle the bell. Then came the construction of the belfry. All the while still more students planted flowers around the area. Already canopied by the great oak trees from which the school had received its name, the scene was so romantic that lore has it that dozens of couples fell in love and proposed to each other on the fabled spot.

On the day of dedication President Peterson led faculty and staff to the new bell tower at the center of campus. The medical cadets stood at attention, uniforms starched and pressed. Excited students and visitors gathered around, craning their necks to watch the ceremony. Deeply and deliberately the bell began to toll—17 times in uninterrupted cadence, each toll representing a year of service rendered to Oakwood by "The Rabbi." Next they unveiled a plaque with an inscription of dedication to C. E. Moseley from the class of 1951. As he realized that the structure and the ceremony were for him, Moseley wept, overcome by the token of love and appreciation.

Brooks's small class of 1951 yielded an unusual number of individuals who went on to build up the Seventh-day Adventist Church much as they had the bell tower. Russell Bates became a fine preacher and leader at the General Conference. The class president and later Charles's brother-in-law, John Wagner, Jr., enjoyed a long career in ministry distinguished by church planting. Harold Cleveland, Leonard Newton, Alvin Goulbourne, A. N. Brogden, and Ralph Hairston all became regional conference presidents. Minneola Dixon and Lovey Davis Verdun became fixtures at Oakwood, giving decades of guidance to the school. Daniel Davis served the church in a number of capacities, but is most well remembered for his work among the youth. Others benefited humanity in their respective fields of medicine, law, business, and education. The bell tower still tolls six decades later, now not only a monument to the deceased C. E. Moseley, but to the heroes of God in training so long ago.

LOVE

"There is the girl I will marry."

The Rabbi had gravely admonished his ministerial underclassmen to wait until they were upperclassmen to start looking for a wife. Charles heeded his advice. However, he did put his first two years to good use for personal development and observation. While a sophomore (after resigning from his job at the dairy) he began attending the optional early-morning prayer meetings at 6:30 on Sabbath mornings. The first time he entered the auditorium he was surprised to find it jam-packed with students—girls on the right, guys on the left. The scene matched his daydreams of heaven, with mellifluous holy melodies filling the air and faces lighted up with godly joy. Silently he vowed to himself, "When the time comes to look for a wife, I shall look among these."

Divine serendipity had it that a very special young woman arrived the year Charles Brooks became an upperclassman—just at the time he was ready for and open to love. Her name was Walterene Wagner. Besides being beautiful, she was friendly, warm, dignified, and yet humble.

Charles was already fast friends with her brothers, John and Jesse, and had tremendous respect for her father, then president of Allegheny Conference. And he had been praying for a suitable helpmeet.

On a warm autumn day in 1950 while he was serving as an usher in the college church, he was walking through the lobby when he spotted Walterene with a wailing infant in her arms. The baby girl, a niece named Jaenette, was crying her little heart out, and a consternated Walterene was unsuccessfully trying to console her. Walking over to the pair with his arms extended, he said softly, "Let me try." She handed the struggling bundle to Charles, who, rocking the child gently, stepped out of the lobby and into the soft fall air. Before he had walked a dozen footsteps the child was fast asleep, nestled in his arms.

Returning to the lobby a short time later with the dozing Jaenette, Charles grinned at the pleasantly surprised aunt. The two decided to walk to John's campus apartment and put the baby to bed. Although two collegians of the opposite sex walking to an apartment for whatever reason was unusual in those days, Charles and Walterene were so trusted at Oakwood that their harmless stroll raised no suspicions. Arriving at John Wagner, Jr's apartment, he lowered Jaenette into her crib. Then Walterene thanked him in her gracious way, and he returned to the church.

God called Charles by name only twice in his life. The first was when He summoned him to the ministry while he sat under E. E. Cleveland's tent in Greensboro, North Carolina. The other was that fateful fall day as he walked back to the college church.

"Charles, that is the young lady you will marry."

The voice was so clear as to be unmistakable. Brooks gladly agreed with the Lord, and as he did a peace and comfort flooded his being. He walked the rest of the way with a spring in his step.

Meanwhile, Jaenette's mother arrived shortly to find her daughter fitfully resting, and, relieved of her duties, Walterene hurried to her dormitory room. Finding her roommate there, she confided excitedly, "I've just been with someone I think I want to spend my life with!"

Suffice it to say, Jaenette Wagner has always had a special place in the hearts of Charles and Walterene Brooks.

The Other Anniversary

If Jaenette Wagner is a person with a special place in the heart of the Brookses, February 3, 1951, is a special date for the couple. On that Sabbath day, unseasonably mild and sunny, Charles and "Rene" (by that time Walterene had become Charles's "Rene") were sitting in a classroom in Moran Hall where Moseley taught homiletics during the week. It was a usual routine of theirs: just enjoying each other's company by reading and discussing Bible passages on the hallowed hours of the holy day. But this time was to be extra-special.

His voice and manner serious, Charles declared his love for her, then explained that he was not just seeking a girlfriend but a life partner. At Oakwood a girlfriend could be for the most part just someone to spend time with, but as a senior ministerial student and editor of the yearbook, duty could be his girlfriend, and he had plenty of that to occupy his time. No, he wanted to be clear that he desired Rene to be his wife, a spiritual partner in the great ministry that God had for them. He commented gravely that many young women who were fond of ministerial aspirants did not savor the prospect of being a parson's wife, but that having made his intentions plain, the time had come for a decision. Charles wanted to be sure that they dreamed the same dream and prayed the same prayer.

A smile tugging at her lips, she waited patiently for him to finish his speech. When he was done speaking, she said, "Charles, my favorite person is my father, a minister. The person I admire most is my mother, a minister's wife. I have three uncles and a brother-in-law who are all ministers, and both of my brothers are studying theology here. I've always and only wanted to be a minister's wife!"

If Charles lived to be 1,000 he would never forget her words that day. He had never been so completely delighted in his life. Here was a woman who pleased him more than anyone else on earth. She was godly, kind, dignified, humble, friendly, encouraging, loyal, reasonable, beautiful— and she was his, and he was hers. They had committed themselves to each other totally on that Sabbath at Oakwood. More than 60 years later both still refer to February 3, 1951, as "our other anniversary."

Uniontown
Upon his graduation in late spring of 1951, the Allegheny Conference hired Charles Brooks. It would be putting it mildly to say that the trial of his life was to leave Rene behind at Oakwood. But Walterene Wagner had come to the South to complete her four-year degree, and complete it she would. Charles's only consolation was that during the summers she would be staying with her family on the campus of Pine Forge Academy, about five hours from where he would be stationed as an evangelist's intern in Uniontown, Pennsylvania. But ultimately, the young preacher would have to wait two whole years before they could unite as man and wife, and unlike Jacob's seven years of labor to win Rachel's hand in marriage, Charles was not on the same farm as his sweetheart. To top that, friends in the ministry warned Brooks that the evangelist he would be working under, one J. G. Dasent, was austere and rigid.

James Gershom Dasent was born to Christian parents on the island of Antigua on July 6, 1879. Educated in law under the British system, Dasent converted to Adventism in his early 20s and became a pioneer minister in the Caribbean, introducing the Adventist message on several islands and serving as the church's go-to man in the region. Among his many converts was his future wife, Christine Estelle Seley, with whom he had five children.

Soon called to the United States, Dasant pastored churches in New Orleans, Washington, D.C., Cleveland, Indianapolis, and Minneapolis. He distinguished himself as a spellbinding orator who specialized in sermons tracing prophecy. Elected president of Lake Region Conference in 1944, he simultaneously became the first Black to hold the presidency of any conference in the Seventh-day Adventist Church and the first person to be elected president of one of the newly formed regional conferences. By the time he arrived in Uniontown to hold an evangelistic campaign in mid-1951, J. G. Dasent had been an Adventist minister for almost 50 years.

While preparing to depart from Oakwood and head north, Charles Brooks had come to dread his first assignment, what with being separated from Rene and being under the rule of a curmudgeonly senior. But alas, Brooks had grown to believe strongly in divine providence, and he knew that the Lord was at the helm. So he made the trip to Pennsylvania a bit trepid, but still optimistic.

When the 21-year-old Charles Brooks arrived in Uniontown and finally met the 71-year-old J. G. Dasent for himself, the two became immediate friends. Dasent was in fact a paragon of thoughtfulness, kindness, and graciousness, the exact things that Charles feared he wouldn't be. His friends' horror stories had no basis in reality, and he could only smile with relief at the grace of God. As the two built up the kingdom of God month after month, they developed a father-son bond, Dasent giving Charles the benefits of his decades of wisdom, patiently instructing him in the science of evangelism. He even worked it out so that his intern could take several trips on the weekend to Pine Forge to see his girlfriend. Above all, though, Brooks became addicted to soul-winning in Uniontown, content with nothing less than leading individuals to the watery grave to arise born again in Christ.

After the success of the Uniontown campaign, Charles Brooks pastored a district that comprised small churches in Wilmington, Delaware, and nearby Chester, Pennsylvania. Before he left Uniontown for Chester, though, he saw Walterene off to Oakwood to start her junior year. It wasn't just a sentimental cliché when they promised they would write each other every day. After a final embrace, Walterene sank into the car headed south, and moments later it glided out of Charles's reach down the highway. When he stepped into the car that was to take him to Wilmington, Charles had no idea that he was embarking on the loneliest year of his life.

Wilmington

A tiny room with a window overlooking the first-floor roof of a leather factory was Charles's abode during his stint in Wilmington. Just mere years after the end of World War II, the city was experiencing its first mass exodus as thousands abandoned Wilmington proper to live in suburbs patterned after those not too far away in Levittown, New York. Most of the city's Blacks, poor and uneducated, were stuck in the inner core, cooped up in dilapidated row houses. Some three years before Rosa Parks's refusal to relinquish her seat on a Montgomery bus, African Americans lived under Jim Crow conditions in the East Coast city, in Charles's estimation a racial climate not unlike that of Alabama.

The church that he pastored in Wilmington was comprised of wonderful saints, but they were mostly elderly. They brought their young grandchildren to church, so there were essentially two age extremes in the congregation. That fact compounded Charles's loneliness. Not only was he separated from Rene, but he had no one his age with whom to fellowship. He also had no car, but that was not a problem, because most of his parishioners lived in one community. So he faithfully walked his rounds, visiting, encouraging, teaching, comforting, and praying.

Brooks's other church assignment was in Chester, Pennsylvania, a city on the southeastern Pennsylvania border, abutting New Jersey and situated on the Delaware River. As with hundreds of American cities, World War II generated explosive industrial job growth, causing Chester to experience a population surge, peaking at 65,000 residents during the period Brooks pastored there. The city's racial demographic then, as now, was primarily Black. Chester was located between Philadelphia, a significant city in African American history, and Wilmington, whose population was on its way to becoming predominately Black.

The Chester church had a layman as its de facto pastor and worshipped in a small rented auditorium. On the Sabbath afternoon that the just-out-of-school Brooks introduced himself to the congregation, his reception was one that an ice pick couldn't have chipped. The members perceived the untried whippersnapper as usurping the position of their beloved lay leader, and they wanted none of it. Charles sat quietly through it all, taking in the spectacle coolly. But even his cool façade was tested when the lay elder began speaking. The man started out in a woebegone tone about the old "fire horses" who were put out to pasture and replaced by the motorized engines and yet, at the sound of the alarm those old stallions were still straining at the gate. Then he related all the sacrifices he had made . . . the worn-out shoes and tattered suits. Next he said dolefully, "Now that you've got this boy here, you don't need me anymore!" By this time the men seemed ready to stone Charles, while the women wept aloud.

"Now the new pastor will speak," the persecuted and unappreciated elder intoned, retreating to the pew behind the pulpit in exaggerated defeat. Charles Brooks energetically sprung up with a wide grin on his face, informing the tiny congregation of less than 25 that his lifelong dream had finally come to pass. He was a pastor! He was so glad to be here! He had big plans! They would do such and such together! Finally Brooks turned to the pitiful elder, who had somehow shrunk even smaller, and announced, "Sir, if all I've heard about you today is true, then I need you! We must work together!" But despite Brooks's youthful enthusiasm, the congregation's response was tepid, and the new pastor made his way back to his lonely apartment a bit dejected.

The next Sabbath Charles hopped onto the bus at the stop near his apartment and watched from his seat's window as the industrial landscape droned by. Disembarking at Third Street, he walked uphill to Twelfth where the auditorium that was venue to his inglorious first Sabbath stood. Early for Sabbath School, he hoped that fact would be a plus in getting some kind of consideration from the members, but the atmosphere hadn't thawed at all. He was neither acknowledged nor welcomed, and sitting upright in his seat, he observed the congregation with as pleasant an expression as he could muster under the circumstances.

In the middle of a tiny elderly member's mission report the auditorium door burst open, and a broad-shouldered hulk of a man appeared with the biggest smile you can imagine. For a brief moment he surveyed the two dozen or so chairs and began charging toward Brooks when his eyes lighted on him. When he reached the startled young pastor he stuck out his ham of a hand and practically shouted, "Pastor, I'm Clarence Reaves. Man, are we glad to see you here! We been needin' you for a long time!"

Well, his was the first friendly face and voice to greet Charles in Chester, and the man was big enough to make up three people and three voices! Brooks stood, grasped Reaves' hand (it was immediately swallowed up), and vigorously pumped it. It was as if the two had known each other for years, and indeed for the next 20 years until Clarence "Bunky" Reaves' death, the two were closer than most blood brothers. This gem of a gent made Brooks's first pastorate away from his sweetheart bearable.

God placed two other saints in the life of the young pastor to brighten those dreary days. The Lyonses had a comfortable home in Wilmington, spacious yet cozy and welcoming, and the door was not only open wide to Charles, but if he did not visit daily, the couple worried that something was amiss. Their abode and fellowship were a relief to Brooks's cramped and cold place, and Mrs. Lyons kindly cooked him two meals a day and ironed his shirts. Just as Charles had a brother in Bunky, the Lyonses treated him like their son.

The Blessing

The two lovers wrote to each other every day that year with few exceptions. Each morning Charles's routine was to wake up, have worship, shower, dress, walk three blocks to the post office for Rene's letter, pore over it, respond, then walk back to the post office and mail his letter. Walterene received an allowance of $5 a month from her parents, which equaled a dollar and change a week. Each month she would use a dollar to buy stamps so that she could mail letters to her fiancé.

On Christmas that year Charles received the best present of all: the opportunity to see Rene. Bunky started to drive him to her house in Pine Forge, but the ice and sleet on the roads were so treacherous that they had to turn back and stay overnight at an Adventist couple's house in Bryn Mawr. Suffice it to say that it was the longest night of Charles Brooks's life! The next morning the sun was so bright that it blinded their eyes, all to the sound of ice falling. But Charles and Bunky wouldn't be denied that day. They torpedoed to Pine Forge, and upon arrival Charles was rewarded with a smile brighter even than the sun and so warm it could melt the ice before it hit the ground. It was his first Christmas with the Wagners.

When John Wagner had to make a trip to Oakwood for a board meeting months later, he didn't have to ask Charles twice to drive, even though it took 16 hours to get there, and even more with the stops Wagner had to make in his capacity as president of Allegheny Conference. Returning north, early on a Sabbath morning he instructed Charles to swing over to the western part of the territory, and as they arrived in Cincinnati, Ohio, he informed Brooks that he was the preacher for the morning. Rightly nervous—he was to speak to one of the largest congregations in the conference and in front of the president and future father-in-law—Charles nevertheless delivered the Word with power, and then redelivered it Sunday in Columbus.

That night Brooks and Wagner drove an hour north to Germantown, Ohio, outside of Dayton, where John introduced Charles to the Wrights, a family of exceptionally talented musicians who blessed the denomination and the world with their gifts. Emanating from the humble church in cornfield country were melodies that could charm angels, and the president and youthful pastor conversed with the members in front of the roaring fireplace that warmed the room. Charles's ties with the Wright family would be deep and strong throughout his ministry, as they would be with the Buckeye state and the many believers who resided there.

A bit later after his trip south with Wagner, Charles bought his first car, a new black Chevrolet, for $1,900. He was understandably elated with his purchase, because for the first time in his life he could drive in the rain without the car leaking. Other pluses that seemed too good to be true were windshield wipers that worked and a heater. One of the first things he did with the car was to have Rene's initials inscribed on the door and to have a set of keys made for her, which he pressed into her hand the next time they met.

Despite the trips and Charles's new set of wheels, the two lovers didn't see each other nearly enough. Then they made the big decision when Rene had just arrived home to Pennsylvania for the summer of her senior year and Charles was running his first tent campaign in Chester. They could not and would not endure another year of separation, they concluded, hands clasped. But how could Rene quit college in a family in which the word "dropout" did not exist? Should they elope? Well, that wasn't an option either, for the conference president's daughter could not be the subject of gossip or conjecture. Neither could Charles. There was only one option. Hands still clasped, they decided that he would go to her parents and ask for their blessing to marry their daughter.

Charles prepared a speech. He would say this and this and that, no, this, then that . . . On the chosen evening he called on John Wagner, a man he had grown to love and highly respect, but who on this occasion filled him with trepidation. Later he remarked that he was "as nervous as a long-tailed cat in a roomful of rocking chairs." As Charles delivered his spiel in the den to a relaxed John Wagner wearing evening robe and slippers, the man smiled patiently, waiting for the conclusion.

When Charles had run out of things to say, Wagner began, "We've been expecting this. Now, son, before I answer I want to tell you something. Everyone knows you and my daughter are serious about each other, so I want to let you know how much I appreciate the way you have carried yourself in this year or so you've been alone. There hasn't been a single rumor or negative comment—"

While he was speaking, Jessie Wagner appeared, a quizzical look on her face. "What is it?" she asked, turning from her husband to Charles. Jessie Wagner was a marvelous woman with enchanting green eyes. Her daughter had been with her in the living room, giggling away, but wouldn't divulge what was going on in the other room. Finally Rene said simply, "You'd better go in there where Daddy and Charles are."

"Kid," John Wagner said to his wife with a pleased look playing on his face, "these birds want to get married."

Mrs. Wagner's face broke into an expression that only a select group of women have pulled off in the history of humankind: a smile and a frown at the same time.

"Oh, Charles, we like you, but Walterene is so close to finishing . . . Just one more year. Can't you—"

"She can still finish, kid," her husband interrupted. As they had a little back-and-forth—wife worriedly but pleasantly voicing objections, husband gamely meeting them—Charles watched, not saying a word. But joy bubbled in his heart. He knew that he and Rene would be married very, very soon.

"All right, then, with our blessing," the wife finally gave in, with an exaggerated resignation, for she was actually beside herself with excitement and pride for her daughter and soon-to-be son-in-law. The smile-frown curved into a full-on smile, the most beautiful sight Charles had ever laid eyes on. Mother Wagner then addressed him matter-of-factly but with much love brimming in her voice and expression: "Charles, first thing I want to tell you is that in this family we do not have in-laws. You are a full member of our family with no difference between the sons I gave birth to." And she treated him as her own son for the rest of her life.

Charles solemnly promised father and mother that by God's grace he would make sure that their daughter finished school.

The next day Charles, Rene, and her mother drove to Levitz in Charles's black Chevrolet. He presented his fiancé with an 18-karat gold engagement watch, as was the Adventist custom in those days. For his gift Charles received a substantial kiss from Rene, while her mother blushed with embarrassment and laughter. They set the big date for September 14, 1952.

In the weeks leading up to the wedding Charles was in the midst of his first campaign in Chester, preaching his heart out from a wooden make-shift pulpit each night in the canvas tent on the corner of one of the city's most depressed streets. Meanwhile, Walterene and her mother frenetically made all the arrangements for the wedding. Although beyond busy and hectic, that time was one of sheer joy for the engaged couple.

I Do

September 14, 1952, may have been a dreary Sunday weatherwise, but only sunshine filled the Ebenezer SDA Church in Philadelphia. Charles Brooks had never known a brighter day in his life. He would be wed to the one person in all the world that he truly loved, and the two would embark on the rest of life together as one.

His soon-to-be father-in-law, John Wagner, was dressed to a tee in a tuxedo, with Wilmot Fordham, Walterene's uncle, also impeccably attired. Both would preside over the wedding. Charles and his groomsmen—Elliott Brooks, Russell Bates, Bill DeShay, Aaron Brogen, Jesse Wagner, Clarence Reaves, and "Pop" Willis—were also dashing in their tuxedos, complementing the beauty of Walterene and her bridesmaids.

Charles and Rene couldn't have kept the smiles off their faces even if they had tried. John Wagner spoke to them solemnly and seriously about their vows that day, but he was joyful as well. When he recited the wedding vows a smile covered his face, while bride and groom beamed from ear to ear.

The *North American Informant,* at the time the periodical of Black Seventh-day Adventists, published this wedding notice in the December 1952 issue:

"Sunday, September 14, at the Ebenezer S.D.A. Church, Philadelphia, Pennsylvania, Walterine Wagner and Pastor Charles Brooks were united in the bonds of holy matrimony, with the bride's father, Elder J. H. Wagner, officiating. Pastor J. H. Wagner, Jr., the bride's brother, served as best man.

"We wish for each of these newlyweds an abundance of God's richest blessings as they share their lives together."

The Honeymoon

The newlyweds started out on their honeymoon on Sunday night to Niagara Falls, drunk on love and giddy about a bright future. But the pall of racism would dampen their joy. The educated and dignified Christian couple stopped for lodging at seven motels along the way and found themselves refused at each. Here the last room had been reserved just before they arrived. There it had slipped the proprietor's mind to switch the vacancy light off when the final room was occupied.

Fighting off anger, Charles motored on northward, thinking that things would change at the next stop. Around 2:00 in the morning he pulled into the drive-up check-in at a motel in New Jersey, the fluorescent lights of the vacancy sign reflecting off the black paint of his Chevy. The owner, a heavyset White man, came out to meet them, hesitating when he noticed their color.

"Sorry, we just reserved the last room to someone who called just before you pulled up."

Charles had had enough. "It's not enough that you lie to us. Now you insult our intelligence. Just have the courage to tell us the truth—you don't want us to stay here because of our race."

"Well, we used to let Coloreds come here, but they got to the place and brought women and—"

Brooks interrupted him. "The greater percentage of your fine White patrons in those rooms are entertaining other men's wives right now, and you're discussing morals?"

Barely missing the proprietor's toes as he roared out of the parking lot, Charles drove and drove, humiliated and incensed more for his new bride than for himself. On a lake just outside of Newark he pulled over and parked. He then made Rene as comfortable as possible in the back seat, while he stayed in the front, trying in vain to doze off. One thing was certain: he would not consummate their marriage in a car.

The next morning, after a restful night for Rene but a sleepless one for him, the newlyweds used a gas-station bathroom to brush their teeth and wash their faces. Charles pointed the car toward East Orange, New Jersey, where his mother was staying with his brother Hugh. He wanted Mattie and Rene to get more acquainted. Sure enough, no sooner had they arrived at Hugh's place than the two bonded, conversing for hours. When Mother Brooks had her boy alone, she quietly confided, "Son, you've married a fine girl. I love Walterene."

Things changed after that. On their way north the couple had safe, clean quarters every night. They marveled at the awesome wonders of Niagara and took in the natural beauty of the Canadian countryside. Next they headed back south to New York City, where they ascended the Statue of Liberty hand in hand, peering out through her crown into New York

Harbor. During those golden days Charles realized how truly blessed he was, for it dawned on him with greater and greater clarity that God couldn't have given him a better woman than Rene. Now his ministry would be different. He would enjoy every place he was assigned no matter where on earth—because he'd be with Rene.

MINISTRY

"I didn't get tired in those days."

The miracles that attended Charles Brooks's first tent meeting in Chester, Pennsylvania, set the precedent for the scores of subsequent evangelistic campaigns. He and a few men from the Chester church pitched the tent adjacent to railroad tracks that cut through the industrial city. Literally across the tracks stood a Sunday church, and no sooner had Brooks begun his nightly meetings than word got back to him that he had become the subject of its pastor's harangues. In a blatant attempt to outdo the Adventist effort, the church across the tracks set up a tent of its own and held meetings simultaneously, during which the minister contradicted what Brooks was preaching!

A few days later a terrible storm swept through Chester. It leveled the competing tent, while Brooks's remained upright. To be fair, the condition of the tents after the storm was not necessarily a divine judgment. As taught him by J. G. Dasent, Charles had taken great pains to condition and maintain the tent ropes (in those days, ropes consisted of natural fibers that contracted in the rain and expanded in the sun), while the minister across the tracks had not. Nevertheless, the contrast of the tents on opposite sides of the tracks was striking.

The day after the storm, a black limousine pulled onto Brooks's lot, the gravel crunching under the tires, notifying Brooks and the other men who were hard at work that they had a visitor. The minister of the church across the tracks emerged from the rear door of the limo. Not recognizing Charles in his sweat-drenched T-shirt and jeans, he began questioning random church members as to how their tent was still standing. "The Lord did it" was their unanimous reply.

The Lord did indeed bless Charles's ministry in Chester. While he was there, the congregation's membership doubled, growing from 22 to

44. The young pastor also made some long-overdue changes, such as shortening the Sabbath service so that it ended at 12:00 instead of 2:00. Brooks's sincerity and obvious love for the Lord gradually softened the hearts of the members, and those who were initially uncooperative became his biggest supporters. Charles even became fast friends with the lay pastor who had opposed his arrival, the two working in tandem in running the church.

In those early days of his ministry Brooks developed a simple philosophy that inspired all of his efforts and was the engine that drove him to four decades of tireless evangelism. While reading the writings of Ellen G. White, he came upon this line: "One soul saved, to live throughout the ages of eternity, to praise God and the Lamb, is of more value than millions in money." Later a stronger assertion caught his attention: "One soul is worth more than all the gold and silver that could be heaped up on this earth." It further amazed the young evangelist to discover this: "One soul for whom Christ has died is worth more than the whole world." By the time he read the following statement, the true spiritual worth of each person had become deeply embedded in his heart: "One soul saved in the kingdom of God is worth more than ten thousand worlds." But the absolute clincher was when his eyes alighted on "One soul is of infinite value." Charles Brooks resolved that as long as God gave him breath he would bring people into God's kingdom, and he would never consider it a failure if even only one person was baptized.

Firstfruit

The firstfruit of Charles Brooks's ministry in Chester was a woman by the name of Lois Padgett. Blessed with exceptional leadership qualities, she was an attractive person both inside and out. A registered nurse, she was married to a physician who specialized in philandering. Lois was the first person to respond to Brooks's call for baptism in the Chester tent meeting, and her husband used her newfound religion as an excuse to get rid of her. Far from grieving over it, she instead accepted Charles's offer to be a full-time Bible instructor with his evangelistic series. She followed the Brookses across the country and was responsible for bringing many into the Adventist Church.

Decades later when he lived in Washington, D.C., he was distressed to receive a phone call informing him that Lois had been hospitalized with cancer. Her leg had to be amputated at once. Charles hurried to Chester's

Crozer Hospital. As the 140 miles sped by, he prayed for wisdom as to what to say to someone who had done so much for God's kingdom.

Arriving at the hospital, Brooks got directions to her room and negotiated the sterile corridors. Expecting to find her in the throes of despair, he was amazed to stare into the face of an angel. Suddenly everything came into perspective: Jesus gives peace even in the darkest situations.

With a smile Lois reached out both hands to the man who had brought her to Christ so long ago. "Now, Elder Brooks, I have had my little cry and now everything is all right. God has comforted me. Now listen, only you must do my funeral. Despite all my years of soul-winning work, I have had no success getting my former socialite or professional friends even to listen. Well, they are going to be at my funeral, and I want you to tell them what I believed. I want them to hear the truth I accepted and wanted so badly for them to accept. You must tell them what I hoped for, about Jesus and the Sabbath that honors Him. Tell them, please!"

Taken aback but greatly honored, Charles promised he would. He walked out of the hospital that day with an even deeper love and respect for the power of what he preached.

Too soon the day came. The old Chester church was not adequate to accommodate the expected turnout, so Lois Padgett's funeral was planned at St. Andrews church, the one that she attended before becoming a Seventh-day Adventist. The sanctuary was packed. As Charles approached the pulpit to eulogize his trusted Bible instructor of so many years, he prayed for tactfulness and clarity. Lois Padgett had charged him with telling her old friends exactly what made her tick—the blessed hope that was in Jesus—and that is exactly what he did that day. The Lord filled the sanctuary, the exquisitely dressed mourners riveted by the words of a eulogy of a kind they had never heard before. What Lois Padgett couldn't do in life she accomplished at her death.

Camden

The year Charles and Walterene were married the conference reconfigured the young pastor's Pennsylvania district and shifted him to a parish in the south end of New Jersey, four churches in all: Camden, Bridgeton, Jericho, and Salem. A standard practice in those days, the assignments kept Brooks busy. He preached at Camden, the largest congregation, on Sabbath in the early morning, then drove to Bridgeton. One Sabbath a month he spoke at Jericho and Salem. On Sunday night (back then many Adventist churches had programs on Sunday night) Charles alternated between the churches, delivering an evangelistic message aimed at non-Adventists whom the members especially invited. Wednesday nights (the prayer meeting service) featured a teaching talk on prophecy. Any given week Brooks would give five or six messages.

Despite this, the ambitious youthful pastor wanted to do still more. In those storied days of his young adulthood, Charles simply did not get tired. No sooner had Brooks wrapped up the Chester evangelistic campaign than he was eager to start another, and he focused his sights on Camden. A spillover city of Philadelphia just across the Delaware River, Camden's population in the early 1950s was roughly 125,000. During that period immigrants came in large numbers from the Caribbean to find work. But the year Brooks arrived the previously prosperous industrial city was beginning its long and painful spiral into decline, with crime rising sharply and a dangerous element invading the once-peaceful streets. Yet the believers in the area were solid, down-to-earth people who loved Adventism and supported their pastor.

Like many urban areas, Camden had strict zoning codes and prohibitions on canvas auditoriums. So Charles petitioned the mayor and the city council for permission to hold religious tent meetings in the city. Both approved his request, but a tiny, feisty, gray-haired woman in city hall blocked it because of her fear of fires. Twice Brooks attempted to persuade her to allow it, but she was adamant that "there will be no tent meetings in Camden while I'm around!"

Brooks took orders from a Higher Power, however, and moved forward with his plans for a full-fledged meeting. He told his church that on such and such a date they would put up a tent. "If someone tries to stop us, be assured that it will not be easy for them to do that." The members fully backed their bold leader, raring to go.

But then word came to Charles from Danville, Virginia, that Pastor Bill DeShay, with whom he had attended Oakwood, was sick and near death. Everything was in place for DeShay to hold a tent meeting, but despite trying valiantly, he was too ill. The doctor gave him two months to live. DeShay had a frank discussion with William Cheatham, Allegheny Conference president, after the grim prognosis:

DeShay: "Mr. President, I've planned an evangelistic campaign here in Danville. The saints have done so much work to make it a reality."

Cheatham: "Yes, I know, Bill."

DeShay: "We can't disappoint them by not holding it."
Cheatham: "Whom do you want to run it then?"
DeShay: "Charles Brooks."

Danville

So off the newlyweds motored to Danville, Charles putting his plans for Camden on hold. In those days audiences spent five or six nights a week under the tent, seated in fold-up chairs on a floor of yellow-tinged sawdust, while the evangelist preached his heart out on a makeshift wooden pulpit, all for 12 consecutive weeks. Charles loved tents. First, they were cheaper than renting halls. Second, one could set them up in the neighborhoods where people lived and where Brooks and his team could be easily accessible. In this way he showed that he was not high and mighty or distant, but that he came to them, to be among them. Also, in a tent one didn't have to dress special—you could come in whatever clothes you had and feel comfortable. That was important because many who attended were either not used to dressing up or didn't have fancy clothes.

Every night when Brooks stepped onto the pulpit he thanked God for the opportunity to preach His Word, for there was nothing he would rather be doing. An added bonus was that his parents, Marvin and Mattie Brooks, got to hear their son preach, since Greensboro was only about an hour's drive away. Also that summer of 1956 the conference ordained Charles Brooks to the gospel ministry along with his brother-in-law John Wagner, as well as Danny Davis, Edward Dorsey, Aaron Brogden, and Jasper Johnson.

At the very start of the meetings Charles had to confront the ubiquitous thorny issue of race. At his home one day a group of White citizens of the town paid a visit to Brooks. Their question was straightforward: may we attend the meetings?

"Of course," Charles replied. In his mind truth had no color, and Jesus wanted all people to be saved. He had never and would never discriminate based on race as to whom he evangelized.

"Maybe you don't understand what we mean," the leader of the contingent said, a worried look on his face.

"Then what do you mean?" Charles asked, wondering what this was really about.

The White man raised himself a little taller and said, "We want you to provide special seating for us."

"No," Brooks immediately responded. He didn't even have to think about it. "You are our brothers and sisters, and you can come in and find a seat like anyone else. If you arrive early you can have your choice of seats, but I am certainly not going to do an evil thing like that."

The entourage turned around, got in their cars, and drove away.

But that wasn't the end of it. Brooks had positioned his tent at the fork of a road, so there was plenty of parking space on either side of the lot. Every night like clockwork the Whites that had visited Charles's home sat in their cars with windows rolled down, listening to the words of truth from the Black evangelist. Although they never stepped foot under the tent, Charles thanked God for them and hopes to see them in Paradise.

Along with running a full-fledged evangelistic effort in Danville, the insatiable Charles sought to do even more. As he was still considering ways to do this, one evening a tall man stood in line to shake his hand at the close of the meeting.

"Hi, Pastor, my name is John Brooks," the man said with a wide grin.

"Well, with a name like that you can't be all bad," Charles said, smiling also. "Tell me about yourself."

"I am a disc jockey at a radio station here in town," John began. "I close the station every night. We have the news and popular music until 11:00. Normally from 11:00 p.m. to midnight we play more music, because the young people who listen to our station have nowhere to go and want to dance. At midnight we sign off and close the station until the next morning."

Charles sensed what the man might have in mind. "That's interesting," he said to the disc jockey.

"I would like you to come to the station and tell everybody what you are telling them out here, free of charge."

"When do you want me to start?"

"Tonight," John Brooks replied, chuckling.

"All right, give me some time to finish up here, and I'll be at the station."

The Lord blessed that night. When John asked Charles to return every night, he readily agreed. Walterene and three others formed a trio and sang every night on the program. Then Charles, sitting at a table with a big microphone in front of him, broadcast the Adventist message. The young pastor had no clue at that early stage that the hallmark of his ministry would be on media similar to this.

Bookie

Around the ninth week of the campaign a 16-year-old girl nicknamed "Bookie" asked to be baptized, but her family bitterly opposed it. Her mother had at one time actually attended the meetings and brought Bookie with her, but all of a sudden ceased coming and became outright hostile, forbidding her daughter to go to them.

A couple days after Bookie took her stand for baptism a letter addressed to Brooks arrived in the mail stating, "If you baptize the young woman, you will wish you had never been born." That night Brooks stood on the podium before the crowded tent, held up the letter, read it word for word to the stunned audience, then defiantly announced, "My orders come from on high and on high alone. The young woman has presented herself for baptism, so guess who is going to baptize her?" The amazed audience answered unanimously, "You!" And Brooks seconded it: "I am!"

The next day he received a phone call from Bookie's mother asking if he could come by and answer some questions. Before he had a chance to pray and ask God what he should do, Charles hopped into his black Chevy and followed the mother's directions to her home.

When he arrived, he was greeted a little too pleasantly by the mother, who was waiting on her screened-in porch for him. She beckoned him into the house. The foyer and living room were empty, but as he followed his host to the den he was shocked to see a roomful of about 30 people, some standing against the walls and others seated on the floor, all looking at him expectantly, with Bookie sitting on a chair in their midst. It turned out that they had been bombarding her with questions about this strange religion spouted by the fiery preacher who had swept into town. The girl was glad to see Charles, who had finally begun praying.

"Brooks," demanded a man who had to be her pastor because of the suit he wore, "we are here trying to figure you out."

"Am I that complicated?" Charles asked with a grin tugging at his lips.

"What are you doing in this town? You call yourself an evangelist, but you are no evangelist! An evangelist seeks people who are lost—and you, you are bothering people who are already saved." Raising his voice, the pastor began gesticulating animatedly. "You should've first ascertained who was saved and who wasn't." As the exasperated minister unloaded on him, Charles was sending up prayers to heaven.

"Sir," Brooks began slowly and calmly, "the Lord didn't instruct me to do it that way. I came down here with a general invitation to all people.

You seem a little hostile in your judgment—have you been to any of the meetings?"

"I'll have you know that I taught religion at a prestigious university," the pastor snapped. "I wouldn't be caught dead in a tent meeting." He said the words "tent meeting" with such disdain that it seemed as if he were spitting something out of his mouth.

"I know you went to a little no-count school in Alabama! And here you are imagining that I'd deign to step foot inside your little two-bit meeting!"

Again Charles respectfully waited until the man had finished, then said, "Sir, it was at that 'little no-count school' that I learned how to rightly divide the Word of truth. You cannot judge my ministry until you attend a meeting. May I show you what I am preaching about there?"

When Charles opened his Bible, a holy solemnity came over the room, subduing even the irate pastor. As he flipped through the Word the pages uncannily fell open to the perfect texts for the occasion. Charles held the gathering spellbound as he shared Bible passages on grace, salvation, the Second Coming, the Sabbath, and healthful living. He closed by pointing out that sin was the transgression of God's law and that anyone violating it intentionally or unintentionally was a sinner and needed to be at his tent meetings.

Then, remembering one of E. E. Cleveland's tricks, he tossed the Bible onto the pastor's lap and issued a challenge: "Pastor, now you have two Bibles. If you find one text that tells me that I am to worship God on Sunday, I'll take my tent down and join your church today."

Flustered, the heretofore-articulate pastor hemmed and hawed, then finally stammered, "W-well, there is one t-text that says n-nobody should j-judge you." He began frantically flipping through the Bible, ending up somewhere in the Old Testament before Charles finally decided to put him out of his misery.

"Are you referring to Colossians 2:14-16?"

"Yeah, yeah, that's it," the man replied, relieved as if he himself had actually located the text. A bit amused, Brooks noticed that the man didn't attempt to turn to the passage. The others in the room also tried unsuccessfully to keep the amusement from their faces.

"Sir, do you truly understand that passage or did you just quote it for effect? I'd be interested to learn what a Bible scholar like you had to say about it."

Once again the pastor looked painfully confused, until Charles offered to explain it. The Oakwoodite covered the ceremonial law, its obligations and its limits, then moved on to the moral law and the importance of its observance. As he spoke, the minister sank deeper into his chair, his upturned face temporarily betraying his interest. Charles finished by showing from Genesis 2 that God gave the Sabbath to humanity for their happiness before sin even entered the world. The 16-year-old Bookie and her mother were staring at him in agreement, and some of the others were nodding as well.

Seeing that Brooks was persuading some of his own members, the pastor seemed to regain his contrary spirit, and springing up from his chair, announced, "Well, I didn't come here to argue. I don't have time for this. I have an important meeting to attend."

"But Pastor," Charles called to the man's retreating back, "you wouldn't leave without prayer, would you?" The minister stopped in his tracks, and reluctantly turned around, gesturing to Charles to do the honors. Before Brooks prayed, though, he had one more thing to add. Scanning the faces in the room, he asked, "What is it you think my church will do against this family and against their precious daughter by telling her the truth? Do you think she will become a prostitute because she comes to my meetings? Oh no, she will be safeguarded. Do you think she will become a thief? Oh no, because the law teaches that thou shalt not steal."

Then he gave a prayer based loosely on Matthew 18:6: "Lord, You said that it would be better for someone who caused Your little ones to stumble to have a millstone hung around their neck and drown in the sea." At the "Amen" Brooks turned to Bookie's mother, father, and finally her pastor. "You will be accountable if you stand in the way of this child obeying God," he solemnly declared with pointed finger, then departed.

On Sabbath morning Bookie and her friend, also a teenager determined to be baptized, jumped out of Bookie's room window in gown and housecoat and ran the 10 blocks to the house where the Brookses were temporarily lodging. Charles instructed Rene to drive the brave girls to Roanoke, Virginia, where the baptism would take place. The others would arrive later by bus.

As the baptismal candidates boarded the bus, Bookie's mother showed up, stalking the tent grounds like a hungry lion, then searching the faces on the bus for her daughter. When she had looked in every possible place, she huffed away.

The baptismal service in Roanoke was the recently ordained Charles

Brooks's first, with the great George E. Peters, then pastor of Ebenezer in Philadelphia, assisting him. Marvin and Mattie Brooks stood proud as their son led 26 people to the watery grave and brought them up in newness of life. One of those baptized was another of their sons, Elliott. That day Bookie and her friend also were among those who started a new life in Christ. Nearly six decades later, now a senior citizen, she has the same love for biblical truth.

***

Miraculously, Bill DeShay revived, beating the cancer and living a rich, full life. A few years later Charles presided over his wedding to a gem of a woman named Corrine. The couple had two sons, and Bill lived to see both of them get married and have children. DeShay went on to pastor some of the denomination's most prestigious congregations, including the Oakwood College Church.

The Brookses returned to Camden high off their successful Danville effort. But when Rene announced to Charles that she was pregnant, his new focus was seeing to his beloved wife and the growing bump that was her belly. The young preacher was continually enchanted by the beauty of his wife, who looked positively radiant as the first, second, and finally third trimesters passed.

The Brookses' physician was the legendary Dr. Grace Kimbrough. Grace Ann Diuguid was born in 1883 and earned her medical degree from American Medical Missionary College in 1906 at the young age of 23. There in Battle Creek, Michigan, she studied under the tutelage of John Harvey Kellogg, as did other Black Adventist female pioneers in medicine, Lottie Blake and Anna Knight. Kimbrough would spend her career in the city of Philadelphia, where she became the first woman chief resident at the Frederick Douglass Memorial Hospital, and received myriad accolades for the expert medical care that she provided for more than a half century to those of all classes and races. Notably, she paid for the voice lessons of a poor young Philadelphian named Marian Anderson, who would go on to become one of the greatest singers of the twentieth century, and whose performance at the Lincoln Memorial in 1939 helped lay the foundation for the civil rights movement. Kimbrough also financed the purchase of the Pine Forge Academy property, as well as other properties in the Allegheny Conference.

Dr. Kimbrough had predicted that Walterene Brooks would give birth in late September or the first week of October of 1954. But the first week of October passed, and the baby remained put. So the Brookses drove to Philadelphia to see Dr. Kimbrough, now in her 70s. After examining Rene, the kindhearted physician declared, "When the apple is ripe, it will fall." Then when she saw the worried looks on the faces of the young couple before her, she added a more specific date: "The baby will come about the fifteenth of October."

On the way back across the bridge to Camden Charles's biggest fear swirled around in his head—that the baby would come while they were driving in the car. Just a few days later "Pop" Wagner, Rene's father, came to help out and be there for his middle daughter. On the Saturday morning of the sixteenth, Rene walked up to her husband in their bedroom and said two words: "It's time."

A terrified Charles sprang into motion, grabbing all of the necessary items, tossing them into the black Chevy, then gently helped Rene into the car. Once they and her father were all in, Charles sped across the Benjamin Franklin Bridge, then hightailed it to West Philadelphia's Woman's Hospital.

"Slow down, son," John Wagner said, adding, "We have plenty of time."

John Wagner was right. The two men sat in a hospital waiting room all Saturday night until finally, early on Sunday morning, a nurse informed Charles that he was father to a 6-pound 14½-ounce girl. Charles was overjoyed, for his wife had brainwashed him into wanting a girl first. They named her "Diedra" after a delightful young woman in their church. Amazingly, the next week Rene's brother Jesse had a daughter, Delvius, and the very next day, Rene's other brother, John, had a daughter, Judy. Later the couples would calculate that all three of the newborns might have been conceived when they were in Atlanta for the Christmas holiday in 1953. The three girl cousins maintained a tight friendship throughout their lives, attending college and going through life together.

**

Charles was in love with Walterene, plain and simple, and although he didn't think it possible, he grew more deeply in love with her after their first child. To behold Rene carry and bear such a beautiful baby girl, all the while being the best wife in the world to him, caused him to go head over heels in love again, as he had done in college.

The two tried to have special dates as often as possible. Because they had very little money in those days, they often had to hold them in their humble little home. But they made the occasions as special as possible.

Making sure little Diedre was sound asleep, the two got ready. Both put on dress clothes. Rene prepared a special meal of dishes they couldn't afford on a regular basis. Charles placed candles on the tables, shut off the electric lights, and put on soft romantic music. The lovers dined on china and silver utensils given them as a wedding gift. The glow from the candlelight revealed joy in their faces that words could not express.

"Many women have done virtuously, Rene," Charles said, staring over his glass into the eyes of his only love, "but you excel them all."

***

In Camden the new father determinedly made plans to put up the tent that the Danville evangelistic series had temporarily (he convinced himself) delayed, and then another in a different location in the city after those meetings ended. While plotting his evangelistic blitz, however, Brooks always sought out one-on-one encounters, as did Jesus while on earth. Because of his personal witnessing, all kinds of visitors showed up at his church. One such visitor was a man by the name of James Williams.

The Sunday after Williams appeared at church, Charles paid him a house visit. A massive muscular man of six feet five, Williams boomed for Charles to come in and sit down. James Williams and his wife sat on the couch across from the evangelist, intently listening to him talk about the Bible. At one point Williams explained that he was being regularly visited by three ministers, all convincing in their own way and all trying to persuade him to join their particular church. Charles smiled. The young preacher welcomed the competition, for he knew he had the truth and always exulted to see it triumph.

"Mr. Williams," he began, certainty in his voice, "it's hard to join my church."

Taken aback, James and his wife stared at Brooks, waiting for his next words.

"You are nowhere near being fit to be a member."

Far from offended, the couple was intrigued. "Well, why not?"

"Because you don't know the truth, and thus you haven't accepted it and aren't living by it."

After that Brooks came twice a week to the Williams home, giving studies to the couple on the distinctive doctrines of Adventism with the aid of slides projected on a screen. When camp meeting season rolled around, Charles invited them to Pine Forge for Allegheny's camp meeting. He procured a tent for the couple, who eagerly joined the thousands of believers on the grounds. It was there that James Williams first told Brooks that he wanted to be baptized. Every night the massive man would sit in the tent listening to the truths of God's Word, his face shiny from tears. Near the end of the meetings, Charles and Walterene went to the Williamses' tent on a quiet Pennsylvania night, the stars twinkling distantly in space. Lights from scores of other tents lit the rural campus as the pastoral couple slipped through the flap of the tent.

In a marathon session spanning three hours, Charles again covered the fundamental teachings of the Adventist Church using James Williams' large family Bible. The tent, which had no light, was cast in a soft darkness. The husband peered over Brooks's right shoulder with a pen flashlight, while his wife stood at Brooks's left. Whenever Brooks cited a text, Williams shone his flashlight on the passage, bringing new meaning to the words of David, "The entrance of thy word giveth light." When Charles had finished covering the doctrine of modesty and demonstrated that the Bible forbids the wearing of jewelry, Williams shone the flashlight on his wife, still standing in darkness. With a resolute look on her face, the woman began peeling off her jewelry. The next day husband and wife were baptized.

In-reach

Charles Brooks also gave priority to in-reach, knowing full well that those who faithfully attended church could be lost as fast as those who didn't attend. After he and church officers concluded a business meeting with prayer, an elder confided to Brooks, "Pastor, there is a man in our church who is there every time you open the door, but he is not a member. Maybe you can see about baptizing him."

As he listened to the elder, Charles was incredulous. He had assumed that particular individual was one of the deacons! Rushing to his car, he headed for the man's house. It was only a matter of minutes before he spotted him sitting on a stool on the side porch of his residence.

Barely putting the car in park before he jumped out, Charles ran to the fence that surrounded the property and called to the man to come to him. Rising from his stool, he hurried over to his pastor.

"I understand you're not baptized yet," Brooks said.

"No," he replied, hanging his head a bit.

"Why are you playing with your soul?" Brooks demanded. "You are older than you look but still on the sunset side of life, and you need to do that which is most important quickly." Charles told him that when he made the appeal on Sabbath he would be speaking directly to him.

"All right," the man said simply, shaking his head agreeably.

On Sabbath no sooner had Brooks begun his appeal than the man got up and came down the aisle. The whole church was emotional, tears and Kleenex everywhere. Just hours later Charles baptized him. Later he baptized the man's daughter, too.

***

Brooks's New Jersey churches were all geared up for the long-awaited tent revivals. The enthusiasm that their vigorous young pastor inspired was truly a thing to behold. Each member did their part to make the meetings a success. Soon everything was complete except for putting up the tent.

But, alas, the Allegheny board voted to reassign Charles Brooks to Columbus, Ohio. Cast down but not destroyed, Charles regretted that he had ever asked permission for something that God had given His disciples permission to do a long time ago: "Go ye therefore, and teach all nations, baptizing them in the name of the Father, and of the Son, and of the Holy Ghost: Teaching them to observe all things whatsoever I have commanded you." His parting words to his successor? "Don't ask anybody for permission—just put up your tent and start preaching."

Columbus

In 1957, at age 27, Charles Brooks began one of the most enjoyable periods in his ministry in the large Midwest city of Columbus, Ohio. The capital of Ohio, it was a center of educational, cultural, economic, and political activity during the late 1950s. With its diverse economy and employment prospects, the population of the city had soared after World War II, reaching nearly 500,000 by 1960. Home to Ohio State University, it was also a vital location for research and learning. Like Cleveland, Columbus was a big city where Blacks flourished despite the restrictions of the times, and the capital boasted numerous African American firsts in the areas of politics, religion, music, arts, and education during the period Brooks pastored there.

Like Columbus itself, Charles's new assignment, Ephesus Seventh-day Adventist Church, also boasted outstanding Blacks. Dr. Lottie Blake (1876-1976) was the first Black Adventist medical doctor. Other legendary physicians in the congregation were Richard Neal and Joe Ryan. Bill DeShay, who served as Brooks's associate pastor, and John Pitts were other notables in the accomplished congregation.

Charles was especially happy about his reassignment to Columbus be-cause one of his older sisters, Theresa, and her husband lived there and attended Ephesus. "Tee" had been the tiniest of the Brooks brood, but the spunkiest. From tot to teen she roughhoused with the best of the boys, and had the battle scars to prove it. At a time when women rarely acquired a driver's license, Tee had learned how to drive a car. After high school she became a nurse and married a sergeant in the military named George Burden. Charles's dependable brother-in-law worked for him during his evangelistic meetings, doing whatever was necessary. In turn, Charles had the privilege of finally baptizing George at the close of one of those series.

When Charles, Walterene, and baby Diedre arrived in town, Tee was there to help them get settled. She graciously showed the family around the city, always introducing Charles as "my baby brother." It got so bad that Brooks had to take Tee aside and remind her, "I may be your baby brother, but don't forget that I'm your pastor." At that, Tee just laughed and laughed.

In Columbus Charles was also able to make good on his promise to his father-in-law. Walterene enrolled at Ohio State University for her final year of college. Tee was kind enough to babysit her niece Diedre while Rene was in class. Rene not only graduated in a year but made the dean's list, earning straight A's. Not satisfied, she earned a master's in education a couple years later.

Little Willie

One of Charles's most memorable experiences in Columbus came from his first evangelistic series there, which he conducted just months after moving to the city. Every night an alcoholic (back then referred to as a "wino") named William Webster, but known by all as "Little Willie," wandered into the tent, disheveled and smelling of stale alcohol. Brooks had a general impatience with drunks, believing them to be on the whole insincere and irresponsible. But Little Willie was persistent, the diminutive Black man even staggering forward at the close of each meeting to shake Brooks's hand, either unaware of or unconcerned about the stench that surrounded him.

After eight weeks of preaching, "decision time" finally arrived. Brooks had faithfully laid out the doctrines of the church, and it was the segment of the series most critical, a time when the devil was especially busy. Willie was still coming, with probably the best attendance record even among the church members. One day Sister Bond, a most diligent Bible instructor, asked to have a word with Brooks.

"Pastor, Willie Webster wants to be baptized."

"Little Willie?" Charles replied incredulously. "He is drunk most of the time. He doesn't know, doesn't understand, what I'm preaching."

"He says he's understood and wants to be baptized."

"No. I will not cumber my records with Willie's name. He is not ready and not sincere."

"At least go visit him, Pastor," she said, a bit of pleading in her voice. And so evangelist and Bible instructor drove to inner-city Columbus to see Little Willie.

Willie lived in one of those houses in which the front door is always open. All kinds of people wandered in and out in a never-ending stream. Charles and Sister Bond attempted to knock, then decided just to walk in. People milled about in the foyer and living room. When Brooks asked for Willie, someone disappeared to fetch him. Moments later he descended stairs that had borne the weight of many feet. Brooks motioned him over to the far corner of the living room, where they could have a modicum of privacy.

"Willie," Brooks began rather sternly, "I understand from Sister Bond that you wish to be baptized."

"Yes, sir."

"Do you understand the things I've been preaching all these weeks?"

"Yes, sir."

Brooks commenced to drill him on the doctrines he had presented. As he suspected, Willie's answers were woefully inadequate. But when Charles corrected him, the man shook his head humbly in agreement.

"Do you believe this truth?" Brooks finally asked.

"Yes, sir."

At that, Charles bore down hard. "Willie, I know you drink. In our church, we do not drink. Do you understand that?"

"Yes, sir."

"Now, if I catch you drinking, I will counsel you and pray with you. But if you continue, I will drop you from the church's roll. Do you understand?"

"Yes, sir."

Charles Brooks would later repent for his toughness and insensitivity, but during that stage of his ministry he had little patience with alcoholics.

On that baptismal Sabbath the Ephesus sanctuary was packed. Charles was at his happiest, this being prime time for an evangelist. God had blessed his efforts immensely, he mused, and now . . . But his musings were interrupted when he spotted Little Willie in the white baptismal suit with the 124 other candidates.

As Charles baptized them "in the name of the Father, Son, and Holy Ghost," Little Willie's form appeared in the baptistry doorway. Brooks beckoned to him, and the man stepped into the pool.

"This candidate really needs your prayers," Brooks announced to the congregation. When the young evangelist baptized Willie, he thought, *Here goes a waste of time.*

As the meetings continued (after the baptism Charles presented more sermons on aspects of the faith, but with lesser frequency: Sunday, Wednesday, and Friday nights), Willie was always found sitting dutifully on the front row. Despite himself Brooks had to admit that he was a pleasant little fellow with a ready smile. Yet he thought to himself, *He'll drop out soon.*

But Little Willie didn't. On the Sunday night meeting a week after his baptism he sat in the front row sporting, of all things, a tie—the knot was loose, Charles noted, but it was a tie nevertheless! As the days went by, he observed that the tie tightened, moving into place. Then one night, several days later, Little Willie entered the tent in a suit—a used suit, Charles saw, but a suit nevertheless! Charles Brooks began to feel a little ashamed of himself.

Calvin Peterson, one of Charles's parishioners, was head of plant services for channel 6 TV. One Sunday Brooks went to visit him at his job to see how he was faring. As soon as he saw his pastor, Peterson said excitedly, "Pastor, guess who's working for me?"

"Who?"

"Little Willie!"

Nonplussed, Charles asked, "Where is he?"

Peterson hurriedly led him up a flight of stairs. At the top the two found Willie vigorously sweeping the hall, oblivious to everything but finishing the task.

Brooks dashed to him and grasped him excitedly.

"Willie, I'm sorry for not believing in you! I just . . ." Charles was in tears. "Forgive me, brother!"

"Pastor Brooks," Willie began, tears streaming down his face too. "I can't begin to tell you what Jesus has done for me. I don't drink anymore. I've got the first job I've had in 20 years. And I didn't even want a job! All I wanted was to run a few errands to get enough for a hot dog and a bottle of liquor. But now, all that's over! I'm going to save up, get me a car, and bring others to church!"

Twenty years later when Diedre Brooks graduated with her master's from Ohio State University, Charles and Walterene were in Columbus for the festivities. They attended Ephesus on Sabbath, and guess who the first elder was? Little Willie! He was fully suited, liquor-free, dignified, diligent, faithful, and matured in the faith. God had turned his life completely around!

In his speaking across the globe, on six continents and in dozens of countries, Brooks has shared the Little Willie story, inspiring thousands by God's power to transform a life. William Webster now sleeps in Jesus. But Charles, and the thousands who have been blessed by his testimony, expect to see Little Willie "in the morning."

The Affirmation
In the same 1957 Columbus evangelistic series Charles Brooks received the ultimate seal that God had anointed his ministry. Almost 10 years before, as a fledgling theology major he had watched with awe as people flocked to the front while his mentor Calvin Moseley preached, but had not yet bidden them come to the altar. As his own meetings approached "decision time," Charles stood under the bright lights of the tent, preaching his heart out. Then, as was his custom, he turned off the lights, and went to the screen to recap his message. Dramatic images of Christ on the cross lit the tent, all the while Brooks telling the crowd what Jesus had done for them.

Suddenly, in the relative dark, the whole back row of the right side of the tent rose as one, silhouettes against the dim streetlight that spilled in from the back. Taught to pray as he preached, Brooks thought, *Lord, have I offended these guests? Are they stalking out because I wasn't loving enough in my presentation? Did I not lift up Thee as I ought?*

Charles's prayer received an instant answer. The 25 figures negotiated out of the row, and began walking toward the front where Brooks stood at the pulpit. As they drew closer, the multicolored light from the screen illuminated their faces. Slowly Brooks recognized each person as someone for whom he and his Bible instructors had diligently labored. Then it struck Charles—this was the manifestation of the power of the Holy Spirit that he had witnessed at Oakwood when Elder Moseley was preaching! Responses without an appeal!

The people who had come up without being bidden that evening would become pillars in the Ephesus church. In fact, Mrs. Sutton, one of Columbus' prominent citizens, and her daughter, Jennie Bouldock, both became church officers. Much later Sister Sutton told her pastor the story behind what happened that night.

She had come to the tent meetings after receiving a handbill that the Bible instructors had given out. The subjects intrigued her, so she telephoned her daughter. "Jennie, listen to this." As she read the sermon titles to her daughter, both became more than a little curious about the whole affair. "Let's go out to that tent and see what this fool is talking about," Sutton said to Jennie. And so they did.

After their first meeting they were hooked, and didn't miss one night after that. Sutton explained to Charles that the Bible-filled messages, totally different from the emotionally driven "gravy" sermons they were accustomed to, had totally bowled over her and her daughter. Both women wrote down each text Brooks cited in his sermon, diligently looking them up after the meeting when they got home. Neither of them was familiar with Scripture, so they spent most of the time simply trying to locate the texts. Mrs. Sutton related to Brooks that often they'd be looking for James in the Old Testament and Isaiah in the New. And so deep into the night the pair flipped through the ancient Book, on a quest to discover truth. They found in every instance that what he had said was in the Bible.

Mother and daughter invited family to the meetings, and before long, a group of some 20 people occupied a row in the rear of the tent. Convicted to follow what they had learned and to give their hearts to Christ, one night as the young evangelist concluded his sermon in his usual way with slides of Jesus, Mrs. Sutton and Jennie Bouldock heard the voice of their Savior beckoning them to come. They didn't hesitate. When they stood, almost all whom they had invited to the meeting accompanied them.

Listening to Sister Sutton's recounting, Charles Brooks was humbled, yet greatly encouraged. Silently he thanked God for affirming him—what he was doing, his efforts—so markedly. So moved was Brooks by the experience that he didn't want to tell anyone—it was that sacred. Only later did he relate it to C. E. Moseley, who served as his mentor long into his ministry. Sister Sutton now sleeps in Jesus after a life full of faith and service.

***

Allegheny Conference set a goal to baptize 1,000 souls in the year of 1957. At 911, it was just short of its goal. The only ministers who baptized 100 or more were the outstanding evangelist George H. Rainey in Richmond, Virginia, at 120, and Charles Brooks with 100. Those were the days of unprecedented growth in the Black church in the United States, and it was the constant public efforts of such evangelists as Rainey and Brooks, along with diligent Bible instructors and church members, that made it possible.

In 1959 Charles's mother, Mattie, died. The fact that she went to sleep in Jesus comforted him. He officiated at her funeral, and for the eulogy recounted her example of faith and obedience. To a large degree, Mattie Brooks was responsible for Charles being a Seventh-day Adventist and entering the ministry. Never before was the great Advent hope so precious with its promise that mother and son would be united again.

Cleveland

In late 1959 Charles Brooks went to pastor Glenville Seventh-day Adventist Church in Cleveland, Ohio. Like Ephesus, it was one of the premier congregations of the Allegheny Conference, so Charles was a bit surprised that president W. L. Cheatham and the conference committee chose him at age 29 to take the place of the great Walter M. Starks, who was transitioning to Dupont Park in Washington, D.C. Indeed, Starks was just the latest in a line of stellar preachers that graced the Glenville pulpit, including Robert Willis, R. T. Hudson, J. E. Cox, and J. H. Laurence.

On the chilly, snowy day of January 3, 1960, Charles, Rene, and Dee-Dee (as everyone now called the child) moved into the old parsonage connected to the Glenville church. Rene was expecting their second child, and as always Charles was the protective husband, shielding his wife from the cold and snow, both of which remained in abundance for the next three weeks.

Cleveland sits along the banks of the Cuyahoga River near Lake Erie in northern Ohio. At first a small settlement in what was then the "West," during the 1820s and 1830s, the construction of the Erie Canal connected it with the Atlantic Ocean, and two decades later railroads reached the town, transforming it into a thriving commercial city. By the last decades of the century Cleveland had become an industrial powerhouse, thanks to such entrepreneurial giants as John D. Rockefeller and Samuel Mather. The metropolis flourished into a social and cultural center, boasting professional sports teams, amusement parks, world-class hospitals, museums and orchestras, and political conventions. However, during the Great Depression and the World War II years Cleveland experienced tremendous economic hardship, and with its population peaking at roughly 1 million in 1950, it would begin to decline at an alarming rate.

Even more than Columbus, Cleveland had always been a vital location for African Americans. Throughout the mid- to late 1800s the city was mostly racially integrated, and Blacks experienced significantly less discrimination there than in most other American cities. Cleveland was also a hotbed of abolitionist and antislavery activity and played an integral role in the Union victory in the Civil War by producing steel and other material for weaponry.

In the early part of the twentieth century Cleveland was a primary location for Southern Blacks migrating north to look for employment and a better life. By 1915 the Black population was about 10,000, and with the increase conditions began to deteriorate for this minority population, African Americans soon experiencing increasing exclusion from jobs, trade unions, health facilities, schools, restaurants, and social clubs. However, World War I again renewed opportunities for African Americans as the demands of war created jobs. By 1930, 72,000 Blacks resided in Cleveland.

The Great Depression reversed the situation again, bringing in its wake extremely desperate times for Black Clevelanders. But again war—this time the Second World War—ushered in a new era. Blacks from the South once more flocked to Cleveland, so that when the Brookses moved to the city in 1960 the African American population had risen to more than a quarter million. In response Whites began abandoning the city in droves, a phenomenon known as "White flight," or, euphemistically, suburbanization. Glenville, the area in which the Black Seventh-day Adventist church was located, had become a congested ghetto with subpar living conditions by 1960.

Although founded in 1918, not until J. H. Laurence arrived as pastor in 1942 did the Glenville church become one of the most vibrant congregations not just in the regional conferences but all of Adventism. The legendary evangelist's first sermon to the church, then on Cedar Avenue with a membership of 189 and an actual attendance of much less, was on the importance of tithing. The homily was certainly effective, for as the church grew by leaps and bounds under the blessing of God and the expert evangelist, the membership financed a large, handsome building at 737 East 105th Street in what was then the thriving section of Glenville. The $69,000 purchase included a parsonage, a large adjoining lot, and enough building space for a church school, with Laurence's wife, Mae, as the first principal. The church was appropriately renamed Glenville. Far from done, Laurence also put on a radio show that aired every Friday night; broke records in

Ingathering totals; and began a church choir of some renown. When Laurence left in 1952, the membership was at 571, making it the largest Black Adventist congregation in Ohio.

Former church elder R. T. Hudson also had a significant pastorate at Glenville. In his approximately five years there he paid off the mortgage and built an elementary school. In early 1957 Walter M. Starks became pastor but stayed for only a short time, transferring to Dupont Park Seventh-day Adventist Church in Washington, D.C., in late 1959. Significantly, during his time the General Conference session took place in Cleveland June 19 to June 28, 1958, and the Glenville choir performed at the services.

The Brookses' relocation to Cleveland bordered on harrowing. First, the arcticlike winter weather left them with a perpetual chill. The family of three drove to Cleveland through a snowstorm that made it seem as if the clouds had turned to snow and were collapsing on the Buckeye State. The couple left behind a house that they had no choice but to put on the market, despite the fact that few bought homes during the winter in Ohio.

Second, their financial situation loomed as ominously as the weather. Walterene, a teacher at the Ephesus school, had to leave her job, cutting the couple's income in half. Charles's salary as a pastor was already meager, and with another child on the way, things were not looking good financially. After a couple weeks in Cleveland, Walterene came to Charles one day and said softly, "Honey, we don't have any bread or milk."

That was one of the many things that he loved about her. She never complained about not having enough money or things or felt inadequate because she couldn't afford this or that. Marriage to Rene was never humdrum or dull. Even in the most stressful of times it was a joy.

This time Charles was alarmed, though. He had a wife and a baby daughter who would soon be hungry. Leaving their parsonage house, he hastened across the driveway to his church office. Once there he sat at his desk and dug his hands into his pockets, pulling out all the money to his name. It totaled 37 cents. Plopping the change on the table, he fell to his knees and began to pray, but strangely doesn't remember closing his eyes. His prayer was full of "You saids." "Lord, You said that You would never leave me nor forsake me." "You said that the righteous would never be forsaken nor His seed beg for bread." "You said that our bread and water would be sure."

In the midst of his prayer he heard a knock at the door. Charles ignored it. But it persisted. Although hating to interrupt a prayer, he rose from his knees. At the door stood one of his members, Sister Guy.

"Hi, Pastor. You told me last week that you have a book that I want to buy."

Charles, still in prayer mode, didn't know what she was referring to.

"Remember," she questioned, giving him the name of the volume.

Hazily Charles recalled a passing reference. Hurrying to his library, he located the book—it was one of the new picture books with full-color spreads—and handed it to the smiling woman. He told her that it was $12, but she pulled a ten and a five from her purse and laid it on top of the 37 cents. Taking the book, she said that he could give her the change later. After thank-yous and goodbyes, Charles closed the door. When the latch clicked into place he broke into tears.

***

Finally, as was the case with his previous assignments, Charles Brooks was initially criticized for his youth. A fresh-faced 29 when he arrived as pastor, the members harbored major concerns about his age. Before him had been capable veterans who had the wisdom of maturity and experience. This Brooks kid wasn't even 30 yet. Well, Charles's inaugural sermon quelled all of that sort of talk before it could pick up steam. His fiery preaching incinerated any talk of any inadequacies.

Evangelism

To say that Charles Brooks hit the ground running in Cleveland would be an understatement. Of course, evangelism was his focus. To Brooks it was the elixir that warmed up a cold church, the force that moved the members from standing on the premises to standing on the promises. With that in mind, Brooks devised a four-point evangelistic thrust: personal, field, reclamation, and public.

Personal: The young pastor instructed members as well as trained leaders to teach members how to give Bible studies most effectively. The church set up a kind of school of evangelism, and in order to graduate with a certificate a participant had to give at least one Bible study to a nonmember.

Field: Brooks and his assistants divvied up territory and marked out team assignments. Procuring 25-30 vehicles, they loaded them with church members gripping gospel literature. Then they blitzed nearby areas and towns with smiling faces, vigorous handshakes, and publications. Instead of merely dispersing the printed material indiscriminately and then moving on, Brooks advised his parishioners to talk to the people, get to know them if possible, and become their friends.

Reclamation: When Brooks arrived at Glenville the congregation had 300 missing members. Alarmed, he immediately mobilized the church to reclaim them, organizing a meeting of church elders, deacons and deaconesses, and spouses. Together with these leaders, the young pastor went through the list of missing church members one by one. Some of the 300 were dead, others had drifted away, and still more were simply unaccounted for. But once they had arrived at a more realistic number, Brooks formed teams—usually husband and wife—and assigned them one, two, or three names from the new list.

Before the teams went out, though, they drilled to make sure their approach was warm and loving, not condemnatory. At the launch of the reclamation campaign, the entire church was in prayer. After a day's work some came back asking what to do when, after identifying themselves as Glenville church members, people cursed at them and slammed doors in their faces. "You wait a couple of days, fast and pray, and go back" came the response from the new pastor. In cases in which urban renewal had destroyed entire blocks, the members sought out relatives, asking if they knew where their family members lived. They also asked neighbors. After this went on for months, the members next wrote loving, pastoral letters, appealing for the missing to return. Eventually Glenville reclaimed seven missing members. Contemplating whether all of the time and effort was worth the results, Charles recalled Ellen White's words: "One soul for whom Christ has died is worth more than the whole world."

Public: Brooks reasoned that those who could not be wooed back to the fold would have to be replaced. His hunger for evangelism had never been greater. To Charles, evangelism was the fountain from which everything else flowed. And so his first tent series in Cleveland would begin in the summer of 1960, mere months after his arrival. The venue was behind a gas station on a massive lot in a run-down area. The other three evangelistic aspects would contribute to the success of the venture, and the entire church was primed to engage in an evangelistic series of unprecedented proportions.

But just as it started, Rene announced "It's time" on a Sabbath morning in July. As she and Charles deposited little Dee-Dee at Sabbath school with her grandmother, Jessie Wagner, they instructed their 5-year-old not to tell anyone what was happening (in the event of "false labor"). The couple later discovered that their daughter positioned herself in a window and whispered to people as they arrived to church that "Mommy went to the hospital to have a baby."

At St. Ann's Hospital Charles anxiously paced the waiting room while the Wagner men, his father-in-law and Rene's brothers, sat talking excitedly. By and by the doctor came and advised the men that they might as well leave—he would call them in plenty of time for the grand event. Then smiling at Charles, he said, "Just relax." But relaxing was the most foreign concept to Brooks's mind at that moment!

The men drove back to the church and to the Brookses' home next door. They stationed Mother Wagner at the phone, Charles instructing her to let him know immediately when the hospital called. His mother-in-law knowingly reassured him that of course she would and that he needn't worry. John Wagner wanted Charles to preach, but Charles insisted that his father-in-law do it instead. Wagner won the day. Quite conveniently, as the family finished their Sabbath meal, the doctor called. "You should return to the hospital, Pastor. No baby yet, but the time is near."

Rene was in the delivery room when Charles and the Wagner men arrived at St. Ann's. Forced to pace it out in the waiting room (back then hospitals did not allow fathers in the delivery room), Brooks had to wait until the receptionist finally called him. Looking at his face, she teasingly said, "Pastor, you are the father of a fine . . . healthy . . . eight-pound . . . 21-inch . . ." (Brooks was dying from anticipation by now) " . . . son." At that he let out a yelp. As he ran to the window, Rene was being wheeled out, smilingly radiantly. A few steps behind her the doctor held the little boy in his arms, the infant's eyes wide open, already taking everything in. Charles and Walterene named their son Charles D. Brooks II and called him Skip. Coincidentally, Skip was born on July 23, Walterene on July 22, and Charles on July 24.

From the start some interesting dynamics developed between Dee-Dee and Skip. A few months before his birth, the Brookses were driving to Germantown, Ohio, when they decided to tell their daughter that a baby was on the way.

"Dee-Dee," Charles said, his head angled toward the back seat, "we are going to have another baby very soon."

There was no sound for a few moments, so much so that Charles and Rene thought Diedre either hadn't heard or understood.

Finally, in a voice barely audible, came the words "You don't want me anymore."

Her parents glanced at each other, and Charles found a safe place on the highway and pulled the car over. Both parents then made it very clear to their daughter that she was their firstborn, and nothing or no one could ever take her place. She was precious to them and besides, the new baby would belong to her!

In retrospect, Charles and Rene decided that they had probably gone a little too far with that last bit. Even though they never noticed any jealousy again, Dee-Dee really believed that Skip was hers. As soon as he could understand her and walk, she bossed him around and ran his life. It didn't end until the day that Skip thoroughly convinced her that he was grown and was no longer under her benevolent rule. But Charles and Rene never had any real trouble from their children, and for this they thanked God every day.

***

After the safe and healthy birth of his second child, Charles was able to focus on the tent series. One day Luther "Bobby" Palmer strode into his office and took a seat. Brooks knew him well. He came from a solid family and had been ahead of him at Oakwood. Well-educated, he had two master's degrees and held a high-ranking position on the Cleveland Board of Education. Having experienced a remarkable conversion, each Sabbath he drove all the way from Oberlin to attend Glenville.

"Your preaching and teaching have greatly inspired me, and I want to be involved in the Lord's work," Bobby stated.

At his last words Charles inwardly grimaced. He had a budget and opening only for a tentmaster—a person who kept up and guarded the meeting tent. But this accomplished man wouldn't be interested in anything like that. It was surely too insignificant for him.

"I'm sorry, but the only budget I have is for a tent master."

To Brooks's surprise, he had barely finished speaking when Bobby replied, "I'll take it."

It stunned Charles. Bobby had a nice home and a lovely wife and daughter! Would he leave that for two months to live in a tent in a dangerous section of town on a salary that was a mere pittance?

Palmer not only became tentmaster, but quickly made himself indispensable to the point of anticipating what Charles needed even before Brooks knew himself. Eventually Charles recommended him to serve as pastor of the other church under his jurisdiction, Bethel on Wade Park Avenue. The man turned out to be as talented a pastor as he was a tentmaster. He held two evangelistic campaigns and followed up by purchasing a beautiful new church home to accommodate the recent converts.

One afternoon Brooks phoned Bobby to tell him that a tornado was possibly heading their way. The evangelist picked up his associate and sped to the tent, the bright sunshine lighting the usually cloudy city. The two must have looked ridiculous as they began tightening ropes and stakes in the gorgeous glow. But just as they finished, Charles glanced at the sky and could hardly believe his eyes.

"Bobby, look!" Brooks shouted.

Palmer followed his pastor's gaze into the yellow sky. To the west it seemed as if someone were drawing a heavy black blanket across the heavens. It was almost apocalyptic how two halves of the sky were completely opposite in color. The nightly meeting was scheduled to start in 15 minutes, but obviously they would have to cancel it for the evening.

Minutes later a terrible storm struck in full fury. In the face of the advancing wind and rain the tent heaved and snapped and popped. Several men from the neighborhood rushed to help Charles and Bobby keep the canvas up, but when they witnessed a tree snap like a matchstick Brooks shouted above the gale, "Let's take it down!"

The evangelist punctuated his words with a kick to the railing; then he and several men turned over the pulpit and covered the piano. They had let down most of the tent walls when, inexplicably, they could see through the open remaining flaps that a group had gathered on the lot, unsure if they should go under the undulating tent or get back in their cars.

Suddenly Charles did not know what to do. What kind of dedication was this? Were people really standing in a vicious storm with raincoats and umbrellas wanting to come in to hear biblical truth? Like the strange sky earlier, here was something else that occurred within the hour that he had never witnessed before.

It then struck Charles like a bolt of lightning from the storm that this was a spiritual battle—that supernatural forces were at play. "Let's pray," Brooks again yelled above the din. As the men huddled, Brooks shouted a prayer, and from the sound outside it seemed as though the storm was getting more vicious. But when Brooks said "In the name of Jesus," the wind immediately quieted, the rain shut off as if someone had twisted a faucet knob, and those standing outside later told the men under the tent that every storm cloud in the sky fled.

Dumbstruck by what had just occurred, the men quickly set out to reverse what they had just done. As they raised the walls, people started streaming in from everywhere. Some had taken shelter in the service station near the lot, others on strangers' porches, and some had braved the torrents and were soaked from head to toe. But all helped set up chairs, and before they knew it, the tent was packed. What a mighty service God gave the people of Cleveland that night! The storm had battered the city, destroying buildings and felling trees. Power lines snaked dangerously in the street—but the canvas pavilion that belonged to the Seventh-day Adventists had survived intact.

***

More miracles occurred during the 1960 Cleveland evangelistic series. Charles Brooks preached so hard and with such vigor that a thoughtful deaconess nightly prepared cold pineapple juice with chipped ice. The young evangelist enjoyed it immensely as it cooled him off in the sweltering heat. On the most important night when he was to present the doctrine of the Sabbath, Charles went through the preliminaries as usual, only to discover that when he rose to speak at the pulpit he could not utter a word. It was as if someone had thrown a handful of sand down his throat.

As Charles stood mute in front of the expectant audience, his mouth moving but nothing coming out, Bobby Palmer rushed to his side with a glass of water. At the same time the song leader sprang forth and led a song to give him more time. Brooks turned his back to the audience and gulped down the water. At length, he could eke out a coarse, raspy whisper. Then he returned to the microphone and delivered his sermon on the Sabbath in a whisper.

Early Monday morning Charles was in the voice specialist's office. After examining Brooks, he then laid down his instruments and said, "Pastor, you are through talking for six to eight weeks." Objecting, Charles, in a raspy voice, tried to explain his job to the physician. But the man would have none of it. "I'm not asking, I'm telling! You could do permanent damage. I do not even want you to talk to your wife except in a whisper. Your vocal cords are devastated and need rest."

Brooks desperately prayed as he drove home. He was in the middle of a series of meetings that he had to finish. But he didn't want to be presumptuous. On the other hand, he didn't want to lack faith. When he arrived at his parsonage home, a letter from E. E. Cleveland lay in his box. Strangely, Cleveland had never before written a letter to Brooks. Puzzled, Charles opened the envelope. The first words he read were "Charlie, I want to tell you how to take care of your throat. Nothing cold by mouth hours before and after preaching. Drink only water from the tap. If there is a throat crisis, use liquid heat without sugar. Do not drink it down fast. Just sip and bathe the vocal cords with hot liquid."

Shaking his head in amazement, Brooks immediately took the veteran evangelist's advice. That evening as he stood in front of the audience and opened his mouth, Charles preached like he had on opening night. He never had another problem with his throat again.

Years later he pulled Cleveland aside after a church function. Brooks didn't tell him what had happened that night with his voice, nor how he had mailed the letter even before Charles himself knew that he had a problem. Nor did he mention the throat specialist's impossible proscription, or his prayer on the way home about the whole situation. Instead, he just asked a simple question: "Why did you write me that letter on how to take care of my voice at the time you did?" A blank look crossed the face of the usually animated Cleveland; then he broke into a grin and said, "Charlie, you know how the Lord is . . ." Brooks let it go at that. He did know how the Lord was.

With the blessings of God, all the efforts of Charles Brooks, Bobby Palmer, and the Glenville members paid off. The first evangelistic series was such a smashing success that the *Review and Herald* published a spread on it, written by Mylas Martin, a Glenville layman who was a journalist:

"New believers who have become members of the Glenville church in Cleveland, Ohio, through a two-month evangelistic effort in the heart of the city now number 132. The 60-day campaign in the teeming Central Avenue neighborhood packed 500 people nightly into the tent, with 50 to 75 persons standing.

"Charles D. Brooks, Cleveland pastor, was the evangelist. His company of tent workers included Luther R. Palmer, Jr., and three Bible workers, Mrs. Mamie Bond of Chicago, Mrs. Rebecca James of Baltimore, and Mrs. Mary E. Kelly of Cleveland.

"It was the fourth big effort in the past five years in this Great Lakes metropolis of one million people, on the shores of Lake Erie, and it resulted in the largest number ever won in the history of Cleveland evangelism.

"One woman, a habitual drunkard, has given up liquor. 'I look at her face on Sabbath mornings and I barely recognize her as the disheveled woman who came to the tent the first night we opened, July 17,' said Bible worker Mrs. Bond. 'She seems a new person.'

"When one young man began attending, his parents forbade him. But he returned again and again, his 16-year-old heart hungering for the words of life. Bitterly opposed, his parents gave him hours of chores to do each day after school. They knew he could not complete them in time to attend the meetings that began at 7:30 p.m.

"But his high school buddies stepped in to help him. Though they had no convictions themselves, they admired his new interest in religion. Each day after school five or six of these boys went to William's house to help him with his chores. That way he finished on time. And each night he was present and on time to hear the Bible preached.

"Several new converts—such as Brother Thomas Fulford and his wife, who have six children, and another brother whose wife deserted him, leaving him with three small boys to rear—are undergoing severe financial crises.

"The recent evangelistic effort has demonstrated that a Spirit-filled campaign for souls can revitalize a church. Ushers, prayer bands, quartets, trios, song leaders, pianists, and substitute tentmasters served unstintingly night after night, pleading with God to make the meetings a success. Their faithfulness was amply rewarded" (Dec. 29, 1960, p. 19).

Charles Brooks praised God for the 132 individuals that the 1960 meetings brought into the church. Yet he knew that it was God's will for all to be saved, and the next summer he looked for the Lord to bring in still more. Brooks was not disappointed. The summer of 1961 the 31-year-old evangelist baptized 179 people. The influx of new converts put the Glenville membership at more than 1,000, making it the largest congregation in the Allegheny Conference. In his final series in Cleveland in 1963 Charles baptized 108. With this, the name of Charles Brooks joined the list of premier evangelists in the Seventh-day Adventist denomination.

Brooks was especially proud that those he baptized stayed in the church. Already the insidious trend of the recently baptized coming in the front door just to walk out of the back a short time later was increasingly manifesting itself. Not so with Charles: he thoroughly instructed his baptismal candidates on the tenets and requirements of the Seventh-day Adventist faith, all the while observing them closely to discern their steadfastness and sincerity. When a member did drop off the radar, the church immediately sent someone to see about them and made every effort to bring them back into fellowship. As a result, Glenville was the very picture of spiritual vitality, with attendance at Wednesday night prayer meetings almost equal to that of Sabbath morning. The academy connected to the church, Ramah, peaked in enrollment during Brooks's tenure, becoming one of the largest in the conference. W. A. Thompson, the conference treasurer, informed Charles that Glenville was the only church meeting its mortgage and paying back the conference at the same time.

Youth

One of the main focuses throughout Charles Brooks's ministry was youth. Having a deep love and abiding interest in young people, he constantly thought of innovative and creative ways to interest them in the life of faith. With this emphasis, Glenville became known as a church for young people.

The Youth Week of Prayer at Glenville was always special. One year Charles Bradford was the speaker, and the members were enjoying themselves after the excellent preaching with a game identifying authors of books. When the moderator asked who wrote a poem titled "The Charge of the Light Brigade," something flashed in Charles's mind. He thought of the Ellen White quotation stating that the neighbors should know where our churches are. The huge crowds that Glenville attracted caused irritation among the church's neighbors, because of cars either taking parking spaces or blocking vehicles in. Although vague at first, a plan soon took shape in the young pastor's mind.

After assembling a group of youth in the church who were natural leaders, he assigned them to count every home on the six blocks around the church. Once the number was determined, the church raised money to purchase a hardback missionary book for each home. Then they chose 200 young people, assigned each a house, and instructed them to bring a flashlight the following night.

The next night they stacked the expensive volumes in front of the Glenville church. After Charles offered a brief prayer, each young person took a book. With book in hand, they were to stand in front of the house assigned them, then, when the signal was given, turn on their flashlights. Two hundred flashlights of varying intensity and hue then lighted the neighborhood and the sky. The spectacle brought the neighbors to their doors as the fingers of light played across the street.

A young person visited each home on the six blocks and announced, "We are the youth of the Glenville Seventh-day Adventist Church. We wanted to meet and greet our neighbors and bring a little gift we thought you would enjoy. We love you. Do you mind if we say a brief prayer for this home?" Soon there were bowed heads and tear-stained faces all over those six blocks.

Returning to the church, Pastor Brooks led a rousing song service. When everyone finally had gotten back, Charles signaled a deacon, who killed all the lights. At that cue the youngsters flipped back on their flashlights and marched across the sanctuary singing "This little light of mine, I'm going to let it shine." The neighborhood was never the same after that night, and neither were the youth of Glenville.

Their pastor wanted the young people to know that they could find true happiness only in Jesus and biblical truth. And he wanted them to realize that Christians had good, clean fun. Some Sundays he had trucks come and unload bicycles on the church lawn, and with their pastor, the kids would pedal toward the lake and the city parks with their tennis courts, baseball diamonds, basketball and volleyball courts, and jungle gyms. The older, more athletic young men rode ahead, making sure the intersections were safe. Around 11:30 a.m. a church van delivered hot and cold lunches. To cap it off, everyone went to Gibson's Ice Cream Parlor, where Brooks stood at the cash register while all the young people helped themselves to the treats. The church picked up the tab.

But Charles's preaching was perhaps the biggest draw for the young people of the church and the community. From around the city and the bordering suburbs, and increasingly from out of state, people flocked to hear the dynamic speaker, who was himself young. He preached Sunday night, Wednesday night, and Sabbath morning. The church sanctuary, which easily seated 1,000, was consistently packed, even the balcony and the downstairs overflow full. When the pastor spoke, the youngsters milling about in the foyer and halls of the church made a beeline to the sanctuary.

Above all else, though, Charles taught the youth to be soul winners themselves. When the big summer tent series began, he declared a moratorium on social activities until the 10- to 12-week meetings ended. The young people were right by their pastor's side, handing out flyers and invitations, singing and witnessing, and even taking part in the nightly programs. Glenville had the most youth of all the churches in the Allegheny Conference, and their youth program was renowned for being the finest.

His Eyes
One story in particular illustrates Charles's love and care for the young people of Glenville.

Gloria Jackson was entering her senior year of high school in 1960. The only Adventist in her immediate family, she was especially close to her

Glenville church family. She was excited about going to Oakwood for college next year, and the future looked bright for her.

But tragedy struck, and it struck hard. Just two months into the school year she came down with a brutal fever and then began vomiting excessively throughout the day. She felt so terrible that her parents rushed her to nearby Lakeside Hospital. After days of close observation, the physicians administered a spinal tap, one then dreaded for its painfulness. When the doctors had determined her condition, they had her moved immediately to a secluded section of the hospital and placed under strict quarantine. Gloria had viral spinal meningitis.

Her illness worsened, and it was feared that she would die. The city's board of health got involved. At the moment Cleveland had only two cases of meningitis among teens, Gloria on the East Side, and another girl on the West Side. The Jacksons were dismayed the day they received the news that the other victim had died.

Gloria lay in her secluded room near death. Because of the highly infectious nature of meningitis, only her parents could visit her, and then only on a very infrequent basis. When they did venture into her room they donned full protective suits, foot covers, gloves, surgical hats, and face masks, their eyes being the only part of their body exposed. Feeling half dead and uncertain of her future, Gloria longed for human contact.

One evening depression swept over Gloria. Was she going to live or die? Had God given up on her? Would she ever see her church family again? With those thoughts swirling in her head, she heard the door of her room open and a figure in the protective clothing step in. At first she thought it was her doctor with more bad news. But when she saw the walk, she knew it was not her doctor. As the figure came closer, she looked into the eyes—just the eyes—and immediately knew who it was. Her mood totally lifted, and she felt like shouting for joy.

Pastor Brooks!

More than a half century later Gloria remembered nothing of what her pastor said other than a brief prayer. But she had not forgotten the kindness and love that Pastor Brooks showed to her, and how it did her soul better than any medicine or medical procedure ever could. His son had just been born, and her pastor was placing his little family at risk by being in the room. But he was there, for her, a member of his church with no power or standing or money. He was deeply interested in her, enough to risk the safety of himself and his family.

In the intervening years Gloria would never forget those eyes, how the whole time her pastor was smiling at her with inexpressible love. This she knew just by looking at his eyes.

***

It was while pastoring at Glenville that Charles Brooks began to gain renown in the Seventh-day Adventist denomination. Tall, handsome, and dashing with a beautiful wife who possessed a winsome personality, the Brookses were something like the spiritual counterparts of the Kennedys, who were in the White House during those years. Their congregations adored them, the members never forgetting the elegant and regal family who led them. The youngsters in the churches looked up to the Brookses, while the adults latched on to the evangelistic initiatives of their visionary pastor, doing what they could to forward his goals.

But Charles Brooks really gained a following because of his mastery behind the pulpit. In a time when Adventist preachers were straight shooters, Brooks was one of the straightest. Infused with raw power, he crisply delivered his sermons in a no-holds-barred fashion, full of Bible texts, precise vocabulary, and compelling stories that lingered in the mind after the voice had faded. The masses of Adventism craved the clear and powerful way he presented truth, and they sought him out as a speaker at youth events, colleges, camp meetings, and revivals.

Church leaders were also taking notice of him. He was proud to be a Black man, but he could also circulate among Whites with ease, and his presence radiated authority and commanded respect. While he served at Glenville the Columbia Union chose him to serve on its nominating committee. Another acknowledgment that he was a force in the denomination was his appointment as a delegate to the forty-ninth General Conference session (in 1962) in San Francisco, California.

1962: General Conference Session, San Francisco, California

Many General Conference sessions have gone down in history as being crucial to the African American Seventh-day Adventist membership. At the third General Conference session, held in Battle Creek, Michigan, on May 17, 1865, the delegates resolved "that a field is now opened in the South for labor among the colored people and should be entered upon according to our ability." At the General Conference session of 1889, also in Battle Creek, the first ordained Black Adventist minister, Charles Kinney, read a letter on July 17 on the progress of his work for African Americans.

Also at that session church leaders discussed the "color line" at length in an attempt to determine how best to reach both Blacks and Whites in the South.

Two years later at the 1891 session Ellen White delivered her talk "Our Duty to the Colored People" to a select group of leaders, reproving the church for neglecting to prioritize the evangelization of Blacks in the South and urging greater effort in that regard. Here are some of that speech's most memorable excerpts:

"The Lord Jesus came to our world to save men and women of all nationalities. He died just as much for the colored people as for the white race."

"The color of the skin does not determine character in the heavenly courts."

"The God of the white man is the God of the black man, and the Lord declares that His love for the least of His children exceeds that of a mother for her beloved child."

"The Lord's eye is upon all His creatures; He loves them all, and makes no difference between white and black, except that He has a special, tender pity for those who are called to bear a greater burden than others."

"The ignorant and the wise, the rich and the poor, the heathen and the slave, white or black—Jesus paid the purchase money for their souls. If they believe on Him, His cleansing blood is applied to them. The black man's name is written in the book of life beside the white man's. All are one in Christ.

"Birth, station, nationality, or color cannot elevate or degrade men. The character makes the man. If a red man, a Chinaman, or an African gives his heart to God, in obedience and faith, Jesus loves him none the less for his color. He calls him his well-beloved brother. The day is coming when the kings and the lordly men of the earth would be glad to exchange places with the humblest African who has laid hold on the hope of the gospel."

"Those who slight a brother because of his color are slighting Christ."

"If Jesus is abiding in our hearts we cannot despise the colored man who has the same Savior abiding in his heart. When these unchristian prejudices are broken down, more earnest effort will be put forth to do missionary work among the colored race."

"God cares no less for the souls of the African race that might be won to serve Him than He cared for Israel. He requires far more of His people than they have given Him in missionary work among the people of the

South of all classes, and especially among the colored race. Are we not under even greater obligation to labor for the colored people than for those who have been more highly favored? Who is it that held these people in servitude? Who kept them in ignorance, and pursued a course to debase and brutalize them, forcing them to disregard the law of marriage, breaking up the family relation, tearing wife from husband, and husband from wife? If the race is degraded, if they are repulsive in habits and manners, who made them so? Is there not much due to them from the white people? After so great a wrong has been done them, should not an earnest effort be made to lift them up? The truth must be carried to them. They have souls to save as well as we."

"Sin rests upon us as a church because we have not made greater effort for the salvation of souls among the colored people."

"You have no license from God to exclude the colored people from your places of worship. Treat them as Christ's property, which they are, just as much as yourselves. They should hold membership in the church with the white brethren. Every effort should be made to wipe out the terrible wrong which has been done them."

Her pronouncements inspired Edson White and Will Palmer several years later to form the Southern Missionary Society, build the riverboat *Morning Star,* and sail down the Mississippi River to the Deep South to educate and evangelize Black people. In the summer of 1898, using the makeshift printing press on the *Morning Star,* Edson compiled and printed "Our Duty to the Colored People" along with a series of Ellen White articles in the *Review and Herald,* and letters from his mother, into a book called *The Southern Work.*

The Southern Work would powerfully transform generations to come. Many other Black and White Adventist ministers credit it with shaping their concept of God's love for all people; the Christian's attitude toward race, ethnicity, and nationality; human equality; and inclusive ministry. In particular, *The Southern Work* was highly influential in the lives of Charles Brooks and other Black Adventist leaders of his time in their understanding of race relations in America and the church, and would inspire their efforts to redress inequality and discrimination in Adventism. In the 1973 book *What Ellen White Has Meant to Me,* edited by Herbert Douglass, Brooks credits *The Southern Work* with renewing his belief in the inspiration of Ellen White:

"But I am black and there was a time when Satan stormed my faith by stinging references to what 'Mrs. White says in *[Testimonies for the Church]* volume 9 about black people?' It happened that even as a youngster I weighed the positive good of all I had read against the apparent narrowness of volume 9, and decided to suspend judgment until I could understand.

"I could not believe that she who would write *The Desire of Ages*, presenting Christ as the Desire of all nations, and who wrote so powerfully of the final triumph when God's people of every race, kindred, tongue, and people would be gathered home, could possibly be a racist. It just didn't make sense that Mrs. White could write with such conviction and power urging the church into jungle recesses and island villages in search of souls, and then believe that the fruit of such excursions could be 'one in Christ' and subhuman at the same time. I couldn't allow my impression of the instrument who penned *Steps to Christ* to disintegrate.

"Would she who wrote with such tenderness, such holiness, such feeling, such sympathy, now break the 'bruised reed'? Could one who wrote with such love now join the hostile oppressor, the inhuman, demon-inspired tyrant against a defenseless people? I'm glad I wondered and did not jump to conclusions. I'm glad I suspended judgment. I waited.

"But I was troubled. Men and women, black and white, were being fed a revolting diet of sanctified racism, and perhaps it did much less harm to the blacks than it did to their white brothers and sisters. It displaced love, nurtured bitterness, extended ignorance, and separated brethren. Many fell by the wayside on both sides of the issue. Could God's servant be responsible for that? Many blacks tried to find a way out. Some just dismissed the issue; but it didn't go away.

"Others questioned: 'Is all that Mrs. White wrote inspired?' To me this is a dangerous approach. It opens the door to skepticism everywhere and solves nothing. One could easily dismiss any counsel or all counsel by simply deciding that one part of this counsel was not inspired. Well, I don't believe that way. I do not think of some words as inspired and others as uninspired.

"I believe Mrs. White was inspired. She was God's chosen instrument. We cannot categorize her writings according to our likes and dislikes. *She* was inspired! *She* was chosen! *She* was special to God and His church, and whatever counsel she gave came from Him.

"I finished school, refusing to lose faith in spite of all the foolishness some people had associated with certain statements in volume 9. I heard painful references applying the statement about the 'amalgamation of man and beast,' to the production of subhuman beings. I endured the insults aimed at black morals and black brains and black worship. I lived with the discipline of humiliation and sustained myself with private thoughts and faith.

"Then one day my wife's father, a saintly minister of God and president of my conference, answered a question for me. His radiant, confident, poised faith was something to emulate. He was a fighter for human rights and dignity, but he was always at peace. I wanted to know whether all this bothered him. He pulled from a special recess in his desk a battered old copy of *The Southern Work* by Ellen G. White and began to read. I cannot tell you how I felt. There it was, God coming through for me and for disinherited peoples of all lands. There was what I had heard at mother's knee from the 'fancy-backed' volume that the Methodist deacon brought— truth, courage, power, judgment, and through it all the sterling quality of the gift and the vessel. I didn't have to surrender one iota of respect or confidence.

"Some time later I got my own copy of this book, *The Southern Work*. I was no longer afraid to investigate, no longer fearful that the whole beautiful thing would come crashing down on me. I should have known better. I think I did.

"Here is a sample of what became clearer to me as the days of study passed:

" 'The white people who embrace the truth in the Southern field, if converted to God, will discern the fact that the plan of redemption embraces every soul that God has created. The walls of sectarianism and caste and race will fall down when the true missionary spirit enters the hearts of men. Prejudice is melted away by the love of God. All will realize that they are to become laborers together with God. Both the Ethiopian and the white race are God's purchased possession, and our work is to improve every talent that has been lent to us of God, to save the souls of both white and black.'—*The Southern Work, p. 55.*

" 'There is to be no special heaven for the white man and another heaven for the black man. We are all to be saved through the same grace, all to enter the same heaven at last. Then why not act like rational beings, and overcome our unlikeness to Christ.'—*Ibid.*

" 'He who is closely connected with Christ is lifted above the prejudice of color or caste.'—*Testimonies,* vol. 9, p. 209.

" 'He [Christ] laid the foundation for a religion by which Jew and Gentile, black and white, free and bond, are linked together in one common brotherhood, recognized as equal in the sight of God.'—*Ibid.,* vol. 7, p. 225.

"These are only a few of the general statements of principle, but all her comments taken in context are essentially incisive, direct, clear, sharp, bold in rebuke, and loving in appeal. Not all that has been written is complimentary to the black race, and certainly not to the white race. But her counsel is practical, timely, and realistic; it is just. The point is, the Lord's servant was what we should expect her to be in her witness: flawlessly pure and true to principle. She said, 'I do not intend to live a coward or die a coward.' Like all of God's prophets, she was first faithful to her calling—to speak for God without accommodating to the ingrained sins of the people. She never compromised.

"The negative, soul-withering impressions too long ascribed to volume 9 are the responsibility then, not of the sacred gift or of the holy vessel, but of misguided persons who want to project their own views and that of a hostile, divided, hate-filled society on the authority of the Lord's servant. In recent years I have cooperated with concerned church leaders to see that *The Southern Work,* so long out of print, was republished and joined the other well-known Ellen G. White volumes. Together, they pull up the slack, exalt the dark valleys of oppression, make low the mountains and hills of pride and superiority, and place the flock of God everywhere on an equality in all nations and among all races. She challenges all to stand equal in Christ Jesus, a common brotherhood of saints.

"I did not have to surrender my faith in Ellen White. Had I found her to be a racist I would have found her to be immoral, for racism is immoral. On the other hand, I did not have to surrender my manhood or my convictions on the brotherhood of man in order to believe in her. No one else can decide for me whether or not I am a man and equal to all other men in that respect. I decided that. The God who created me said so, and as surely as I am born, Mrs. White confirms it. She was a champion of human rights. She spoke up when it was unpopular to do so—even dangerous. The pioneers of our faith joined her and risked much for this principle. I am grateful now that our church stands on this principle, supports this principle. We are officially and forever with her on this question. Anyone in the church showing weakness in this area is out of step with the church, out of agreement with what she wrote, and out of harmony with God. Such deserve our pity and our prayers.

"Ellen White is my friend. I believe in her as a person, a prophetess, a servant of God. The church moves ahead as it moves back to her God-given counsel. 'Believe his prophets, so shall ye prosper' " (pp. 38-42).

In fact, Brooks believed in *The Southern Work* so strongly that he would be instrumental in its reprinting by the Ellen G. White Estate in 1966.

***

Still more General Conference sessions were pivotal to the Black cause in the Adventist Church. On February 11, 1895, versatile White minister and evangelist Harry S. Shaw (Shaw often passed for Black in the South, and took advantage of his ability to blend in with both races) delivered a talk on the work among African Americans, affirming the importance of evangelizing Blacks and their equal humanity. Provocative for the time, Shaw mused, "A large majority of the inhabitants of the world are colored people. But some have said, 'I wonder why it is that the Lord made the black man black'; but I wonder why in the world he made the white man white. The mystery to me is, why he didn't make all of them colored." Quoting from "Our Duty to the Colored People," Shaw continued: " 'The character makes the man.' I am glad the Lord said that. It takes the character of Jesus Christ, too; and the character of Jesus Christ in the black man is the character of Jesus Christ, notwithstanding." Shaw then followed up with a lengthy excerpt from Ellen White's 1891 address.

In later consecutive sessions in the late 1890s and the first decade of the 1900s Edson White reported on the progress among Blacks in the South made by the Southern Missionary Society. His reports were impressive in the fact that he always presented tangible fruits of the Society's efforts—number of converts, schools, books distributed, and SMS workers—as well as impassioned appeals for more laborers. He also encouraged, often dogmatically, intelligent and considered methods of reaching African Americans, knowing from experience that sporadic, halfhearted, and ill-laid efforts were doomed to failure.

In 1909 at the thirty-seventh General Conference session in Washington, D.C., church leadership established the Negro Department to "advance the work among the Colored people." Other conferences would follow suit and establish departments dedicated to African American concerns and missions. By 1918 the denomination had appointed distinguished lawyer William H. Green as the first Black director of the Negro Department, a position he held until his death in late 1928. His successors were all prominent Black ministers: George E. Peters, Frank L. Peterson, Calvin E. Moseley, Harold D. Singleton, and Walter W. Fordham. After several name changes, the department was discontinued in 1978—the formation of regional conferences in the 1940s and increasing Black representation in church leadership in the intervening years making it redundant.

At the General Conference session of 1922, held in San Francisco, California, one of the most effective evangelists of any color in the church for the past decade, Jamaican James K. Humphrey, delivered the evening sermon on May 23. Humphrey and his congregation, the First Harlem Seventh-day Adventist Church, would eventually be disfellowshipped in 1930, an event that served as a catalyst for the formation of regional conferences. But in his talk at the 1922 session Humphrey announced his loyalty to the church:

"In 1905, a brother came to my house and urged me to cut loose from this denomination. That man was about twenty years my senior. I flatly refused to do it. I had been only three years in the truth. I refused then to do it, and I refuse now to do it. I gave him my reason. I told him that I had never seen in the Word of God a precedent for any man, under any circumstances whatever—of hardships and trials and troubles, of wrong treatment by his brethren—never a precedent for any man to turn aside from God's organized plan of work, and succeed. I therefore said, 'I cannot go with you.' "

Laymen's Leadership Conference
Perhaps the most pivotal General Conference session for African Americans was the 1962 one in San Francisco. As a delegate Charles Brooks participated in the monumental events that took place there, and a prominent member of the Glenville church was a key player in the drama that unfolded.

The formation of Black, or regional, conferences did not remove racism and discriminatory practices and policies from the Seventh-day Adventist Church. Throughout the late 1940s, 1950s, and early 1960s Blacks continued to be excluded from attending predominately White Adventist schools and churches. Meanwhile, in the United States the civil rights movement had begun and was gaining momentum, especially in the late fifties and early sixties.

Lay Adventist Frank Hale, Jr., in 1960 an English professor at Wilberforce University in Ohio, was active in secular circles in combating racial prejudice, segregation, and discrimination. His discovery in May 1960 of a policy that restricted a limit of three Black students for an enrollment of 300 at an Adventist academy in Michigan convinced him that he should also turn his attention to inequality in his own denomination.

Other developments sharpened in Hale's mind exactly how he would go about addressing the complex and stubborn issue. On February 26, 1961, he invited nine (six women and three men) activist-minded Ohio Adventist Black laypersons—including the influential journalist Mylas Martin of Glenville, whom Charles Brooks pastored—to meet at the Neighborhood House in Columbus, Ohio. Martin was the first student to enroll at Pine Forge Institute when the Black school in Pennsylvania opened in 1946, and he attended Oakwood for a brief time with Brooks. After he graduated from Case Western Reserve University, Martin began a career in journalism. When the Brookses arrived at Glenville, Mylas was already a minor celebrity in the city.

Taking the name "Laymen's Leadership Conference" (LLC), the group of 10 set down specific goals that the new organization aimed to accomplish, among them discontinuing closed admissions policies and quota systems in Adventist schools; hiring teachers based on qualifications; welcoming people of all races and colors to all SDA churches; establishing institutes to develop techniques and strategies on the improvement of race relations; and following the biblical principles and those of Ellen G. White on matters of race. The final resolution was "to move with all deliberate speed on the solutions herein mentioned."

Exactly a month later the LLC met again and added 10 more individuals. The meeting approved a brochure with information about the LLC and how to start a local chapter as well as a bank of quotations from *The Southern Work*. Soon the movement gained momentum, thanks mainly to the justness of its cause, the charismatic and decisive leadership of Frank Hale, and the vigorous force of Mylas Martin.

In a matter of months the LLC was well on its way to being a truly national organization, carrying its message to regional churches across the nation and insisting on a formal meeting with General Conference administrators at the Spring Council of 1962 that would take place before the GC session of that year. Indeed, the controversial organization had already commanded the attention of the church's top leaders who then sought to respond to Hale and Martin. At the same time hundreds of letters poured in from faithful Black Seventh-day Adventists describing the racism they constantly had to endure. For example, they were being denied services from institutions that their tithes and offerings helped to make possible.

The reaction to the LLC among Black Adventists was generally supportive, but opposition developed in some quarters. E. E. Cleveland agreed with the aims and objectives of the group, but thought their way of going about them was Machiavellian. Frank L. Peterson, who in a surprising twist would later benefit from the efforts of the LLC, staunchly resisted against the group. His letters to Frank Hale, to whom Peterson was a mentor when he was president of Oakwood and Hale was a professor there, are profoundly compelling. Peterson strongly urged his protégé to dismantle the LLC, because it would "bring the church into disrepute before the world." Hale responded just as persuasively to Peterson's points, and, in a memorable line, wrote on May 3, 1961:

"If the General Conference, the union conferences, the local conferences, the publishing houses, the evangelists, the ministers, the missionaries, and the educational and medical institutions would all combine their powers to erase the smudge of racial segregation and discrimination among us, the whole system would crack and crumble overnight. Such a challenge is for us the living! I have no other plans but to accept this challenge."

Meanwhile, Hale, Martin, and the rest of the LLC prepared a letter and flyer for mass distribution and sent it to their regional constituents. The material stated in part that Seventh-day Adventists championed reform in the areas of diet, health, dress, amusement, music, religious liberty, et al, in a straightforward manner and without apology or concern whether such teachings were counter to the prevailing culture, all because of their belief that the values they presented were biblical. Yet with race relations Adventists had a passive, laissez-faire, it-will-change-with-time attitude and seemed to have little interest in altering the situation. In the meantime, tithe-paying Black Adventist Christians continued to suffer unspeakable injustices. This state of affairs had to be challenged and action taken immediately.

The General Conference met with the LLC on October 23, 1961. The LLC board voted that Hale, Martin, Burrell and Bonnie Scott, Mrs. Willie Dodson, and Mrs. John Richard Ford represent the organization and also voted nine recommendations to present to the church officers. Seven men represented the General Conference, among them Frank Peterson, Neal Wilson, and Walter L. Cheatham. The LLC contingent articulated their reason for existence and what they felt needed to be done in the form of the nine recommendations. The church administrators, for their part, carefully questioned the laypersons. The session had some immediate impact, for four days later the Fall Council, on October 27, 1961, released to the press an official statement affirming the equality of all people.

Frank Hale's organization knew, however, that words and sentiments were cheap indeed, and so pressed on in their fight against institutional racism in the church. The letters documenting racist episodes continued to inundate the LLC's Oberlin office and lent even more urgency and purpose to the group's activities. Meanwhile, communication between Hale and GC officials continued, church leaders more than a little trepid about what LLC might do at the General Conference world session in San Francisco in the summer of 1962. Unfortunately, the LLC and GC leaders failed to meet again before the start of the meetings on July 26. When a GC official informed Hale on July 2, 1962, that the desired discussion would not occur, he later remembered that he "lost no time in informing the LLC executive officers of that decision. The die was cast. I knew now that it would be necessary to go directly to the press in order for any meaningful dialogue to occur between LLC officers and the president of the General Conference. . . . His final slap in the face was glaringly unacceptable."

Frank Hale flew to San Francisco on July 26, 1962, the morning that the GC session commenced and with several assistants set up headquarters in a conference suite in the Jack Tar Hotel. When Mylas Martin arrived, he and Hale decided to hold a press conference with Bonnie and Burrell Scott, whose daughter had been denied admission at Mount Vernon Academy in Ohio. The press conference was effective: some of the nation's most prominent newspapers headlined the story, among them the New York Times ("Adventist Head Asks Patience of the Church's Racial Critics"), San Francisco Chronicle ("100 Pastors Open New Fight on Adventist Bias," "A Fervent Plea for Adventist Integration," and "Adventists Challenged to End Racial Segregation"), San Francisco Times ("Church Academy Hit in Race Issue"), and Oakland Tribune ("Negro Adventists Press Integration"). Additionally Time, Newsweek, Jet, and other magazines ran similar stories. Telegrams, letters, and telephone calls of support inundated the LCC headquarters.

The General Conference leadership designated F. L. Peterson as their official spokesperson to address the response LCC was generating. Once again, Hale was dismayed that his mentor was positioning himself, in Hale's opinion, in the way of progress and being used to "minimize the impact" of the LLC. The LLC held a rally on July 28 at the Jack Tar Hotel with more than 1,000 in attendance.

"The ballroom was peppered by a swirl of electric energy, joyous anticipation, and a frenzy of excitement and racial pride, as those gathered there could not overlook the fact that black Adventists were redefining due process beyond any intentions that traditional decision makers either anticipated or could endorse," Hale later described the scene.

The speakers on that occasion were Mylas Martin; Bonnie Scott; J. Estelle Barnett, a 76-year-old retired layperson from Columbus; and Frank Hale as the keynote speaker. Among other things, Hale presented a letter to the General Conference calling for immediate total integration. On that same day, the church elected Frank Peterson as one of four vice presidents of the General Conference, the first Black ever to hold the position.

If the inaugural press conference was effective, the rally was doubly so. American media trumpeted the story. Nearly 100 Black Adventist ministers, led by Charles Bradford, lent their full support to the LLC. General Conference President R. R. Figuhr spoke on race relations several times at the session. The LLC sold almost 3,000 copies of *The Southern Work* within four days, and later the Ellen G. White Estate republished the volume. Frank Hale considered the election of Peterson to be at least partly owing to the efforts of his grassroots organization. Most important, though, it had directed the attention of the world church to the unacceptable racial realities in Adventism.

Charles Brooks and the Session
Being chosen as a delegate to the General Conference session in San Francisco portended a new phase in Charles Brooks's ministry. The young evangelist actually halted a campaign he was in the middle of to attend the meetings, something he was loath to do. But being in touch with the worldwide church and taking part in its functioning was essential to him, so he flew to the City by the Bay in late July 1962, as did the other 1,314 delegates from around the globe.

Occasions such as the GC sessions every four years reminded Brooks of the strong providence of God in raising up this grand movement. He marveled to see people of all colors and backgrounds come together with one common purpose and goal. The activities and messages during the week or so caused him to renew afresh his commitment to preach what his mother, then he and his siblings, and finally his father, had embraced not so many years before. Since then, his overriding passion had been to tell others about it, and God had richly blessed his efforts.

Although Brooks was not directly involved with the Laymen's Leadership Conference, he stayed abreast of developments and noted their progress as one of the greatest grassroots movements Adventism had ever seen. His parishioner, Mylas Martin, was of course instrumental in it, and Frank Hale, at 35 years of age, was already a force to be reckoned with.

Hale, Martin, and their LLC were not the only Black leaders meeting and effecting change at the 1962 session, however. Charles Brooks, along with other young Black ministers Jesse Wagner, Jr., Earl Cleveland, Charles Bradford, Burrell Scott, and Aaron Brogden, held a separate meeting of their own, strategizing how to improve the racial situation in their denomination. Each man agreed to do his part in personally influencing church leaders and constituencies at the session, not like the LLC with its press conferences and rallies, but behind the scenes, obtaining airtight promises. Because of E. E. Cleveland's clout and expert negotiating skills, he emerged as the leader of the small group, leaving the strategy session with the heaviest burden to achieve results. He didn't disappoint. Charles Brooks believed that it was primarily the backroom maneuvering of Cleveland that resulted in the election of Frank Peterson.

But Charles and the others also did their part in budging a stubborn church. Personal contact and forged alliances put pressure on top leadership, jumpstarting the vehicle of change. As noted earlier, after the session Brooks was instrumental in republishing *The Southern Work,* a book that ensured progress by its very distribution.

Brooks always held the truth to be most important. With countless other Black church leaders and ministers who facilitated the diversification of Adventism (significant numbers of people of color becoming Adventists, both in the United States and overseas), he was highly attuned to the developing racial dynamics. To be sure, Black leaders such as Brooks, Cleveland, Henri, Fordham, Wagner, and others boldly denounced racism where they encountered it in church administration. Yet at the same time they were extremely careful to not disclose such injustices to their lay members, who often did not have the grounding in the faith and the far-sighted perspective that they had as pastors of the flock. Early leaders such as G. E. Peters and W. H. Green could not dine in the General Conference cafeteria because of their color. Like Christ they endured insults silently, with grace and forbearance. But their real valor and love for the church appears in the fact that they did not grow bitter and divulge such egregious slights to the Black membership.

Charles Brooks was especially careful of this because he grasped early on that one's allegiance to Jesus and biblical truth trumped how one was treated by those who were supposed to be following Jesus and the truth. To recount racial wrongs to certain members might cause them to lose their connection with Jesus. That was to be avoided at all cost. Little did Brooks know that his next assignment would give him a prime opportunity to address the embedded racism in the church, and to show God's people a better way.

UNION

"How best to teach others than by example?"

O ne of the most important developments at the 1962 General Conference session as far as Charles Brooks's career was concerned was the election of Neal C. Wilson as president of the Columbia Union Conference.

The son of missionaries Nathaniel and Hannah Wilson, Neal Clayton was born on July 5, 1920, in Lodi, California. Exotic places and people that he encountered in the mission field filled his youth as he lived in Africa, Asia, Australasia, and North America. Wilson graduated from Pacific Union College in 1942, marrying Elinor Neumann that same year. The couple had two children, both of whom dedicated their life to denominational service. In fact, Neal's son, Ted, would also become president of the worldwide church.

Neal first served as pastor-evangelist in Wyoming, where, like Charles Brooks, he pastored churches while running tent campaigns in the lonely state, which at that time had a population of a little more than 250,000. It wasn't long before the church asked Neal to serve as a missionary in the Middle East, because of his vast experience in various mission fields as a youngster. In preparation for this he took the Arabic class at the Seventh-day Adventist Seminary in Washington, D.C.

The Wilsons—now a family of four—lived in Egypt from 1944 to 1958. At this early point in his career he was already displaying exceptional leadership qualities: the ability to establish rapport with people, memorizing their names and small details; being an astute and shrewd observer of cultures, establishing consensus among diverse groups; and the skill of getting others on board to accomplish goals. Church leaders, noting this, made Wilson superintendent of the Egypt Mission, and later president of the Nile Union Mission, all while still a young adult. Also, like Brooks, Neal Wilson constantly promoted evangelism, experiencing record baptisms in the region because of such an emphasis. Far from restricting his efforts to Egypt, Wilson pioneered the message in the Sudan and Libya, planting churches and assisting in the establishment of missions and medical facilities.

The Wilsons relocated to California, where Neal spent a brief time working for the Central California Conference; then he went to the Columbia Union Conference in 1960, where he was the religious liberty secretary until elected president at the General Conference session in 1962. During that year the paths of two of Adventism's most dynamic young ministers merged.

In 1963 the Columbia Union held a constituency session in Atlantic City, New Jersey, and it proved no less divisive than the GC session in San Francisco. As a member of the constituency, Charles Brooks took an active part in the meetings, unaware that his voice would soon be raised the loudest in protest.

When the constituents turned their attention to choosing a lay activities secretary for the union, Brooks nominated Doug Simons, an African American minister who had a fine service record and one whom Charles knew would be a good fit for the job. Across the room a White man nominated a White minister for the position. When no one offered any more nominations, the board took a vote on the two nominees. Simons received only 3 votes out of 21. Immediately sensing what had happened, Charles was outraged. He was one of the three Blacks on the committee.

His anger only increased when one of his White counterparts rose to lecture the three disappointed Black men on the democratic process. In a patronizing manner he explained to them that a person was elected for a position when they received the majority of votes. When the individual at last sat down, Charles immediately rose with a retort:

"We don't appreciate being lectured on the democratic process. I pastor the largest church in the Allegheny territory, Elder Cheatham is a conference president, and this man is a highly successful entrepreneur," he said, gesturing to the two other Black men. "It is quite obvious that the democratic process will never work for us as long as we are in the minority!"

There was such silence in the room that one could hear the proverbial pin drop. Many of the White leaders shifted in their seats uncomfortably, while others suddenly found the tabletop in front of them engrossing. But Brooks wasn't finished.

"There are three votes for Elder Simons. Can you guess where the three votes come from?"

No one dared look at Cheatham or the other Black individual, but everyone knew that they were the ones.

"On the other hand," Charles continued, "I can't blame you who voted 18 to 3 for the new secretary. That's understandable, because you attended school with him and were on the same baseball team. But you do not know Doug Simons. You voted your knowledge, and that is why the democratic process will never cure the problem."

It was true: they had very little inkling as to who Doug Simons was but knew their own nominee very well. What if Simons was the better man for the job?

With authority in voice and manner, Brooks ended, "We must do right because it is right."

Although the Black contingent left dejected, they would eagerly watch to see if things improved with the new president, Neal Wilson.

The Call

A few weeks after Atlantic City, to Charles's surprise he received a letter from the Columbia Union Conference in which Wilson asked him to join the conference staff as field secretary. Cheatham had told Charles that after the constituency meeting in Atlantic City, Wilson had asked a committee of officers what kind of individual the union should have. "Do we need a 'yes man'? Or do we need someone who will courageously speak their mind and stand for right?" Neal deftly persuaded the officers that Charles Brooks was the person for the job.

If Brooks accepted, he would be the first Black at the union conference level who was not just in charge of the "Black work." Yet without even thinking about it, Charles turned the offer down. An office was not for him. He needed to be winning souls on the front line. Twice more Brooks received official letters from the union, each one more urgent and imploratory. And twice more he declined the position.

The next offer came in the form of a phone call from Wilson at the Allegheny camp meeting at Pine Forge Academy, where Brooks was scheduled to preach. While Brooks was in a field putting up a tent in the blazing heat, a car slowly veered off the road and stopped within 10 yards. The camp meeting staff had brought a field phone, and one of them held it up for Charles, indicating that he had a call. It was Neal Wilson. He wanted

C.D. as a student at
James Dudley High School

EXCEPT WHERE INDICATED, ALL PHOTOS COURTESY OF C. D. BROOKS

THE JAMES B. DUDLEY HIGH SCHOOL.

Panther's Claw Staff

Extreme top to right: Mrs. Angeline Smith, adviser, Adolphus Millings, Hazel Robinson, Jecelyn Bailey, Mildred Brown, Dorothy Henderson, Frances Millings, Doris Gill, Charles Brooks, Sallie Carew, Essie Meadows, and James Hargett; Elizabeth Mintz, editor-in-chief, center.

C.D., editor of the Oakwood 1951
yearbook *Acorn*, working at his desk

COURTESY OF OAKWOOD UNIVERSITY ARCHIVES

Staff of James Dudley High School
student newspaper, *Panther's Claw*. On
the top is Angeline Smith, C.D.'s English
teacher. C.D. is third from bottom on
the left.

C.D. in 1951 as an evangelistic intern for J. G. Dasent in Uniontown, Pennsylvania

RUSSELL W. BATES
Major: Religion
Minor: History

AARON N. BROGDEN
Major: Religion
Minor: Business

CHARLES D. BROOKS
Major: Religion
Minor: English

HAROLD L. CLEVELAND
Major: Religion
Minor: History

The 1951 Oakwood *Acorn*

Walterene Wagner in 1951

Wedding day,
September 14, 1952

Marvin and Mattie Brooks

The Brooks brothers at C.D.'s wedding. Left to right: Marvin, Jr., C.D., Hugh, and Elliott ("Rock").

Left to right: C.D., Marvin, Jr. (brother), Marvin, Sr. (father), Hugh (brother), Elliott (brother)

C.D. and Walterene on their honeymoon at Niagara Falls, 1952

Diedre Brooks, 1955

Left to right: (back) John Wagner, Jr., Walterene Wagner Brooks, C.D.; (front) Diedre Brooks, Judy Wagner, 1959

C.D. and son Skip, 1966

"The Rabbi," C. E. Moseley

C.D. with young people of Ephesus church in Columbus, Ohio, 1957

C.D. with the recently baptized at
Ephesus church, 1958

Neal Wilson, president
of Columbia Union
Conference, 1962

COURTESY OF GC ARCHIVES

Newark, 1966: the first
integrated campaign with Alvin
Stewart, associate evangelist

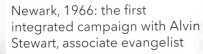

C. D. Brooks preaching, 1965

C. D. Brooks
in Guadalajara,
Mexico,
answering
questions

A BRIGHT HOPE
FOR A DISMAL WORLD

Will we be happier for seeing the other side
of the moon, or strolling in the meadows of
Mars, or exploring the rings of Saturn?
A subject Philadelphia cannot put off . . . A
matter you cannot turn aside . . . .

CHRIST IS OUR ONLY HOPE

CHARLES D. BROOKS, Speaker

Flyer for evangelistic meeting in
Philadelphia, 1964

C.D. around the time he started working at Columbia Union Conference

C.D. at a youth rally encouraging involvement in Mission '73

Hope Pavilion, Chicago, 1973

C.D. looking at sign in front of Hope Pavilion, Chicago, 1973

C.D. instructing baptismal candidates during Chicago campaign, 1973

C.D. and H. A. Lindsay baptizing Chicago campaign converts at Shiloh church, 1973

Chicago '73 team in front of tent. On Brooks's right is college roommate Russell Bates. Delbert Baker is on far right.

▲ The Breath of Life Heritage Series, 1974

◄ C.D. speaking with scriptwriter Louis B. Reynolds, 1974

▼ Advertisement for the Breath of Life campaign in Atlanta, 1977

CHARLES D. BROOKS Speaker

Breath of Life CRUSADE '77

WALTER ARTIES Special Music

Introducing

Breath of Life with Charles D. Brooks as speaker and Walter Arties as soloist, with the Breath of Life quartet. This telecast presents the message of salvation through a unique evangelistic thrust called the Heritage series. Numerous soloists and choral groups also appear.

You don't want to miss this exciting new television series.

Breath of Life CRUSADE '78

'DCA CHANNEL 20 - 8:00 A.M. Each Saturday

CHARLES D. BROOKS DIRECTOR · SPEAKER

Breath of Life campaign promotion at the Warner Theatre, Washington, D.C., 1978

C.D. during
Breath of Life
filming, 1975

Breath of Life
team, 1975

Breath of Life
advertisement,
1979

Breath of Life

with **CHARLES D. BROOKS,** speaker
now on television each Saturday
WDCA CHANNEL 20
8:00 A.M.

**CHARLES D.
BROOKS**
DIRECTOR · SPEAKER

C.D. speaking with translator at the 1975 GC session in Vienna

In the summer of 1984 C.D. led the Breath of Life team on a tour of the Holy Land. Here he is at the tomb where Jesus was believed to have been laid.

Media giants: C.D. with George Vandeman (standing) and Dan Matthews (seated), 1984

C.D. speaking at the Palau High School for the Breath of Life campaign in Palau, 1981

C.D. with fellow ministers, c. 1984

C.D. in 1983

C.D. and Reggie Robinson at the
MLK induction ceremony, 1994

C.D. and Walterene
in the early 1990s

The Brooks family.
Left to right:
Brandon Tramel,
Samuel Tramel,
Diedre Brooks
Tramel, Bradley
Tramel, Charles
"Skip" Brooks II,
Walterene, C.D.,
Detra Brooks

Christ of the Narrow Way, by Elfred Lee, 1991. C.D. is seventh from the front.

Honorees at the MLK induction ceremony, 1994

C.D. final campaign with Breath of Life: Phoenix, 1995

At a ceremony honoring Neal Wilson. Left to right: Harold Lee, Maurice Battle, Ted Wilson, Elinor Wilson, Neal Wilson, Augustus Cheatham, C. D. Brooks, Calvin Rock, 1995

C. D. Brooks, E. E. Cleveland, and Charles Bradford cut the ribbon
at the opening ceremony of the Bradford-Cleveland-Brooks
Leadership Center on October 22, 2007.

Bradford-Cleveland-Brooks Leadership Center

At the Breath of Life reunion on November 3, 2012.
Left to right: Walter Arties, C. D. Brooks, Walter Pearson, Carlton Byrd.

to know if Brooks could at least come to the union office to talk it over. Politely Charles told Wilson that he felt he wasn't suited for the position. The Lord had explicitly called him to do evangelism, and he could not do that cooped up in an office.

"Well, if you won't come to me, then I'll have to come to you," Neal said.

Standing out in the sun with no shade, Charles felt himself being toasted to a crisp while talking with the union president. But while he still had the field phone, he called Rene back in Cleveland. He shared with her what had just happened and suggested that they at least pray about it. At that the two sent prayers heavenward, petitioning the Lord's wisdom and direction.

After handing the phone back to the worker in the car, Charles pondered Wilson's persistence. An incident from five years before came vividly to his mind. The Glenville church had hosted a Columbia Union Conference officers' meeting. As the host pastor Brooks oversaw the arrangements and was privy to the dynamics of union administration. Neal Wilson was religious liberty director of the union at the time and had warmly greeted and conversed with Charles, asking him about his time at the church and his evangelistic meetings, and generally taking an interest in the young pastor.

The other White leaders, though, Charles noted, looked downright uncomfortable. It was obvious that they were not used to dealing with Black leaders. In fact, they didn't seem to know how to relate to Black people at all. Charles could feel the tension in the air.

When the meeting concluded at 5:30 in the evening, the officers seemed relieved and quickly fled the premises. It gave new meaning to the phrase "White flight," something occurring in cities all across the nation during those years. As was his custom, Charles began to walk around the church premises to check on things.

As he started down a corridor to the fellowship hall he stopped short when he saw who was sitting on the piano bench, talking to several laymen of his congregation. It was Neal Wilson! The White man was obviously in no hurry to escape, totally at ease around Blacks. Brooks was amazed. After he finished with that conversation, Neal Wilson had again spoken with Charles, even discussing regional conference pastors and leaders, about whom Wilson was surprisingly knowledgeable.

After praying with his wife, Charles got back to work in his dirty overalls and sun hat, hammering in tent stakes. The young pastor lifted the hammer up and drove it down on the peg, a sharp metal-on-metal "thwack" echoing across the grounds. Occasionally the men broke for a break, but for the most part the country-raised Brooks could work in the heat indefinitely.

About 5:30 the cafeteria served dinner, and Charles strode over with the other workers. Dusty, sweaty, and tanned from the sun, the crew was a sight to behold. The coolness of the cafeteria was a much-appreciated respite, and the men began to get in line. As Charles headed toward it to get his food, someone tapped him on the shoulder, indicating that he had visitors. He turned around, scanning the cafeteria to see whom the messenger was referring to. Then he spotted them: at a table in the midst of the cafeteria sat Neal Wilson and Carl Weiss from the Columbia Union. Charles quickly did the math in his head. Wilson had called him from Takoma Park about 2:00 p.m. It was 5:30 now. The man must have hung up and got in his car immediately and driven to Pine Forge, Pennsylvania!

Somewhat embarrassed by his appearance, Brooks hurried over to the men. After warmly greeting him, Wilson asked Brooks to sit with him and Weiss once he got his food. While loading up his plate, Charles was praying. Conference work was so far from his mind that he and Rene had not prayed about the offer except over the phone a couple hours before. God had to want him out winning souls, right? Nevertheless, as he was gathering his utensils, he had that unmistakable impression that could be only from the Lord. He knew what he had to do.

Charles sat across from the union officers. Carl Weiss, the money man, promised Brooks a higher salary, more per diem, and more perks, all in an effort to entice him to accept the offer. After a few minutes Brooks stopped him. "I don't need coddling," he said. "My wife and I have decided to come."

Immensely pleased, Wilson smiled widely and said, "Praise God for you, C.D." Wilson called Charles Decatur Brooks "C.D." to distinguish him from the renowned singing evangelist Charles Lee Brooks, known as "C.L.," who also resided in the Columbia Union. Unwittingly Neal had coined a nickname that would be synonymous the world over with Bible-filled preaching and evangelism.

The Move
A couple of weeks later Charles Brooks flew to Washington, D.C., to look for housing. The Columbia Union Conference office was actually located in the General Conference headquarters on Carroll Avenue, a thorough-

fare that separated Maryland and the District of Columbia and confusingly gave the General Conference, the Review and Herald Publishing Association, and the Columbia Union Conference addresses in both jurisdictions.

The most obvious place for Brooks to search for housing was the neighborhood in which all of the Columbia Union employees lived, which was conveniently in Takoma Park near the headquarters. But racism reared its ugly head when he learned that a city ordinance precluded Black families from living in the neighborhood. Outraged, he informed Wilson that he had no time to look for housing and was returning to Cleveland to do evangelism. The next day Charles was on a plane headed toward the Midwest.

Not much time had passed before Neal phoned him.

"C.D., we have found a lovely place for you. Because we travel a lot here at the union, we want our wives to be as comfortable as possible. It is especially important for them to have nice kitchens. This home has a beautiful refurbished kitchen. Your kids can also have rooms of their own. Can you fly in to look at it?"

It turned out that Neal Wilson had personally searched for and found a home for the Brookses. When C.D. flew in to see the house, he was pleasantly surprised at the elegant home on Varnum Street in Northwest D.C., near Rock Creek Park and Carter Barron Amphitheatre. Many embassy families resided in the lovely neighborhood, and the Brookses would end up positively delighting in it. At the same time, they couldn't help being puzzled that their residence was bigger and better than that of any other of the Columbia Union staff, including the president.

Glenville was the last church that Charles Brooks pastored. He left it the largest congregation in the Allegheny Conference, after finishing a tent series that resulted in 179 baptisms. By the time C.D. transferred to the union, he was among the most prolific pastor-evangelists in the history of the denomination when it came to baptisms in a given decade. His pastoral career spanned a dozen years, each storied in its own way. The accounts of Little Willie, Bookie, Big Luke, and others would be retold time and time again. Brooks left Glenville in the capable hands of his friend and former classmate, Aaron Brogden.

Columbia Union

The Brookses' transition year of 1963 was also transformative for the nation, much like 1863 had been a century earlier. Diverse crosswinds blew that fated year, scattering the seeds of change and revolution across the country. Americans were no longer confined to the earth, having broken through the planet's atmosphere and reached into space. The social fabric of the U.S. was also punctured, the civil rights movement reaching its peak with the March on Washington on August 28, 1963. The Vietnam War, a protracted and costly conflict in terms of human casualties, morale, natural resources, and monetary expenditure, was quietly ramping up, soon to gain the attention of America's youth, resulting in demonstrations and riots that revealed a sharp division among the American population. That fated year would end with a devastating and deeply saddening occurrence.

It was not even a week before the family moved to Washington and had settled into their new home that Brooks was holding a Week of Prayer for Walter Starks at Dupont Park. On Friday afternoon of that week, Charles and his brother-in-law John Wagner were cooking the Sabbath meal, as both of their wives were out together. As Brooks was vacuuming in the living room he could faintly hear the phone ringing.

"Are you watching TV?" a voice on the other end demanded, bordering on hysterical.

It was one of his friends. Charles hurried to the TV and switched it on. A red-faced and flustered Walter Cronkite materialized on the screen. "The president has been shot!" he announced. "There is chaos in Dallas. President Kennedy has been rushed to Parkland Memorial Hospital."

Suffice it to say, that Sabbath was a sad one for the Brooks and Wagner families. Despite the turmoil in the nation, though, the Lord still blessed marvelously at the Week of Prayer. That Sabbath many were baptized for the first time, while others were rebaptized. For Charles, the joy of winning souls eclipsed the sadness over losing a popular president.

Brooks flew back to Cleveland alone to tie up some loose ends. They had just placed their house on the market, and he decided to spend a final night there. Restless after a couple hours alone, Brooks went outside to be around people. He found himself walking to the Cleveland Municipal Stadium (now Browns Stadium) to watch Cleveland's team play football. It was the year that the squad's famed running back Jim Brown broke the record for most rushing yards in a single season.

Charles sat in the stands, enjoying the warm sunshine and the people surrounding him more than the play on the field. Suddenly the person sitting next to him, who had a little radio tuned to the play-by-play, burst out, "Lee Harvey Oswald has just been shot!"

What madness this all is, Brooks thought to himself. He tried to block it all out of his mind, yet he knew that after the game he'd have to go home alone. There he listened to the sad news and heard the "Navy Hymn" played again and again. It was November 24, 1963.

New Heights
That month Charles commenced as the field secretary of the Columbia Union. His responsibilities also included that of union revivalist and assistant secretary of stewardship and church development. Walterene joined the faculty of the Dupont Park Adventist School as a teacher, a calling that she excelled at wherever she went.

Neal Wilson primarily brought C.D. to the union because he knew that the brilliant minister would be exceptional at his new post. But he also had other reasons. First, he wanted to obliterate the racial barriers in the church, and he set about to accomplish it with strategic and sure strokes. Frankly, a man of Brooks's caliber would show the often-prejudiced White Adventist world the sophistication and refinement of Black Adventism, assuring them that not only could their ministers lead Blacks but could lead Whites and other races just as well as their White counterparts. Wilson also wanted to broaden C.D.'s ministry, making him not just a "regional preacher," but a global evangelist. But that could never be a reality as long as Brooks pastored only Black churches.

His first assignment in his new post was as keynote speaker on human relations at four conferences. The audiences were massive, usually numbering between 2,000 and 2,500 people, and were equally mixed with Blacks and Whites. Knowing how delicate his topic was ("human relations" was a euphemism for "race relations"), Brooks made sure his talks were careful and sensitive, but as usual—and as was his trademark by now—he held no truth back.

C.D. handled the talks superbly, so much so that E. E. Cleveland phoned him one day to say how happy he was at the good reports that he was hearing. But, in true Cleveland fashion, the wise evangelist added that if Brooks made a mess of it, it would be a long time before someone with their skin color got chosen for such a position again. Cleveland recognized that he and other Black men in similar positions represented the entire Black race to Whites, and if Brooks blew it, things would be doubly hard for those who followed him and possibly for all of Black Adventism.

As C.D. traveled across New Jersey, Pennsylvania, West Virginia, and

Ohio, he felt encouraged by the reception of the members to the message of racial equality in Christ, the brotherhood and sisterhood of all believers. The meetings he held were candid and the speeches hard-hitting. One of the questions Brooks heard most often was "What do Black folks want?" When C.D. told them, some White attendees would approach him afterward to confess, "We didn't know. . . . We didn't understand."

Occasionally Wilson accompanied him on the circuit, both as a show of support and because he genuinely admired him and wanted a friendship. Whenever Neal would get into Brooks's car he'd say, "Charles, if we come to a hotel and you can't stay, then I can't stay. And if we stop at a restaurant and you can't eat, then I can't eat." Brooks found Neal Wilson to be a man of his word, and his confidence in the leader grew.

Wilson went to bat for C.D. on more than one occasion, standing in full support of his dynamic field secretary. One year at the Potomac Conference camp meeting Wilson asked Brooks to speak at the divine service in the main pavilion. The place was packed with almost 10,000 people on hand. Unbeknownst to Charles, the union president would introduce him. Wilson's presentation was so elaborate and complimentary that Charles felt embarrassed. When Neale finished and turned to shake his hand, he mouthed to Charles, "These people need the truth."

So C.D. gave it to them.

Monday morning back at the office the phone rang. It was Neal Wilson.

"C.D., you need to come down to the office!"

When Charles arrived, Wilson confided to him, "There is something I couldn't tell you until now. The people objected strongly to my suggestion that a Black man speak at camp meeting." Then he waved his hands dismissively. "But I told them there isn't a corner of our union that C. D. Brooks is not welcome in. Make your peace with that."

The very next camp meeting season Charles received five invitations to speak. Between engagements the speakers sometimes took a break in small makeshift rooms. When people passed by, the person inside could hear their chatter. C.D. was in one such room between messages and heard things about himself that he had never experienced before.

By and by a female voice announced, "Listen, you all can go where you want to, but I'm going to hear this nigger one more time."

Far from being upset, C.D. was actually tickled by it. Instead of considering her comments to be hostile toward him, he just thought she was being honest. Determined to see who it was, Brooks exited the room. As the woman who made the comment saw the young Black man, she lit up and ran to him, grabbing his hand. "Let me tell you something," she said. "I planned to get my hair done tonight, but I've made up my mind that I ain't getting my hair done until you leave here and I've heard all your messages."

***

Such reactions vindicated Wilson's plans in bringing C.D. to the union. Brooks recognized that Neal was of a rare breed, and gained tremendous respect for him. Later Charles would confess that Neal Wilson was one of the greatest men that he had ever known. At one human relations summit C.D. expressed his full support for the agenda of Neal Wilson in these words:

"The Bible says that we should be the head and not the tail. In terms of loving one another and human relations in the church we are certainly not the head but the tail, and we are dragging. If America ever does an about-face and retreats from the race question, we will be in the vanguard of those who retreat. But I believe God has raised up Elder Wilson for such a time as this to right this wrong. Will you join him in fulfilling God's purpose for this church?"

C. D. Brooks's human relations seminars were so successful and effective that other conferences and unions replicated them. Invitations poured in for him to train facilitators. The General Conference used Columbia Union's field secretary's program in toto to formulate its own civil rights policies. Slowly but surely the denomination was coming around—a large part of it owing to dynamic leaders such as Charles Brooks and Neal Wilson.

***

That is not to say that there were no bumps in the road. During their first holiday in the Columbia Union, the Brookses went to a Christmas program for the employees. Deirdre and Skip laughed and laughed at Carl Weiss, who made a pretty good Santa Claus. Everyone was carefree and festive, enjoying each other's company and the warmth and goodwill that the season brings.

At the festivities someone introduced Charles and Walterene to a young couple from Tennessee with small kids who would be joining the Columbia Union family. C.D. noticed that they acted a bit odd and uncomfortable, but chalked it up to their being new and maybe a little shy. But the next day at the office the individual didn't report to work and had disappeared. Later Brooks found out that the man had hightailed it back to the South, informing Neal Wilson that his wife and children were very upset about being at a party with a Negro family and that he had to decline his position at the union. "If you feel that way," Wilson told him, "we don't need you here at Columbia Union."

A Pioneering Wife

C.D. was not the only pioneer in the Brooks family. Walterene was also making her mark in just as powerful a way in breaking down barriers of race in the Columbia Union. Named after her uncle Walter (W. W.) Fordham, Walterene shared her namesake's determination and courage. Fordham had led a student strike at Oakwood Junior College in 1931 that had resulted in improved conditions, a more integrated faculty, and the school's first Black president, James Moran. Ironically, it was Moran who persuaded Walterene to teach at Dupont Park Elementary School when the couple moved to Washington.

After five years at Dupont, the Columbia Union asked Walterene to teach at Sligo Elementary. It was more than just a job offer: Sligo's teaching staff was all White, and she would be the first person of color on the faculty there. Walterene was reluctant, since she and her kids were happy at the all-Black Dupont. But she believed God was leading her to do it, so she did. It was as simple as that. Like her husband, she wanted to be only where God wanted her to be.

And so in August 1968 Walterene started teaching fifth grade at Sligo. It was her favorite age. The class was disproportionate, though: 30 boys and only eight girls, all White. On the first day of class one of the boys challenged her, not obeying an instruction. Walterene fastened her eyes on him, and from then on the boy was her best pupil.

The Brookses were looking racism in the eye, and slowly but surely it was backing down.

1964: Philadelphia

Charles hadn't been at the union for even two months before he was raring to hit the sawdust trail again. He had the bustling city of Philadelphia in his sights, and it was going to hear the truth from him one way or the other. Brooks told Neal Wilson of his plans to conduct a massive tent effort in the City of Brotherly Love.

"C.D., we didn't call you here for that," Wilson began. "We want you to teach others how to do that."

"God specifically called me to do evangelism, Neal, and I have to do it," Brooks said resolutely. "Besides, the best way to teach is by example. All who are interested can come and watch how I conduct the meetings." When Wilson saw the look on Charles's face, he acquiesced. So in the summer of 1964 Brooks and his small evangelistic team descended upon Philadelphia.

Perhaps the most important city in the United States along with Boston during the American Revolution, Philadelphia was the second capital of the fledgling nation. In those early days of the Republic it was a center of commerce, trade, industry, religion, politics, economics, education, and social reform. That continued into the early twentieth century, when its neighbor to the north, New York, and neighbor to the south, Washington, D.C., eclipsed it. The city's population peaked at more than 2 million in 1950, and began a steady decline in the years following.

"Philly," as the city was known colloquially, had always been among the most important cities for Blacks in the Union. African captives bore the yeoman's burden of building the city in the years after their arrival in the late 1600s. But Philadelphia quickly became a "free city" in a "free state" with a no-tolerance law for slavery, and escaped Blacks from both the South and parts of the North fled to it for freedom. A center of the growing antislavery and abolitionist movements in the early- to mid-nineteenth century, it was more responsible for the eventual abolition of slavery than any other city save Boston and Washington.

Since its emergence as a major city, Philadelphia has boasted one of the most thriving and sophisticated Black populations in America. Although a typical American city in terms of racial hostilities and flare-ups, Blacks nevertheless prospered in Philadelphia after the Civil War. It became home to many thousands of ministers, teachers, politicians, doctors, musicians, entrepreneurs, writers, artists, and skilled laborers. By the dawn of the twentieth century Black Philadelphians numbered more than 62,000. The succeeding decades witnessed a doubling of the number as Blacks migrated from the South in search of jobs, rising to 135,000 in 1920. At the time of Charles Brooks's arrival in 1964, the Black population had reached 600,000. Little did the eager evangelist know that one of the biggest race riots in American history would take place there at the end of the summer.

***

The Brooks team could not find a lot in the vast city, because acres of old homes were being torn down to facilitate urban renewal, and often ownership of these properties was in limbo. But he kept searching, scanning the endless thoroughfares, talking to people, contacting church members.

"Elder Brooks," one such church member said to him excitedly one day, "the man who is second in charge of urban renewal is an Adventist."

The words had barely escaped his mouth before Charles was speeding to city hall. He parked smack in front, hopped out of his car, and jogged into the building without even glancing at the parking meter. Inside, he looked up the Adventist's name on the directory, bounded up to his office, and told his secretary that C. D. Brooks was here to see him. The man was in and was gracious enough to meet with Brooks.

"God put you here because I am here to run a campaign this summer and we need you to help us secure a lot," Brooks told him.

Startled by Brooks's directness, the man managed an "All right."

C.D. then explained to him the type of site they needed, namely, one in a central location and large enough to house a humongous tent and a parking lot to accommodate the nightly visitors.

"I know just the place," the city official replied, immediately catching on to C.D.'s vision and becoming excited himself. "Why don't you go to Girard Avenue and Broad Street, where there are acres of land that have been cleared for housing? You can have any of those lots you want."

"Great. What's the cost?"

"One dollar per month."

***

Brooks's evangelistic team chose a site just hours later, and pitched their tent the next day. Church members gave a hand, cleaning the premises and posting signs advertising the meetings. The place turned out to be the optimal location, clearly visible on a boulevard that tens of thousands passed through daily, with plenty of parking.

On the opening night the tent was standing room only. The stature of C. D. Brooks even at his young age inspired hundreds of church members to get involved with the groundwork for the evangelistic series—Bible studies, visitations, passing out flyers, spreading the word—because everyone knew that it would be a soul-winning extravaganza. With knowing looks, church members said to each other, "Brooks is in town." The city was to be taken by storm, and the members wanted to be a part of it. No sinner was safe.

Unbeknownst to C.D., Neal Wilson showed up on opening night, just one face among the thousands in a tent deep in the heart of Black Philadelphia. After a powerful message that riveted biblical truth in their minds, the audience thoughtfully dispersed. When the tent had all but emptied, the solitary figure of Neal Wilson remained, waiting to congratulate his friend. "C.D.," he said, "you don't ever have to discuss doing a tent meeting with me again."

***

Brooks introduced the seventh-day Sabbath on the Sunday night of August 30, 1964. Two nights before, on Friday, August 28, two White officers had attempted to break up a domestic dispute at the corner of 22nd Street and Columbia Avenue, an overwhelmingly Black area known as "The Jungle" and a mere nine blocks away from Brooks's tent. The commotion drew a rambunctious crowd that began chucking rocks, bricks, and pieces of cement at the officers. As a rumor circulated that the police had beaten a pregnant woman to death, a full-fledged riot erupted across North Philadelphia. Order did not get restored until September 1, after looters had pillaged local businesses, arsonists had razed numerous shops and buildings, and general mayhem had run its course.

In light of the burning and looting, law enforcement officials petitioned the pastors of local churches via radio announcement not to have services on Sunday. Knowing the risk of violence, thievery, and arson, Charles asked for divine guidance as to how he should proceed. He was planning to present the controversial subject of the change of the Sabbath that night. "Lord, help me, because it is never easy to preach about the Sabbath, yet I dare not dishonor You with lack of faith!" God impressed Brooks to go ahead with the meeting during that dreadful time for the city.

That night, as the crowd swelled, Brooks laid everything on the pulpit. The raging fires just streets away lit a fuse to his message. Jesus and His soon coming was the only hope for the world, and Charles told the attentive crowd so in no uncertain terms. While preaching, Brooks noticed in his peripheral vision police cars pulling into the lot, turning off their engines and lights. He rejoiced—the Lord wanted the officers to hear this message also. Many under the tent that night claimed that Brooks's sermon was the greatest they had ever heard. Historians now cite the 1964 Philadelphia race riot as a pivotal event in the civil rights movement, but heaven recognizes August 30, 1964, as a pivotal night in the Advent movement.

***

The evangelistic series faced still more dangers. Brooks had warned the tentmaster, his nephew "Bubby" Wagner (later a distinguished medical doctor), to avoid mixing with the crowds of volatile youth in the neighborhood. "Never run toward trouble; always run away from it" was C.D.'s simple advice.

On a humid night as Charles rose to preach, a raucous commotion began coming from Girard Street, right across from the tent. It turned out that 20 to 25 youths had decided to have a rumble. From the vantage of the pulpit Brooks saw Bubby sprinting toward the imbroglio, and thought to himself, *That boy is doing exactly what I counseled him not to do!* As Bubby neared the crowd a gunshot rang out. At the sound Bubby performed a swift U-turn and ran so fast back to the tent that his jacket actually waved in the wind like a superhero's cape. Stifling a laugh, Brooks kept on preaching. The tent congregation was so riveted by what C.D. was saying that they didn't even look around after the gunshot.

Another time he was driving around the city and decided to drop by the tent. Later he couldn't figure out why he had on the spur of the moment stopped there, but the events that followed indicated God's direction. When he pulled into the parking lot, he saw a crowd of street toughs confronting Bubby—15 to 1, by Brooks's estimate. The evangelist stepped in between the opposing factions.

"What's going on?" he questioned, scanning their faces. The youngsters looked surly, itching for conflict. But they remained silent.

"They threatened me," Bubby explained.

"Fellas," Brooks said in a placating tone, "we are not that type of people here. We are Christians. We don't fight and cause trouble. Our mission is peaceful, and we mean everyone only good." At this the boys lowered their eyes, studying the ground.

"Now move on," Charles commanded. Then softening again: "And let's be friends."

En masse they lurched away, all doing a tough-guy street walk.

When they were out of earshot, Bubby said, "Uncle Charles, they told me that they're coming tonight to burn our tent down!"

After the evening service C.D. stationed three men to stay the night. It was a peaceful, uneventful night.

A few days later one of the street toughs who had been involved in the confrontation came by the lot and was quite friendly to Wagner. Bubby asked him why they hadn't come to the tent the other night as they had threatened.

"Oh, we did come" was his reply. "You just had all those men standing around that tent!"

When Bubby related it to his uncle, C.D. thought of the text "The angel of the Lord encampeth round about them that fear him, and delivereth them."

***

The Lord blessed C. D. Brooks, and he baptized more than 300 during the Philadelphia meetings. They were not fly-by-night, in-and-out conversions, either, for before Brooks would baptize anyone, he had them thoroughly vetted and tested to see if they were genuine in their profession and fit to join the church. The standards in Adventism—yes, God's standards—were high, and Brooks refused to water them down or compromise them one iota to get a baptism. He'd rather baptize no one than be guilty of that.

One of the personal highlights of the series for Charles was his older brother Elliott's ("Rock") decision to be baptized. That day he, along with his wife and kids, made the greatest decision that a person ever can: to go all the way with Jesus. Later Elliott told C.D., "Chuck, it wasn't your preaching that got me. It was thinking of the times Mom would take my hand and point upward, telling me that she was praying that I would accept Jesus into my heart." Mattie Brooks, although now dead, yet spoke.

Rock turned out to be one of God's jewels, becoming the first elder of the North Philadelphia church just six years after his baptism. His conversion was so striking that it even led his little brother evangelist into a closer walk with the Lord. Years later when Elliott was gravely ill, Charles drove up to Philadelphia on Sundays and just sat in the hospital room, discussing old times and life in Christ with Rock. During one such meeting his face lighted up as he remarked, "Even if the Lord doesn't heal me, Chuck, look where I am headed." Following Elliott's death, the North Philadelphia Seventh-day Adventist Church named their fellowship hall in his honor.

It turned out that C.D.'s city hall contact was a nominal Adventist, somewhere between lukewarm and leaving the church. But he began attending the meetings and renewed his walk with Christ. Years later when he lay in Philadelphia's Temple University Hospital dying from cancer, he sent for Brooks. The circumstances were vastly different from their first meeting in 1964, but the men's respect and admiration for each other had not abated. They worshipped and prayed together, and when the man breathed his last, Charles was sure that he would see him and his brother Elliott again in the kingdom of God.

Big Luke

The makings of another amazing testimony occurred during the Philadelphia campaign, a real-life drama of immense proportions.

A giant of a man, Big Luke was a giant of a sinner. He sold drugs and was on drugs. When in the evening he walked through the neighborhood to his house, the kids ran from him with terror in their eyes. As husband, Luke thought it his duty to knock his wife down the first thing he got home. He was angry at everyone, and everyone was afraid of him. Big Luke was about as far away from Jesus as a person could get—so it seemed.

One day he walked into his home and found his wife reading the Bible. He tore into her, grabbing the Bible and hurling it across the room. Then he went upstairs, sat on his bed, and fumed. For some reason his mind turned to God, and he grew only more upset.

"God," he managed, almost too angry to think, "if You are real, as people claim You are, I have something for You to do. And if You exist, it shouldn't be too hard for You to pull off."

Retrieving his wife's Bible, he snarled, "I'm going to sling this Bible against the wall. It's going to fall open, and whatever I touch, I want You to speak to me through it. This is Your last chance!"

Luke threw the Bible against the wall, and it bounced and hit the floor messily, its thin pages crumpling and bending. Then almost miraculously it righted itself and neatly opened to a spot almost in the middle. Hurrying over, and without looking, he placed his finger on the page. Then he grabbed it up and read the passage his finger lay on:

"I am the Lord, and there is none else, there is no God beside me."

Awed by the simplicity and power of the words, and more so that the Lord had taken him up on his blasphemous ultimatum, Big Luke gave his heart to Jesus right then and there.

His change was absolute. He began treating his wife like a princess. The neighborhood kids, instead of fleeing from him, were now drawn to his Christlike demeanor.

But his previous life kept beckoning him back, for he was heavily in debt and desperately needed quick money. So he said to his wife, "You know I'm changed, but I need to get some money to feed you and the kids and to pay these debts. Now, I have connections. If I can get one last package of drugs and sell it, I will have enough money to pay our debts and to get us out of the jam we're in." His wife, seeing the logic in his plan, agreed.

So the two hopped in their car and set out to South Street just beyond the train station where Luke's contact lived. Although it was a clear day, a gray cloud hovered in the sky. Luke couldn't shake the impression that it hung directly over his car, despite how fast he drove. As he turned onto South Street, a bolt of lightning flashed from the cloud so close that he was certain it had struck the front of his car. Mashing the brakes and throwing the vehicle into park, a wide-eyed Luke looked at his wife.

"What was that!" he yelled, beside himself.

"I don't know," she replied, equally shaken.

"We better rush, get our drugs, and get out of here!" With that, he put the car in drive and hightailed it to his contact's place.

No sooner had he got a block down the boulevard than *wham!* The lightning flashed again, this time so close that Luke and his wife could see in high definition its surreal metallic gray-white tentacles. The car shook violently, teetering back and forth.

Luke didn't need a third encounter. He performed a U-turn in the busy intersection and got out of there as fast as his vehicle would go. But what happened next was perhaps the most unbelievable thing of all: the dark cloud disappeared and the sun came out. He and his wife never bought, sold, touched, or even looked at drugs for the rest of their lives.

C. D. Brooks was happy to baptize them a few weeks later.

1966: Newark

In 1966 C. D. Brooks became the first secretary of the Columbia Union's newly established Ministerial Association. The promotion, which was in effect a creation of a job tailored just for Brooks, was a rare phenomenon in Seventh-day Adventist governmental structure. Yet the primary task in his job portfolio did not change: evangelism.

Brooks next set his sights on Newark, New Jersey. With almost a half million residents in 1966, it was the largest city in the Garden State, located just eight miles from the financial capital of the world, downtown Manhattan, and a vital port city itself. Some of the world's wealthiest companies and most prestigious educational institutions called the metropolis home. It was in Newark that an unprecedented event in Adventism would take place.

The historic Newark Symphony Hall on 1020 Broad Street was the venue for the evangelistic meetings, becoming a hive of spiritual activity on a boulevard of secular hustle and bustle. During that 1966 summer evangelistic series Symphony Hall garnered another bit of history, for it was the site of the first official joint evangelistic series in the Seventh-day Adventist Church by both a Black and a White evangelist. The Columbia Union Conference executive committee passed a motion for Alvin Stewart, White pastor of the Newark church, to serve as assistant evangelist to C. D. Brooks. Other White ministers joined their counterparts from the Allegheny East Conference in the planning, operation, and running of the meetings.

C.D. found Stewart to be most cooperative and supportive. The two were a model demonstration of the power of evangelism to totally sweep away racial barriers and turn diversity into an asset of the gospel. Unbeknownst to Brooks, it was yet another strategy of Neal Wilson's to accomplish this very end by demonstrating to the denomination that Black and White leaders could successfully work closely together. A lengthy object lesson, the meetings lasted two months, from July 17 to September 11.

The preparations and advertising were spectacular. Even though only about 20 members from the White churches attended, the Blacks in Allegheny East came out in large numbers to support the meetings. The series' flyer featured the speaker and his associate, along with the lines "Intelligent services! Clear satisfying lectures! Unencumbered by big money appeals. Bring your Bible!" Under "Special Features" was "Stereo Meditations, Motion Pictures, Free Scripture-filled Literature," and "Prayer for the Sick." Some of the topics of the first week were "The Second Coming of Christ," "Born Twice or Die Twice," "Amazing Grace—How to 'Get Religion' Instantly," and "The Devil's Vacation! He Didn't Plan It—It's Planned for Him!"

The devil was furious about the evangelistic series, of course, not only because it would pry souls from his grasp, but because of the racism-defeating approach it employed. So he set about his fiendish work, his unplanned vacation no doubt in his mind.

The conferences sponsored advertisements for the meetings on the sides of city buses. They were printed on panels of heavy cardboard, six feet high and 10 feet long. The church really went all out in financing these ads, paying top dollar for the coveted exteriors of the buses. One day C.D. decided to take the bus to the hall instead of his own car. As he waited at the stop, he was amused to see his face blown up three times its natural size on the side of the bus. But when the bus got nearer to the curb, his light-heartedness turned cold. Scrawled across his forehead in all capital letters was the word NIGGER.

***

Satan struck in other ways, too, but his chicaneries were always frustrated. When Charles and Alvin Stewart arrived at the large civic auditorium, they discovered very quickly that the custodian of the hall took his job very seriously, to the extent that he was brusque and unhelpful. Once Brooks arrived early before the meetings began (as was his custom) and turned on the lights. The surly individual told him in no uncertain terms that it was not Charles's responsibility and that it must never happen again. C.D. apologized and made sure that was the last time he did that. For the life of him he couldn't figure out why the custodian was so mean to Adventists. He wondered if the White man had racial hang-ups.

Because the job required that he make sure that everyone strictly observed fire codes and the like, the custodian had to sit through the meetings each night. Almost imperceptibly, as the series wore on and night after night C.D. laid out the gospel of Jesus in plain and powerful language, a change in attitude came over the custodian. The formerly uninterested and insolent expression slowly transformed to an open and interested one. His formerly hostile posture now relaxed, and he leaned forward in anticipation. When he couldn't attend because of other duties, he rigged the speaker to play in his office. The Lord was working on him.

As decision time neared, the custodian approached C.D. one night after a meeting.

"Pastor, I have had this job for a long time, and I have seen evangelistic groups come and go," he said with a pensive expression. Naming some of the denominations he had worked with, the man shared a series of unfortunate experiences of abusive ministers, dishonest evangelistic practices, exploitation, and suspect money management. He also intimated how they had generally treated him like dirt because of his lowly status. All of it from professed Christians. One particular story shocked Brooks.

A "Christian" group purporting to possess the gift of healing had rented Symphony Hall several summers before. One day a man brought his young daughter from many miles away to be healed. Carrying the crippled girl into the building, he went from office to office along the corridors circling the auditorium, looking for one of the ministers. When he couldn't find anyone, he knocked on the custodian's office door, daughter in his arms, and asked for help.

The custodian led him to a conference room where the Christian leaders were. He politely knocked on the door, and a voice shouted for him to come in. Inside, a group of leaders were intently counting stacks of bills piled on a long table, money collected in the meetings. They paused from their tallying, glancing up with irritated expressions, since it was not yet program time. But the father and daughter had come a long way and were desperate for help.

A big stack of money in front of him, the nattily dressed evangelist told the man to come back during the 7:00 to 9:30 meeting and not to disturb them another minute. At this, like any good father, the man pleaded for his daughter, but the answer was the same. As the man joined his child in pitiful sobs, the evangelist and his cohorts went back to counting their money, oblivious to the tears. With an utterly disgusted expression, the custodian spat out the last few lines of the story.

"When word came that you were renting this place, I figured you'd be just like the rest of them," he said, anger still filling his face. "Truth is, I kept waiting for you Adventists to act like all the rest of the Christians." He pronounced the last word sarcastically and with no small amount of disdain.

"I heard you say when you were lifting the offering that there are huge expenses and that if you would like to help, feel free, but that if you can't or don't want to, you'd understand; just don't stop coming." The custodian's face softened to one of surprise as he was reliving the moment. "I couldn't believe it—I didn't think this was possible. I couldn't believe that you weren't manipulative and begging for money."

The custodian's face then turned resolute. "Now, Pastor," he said, "you have announced a baptism. I want you to baptize me."

C.D. couldn't believe his ears! The power of God was truly at work!

Where to have the baptism created a slight problem. If the ceremony was far from Symphony Hall, then the nightly crowd would probably drop by half. No public pool was large enough to accommodate so many people. Such a thing was prohibited in lakes and ponds in the park. And the natural shoreline was either too dirty or too deep.

And so Brooks came up with the idea of installing a backyard swimming pool on the stage of Symphony Hall. A thick plastic sheet underneath it would protect against spilled water or condensation damaging the wood floors. Brooks and Stewart would stay in the pool baptizing, while the candidates would file in two by two. Meanwhile, the crowd could remain in their normal seating.

"Leave it to me," the custodian said confidently when C.D. told him of his plan.

On the day of the baptism, sure enough, a humongous swimming pool occupied the stage. Immediately behind it was a magnificent waterfall cascading into the pool, with artificial palm trees surrounding it. The man had truly made the stage into a garden of beauty. Later C.D. found out that the pool and the props were the custodian's own, right from his own backyard. At that service C. D. Brooks baptized him into the Seventh-day Adventist Church, along with 129 others.

1967: Egypt

Doing the seemingly impossible was becoming the norm in C.D.'s ministry. While aware of it, the young union staff member acknowledged it only in passing, and when he did, he remarked simply, "Praise the Lord." Brooks knew it was never about him—so he never made it about him. It was about Jesus—Jesus had brought his mother into biblical truth so long ago, then her family, and next called him to the ministry under a tent in the South. Jesus had led him from dentistry to the ministry, placing him under truth-presenting teachers at Oakwood. Jesus had guided his ministry, unleashing the Spirit's power to win others. And Jesus had called him to the Columbia Union. All he was or ever would be was because of Jesus. On this C.D. never wavered.

In the Middle East God again used him to set a record. At the dawn of the new year of 1967, the North Carolinian flew to Cairo, Egypt, on a mission to reach the people of an ancient land. Egypt was in its tenth year of leadership by the charismatic but controversial Gamal Abdel Nasser. Unknown at the time was that just months after Brooks's evangelistic effort in the capital city conflict would explode between Egypt and her biblical enemy, Israel, in what became known as the Six-Day War.

The Middle East Division of Seventh-day Adventists was having a difficult time gaining any sort of foothold in the Arab nation, as leading Muslims to the Christian faith was extremely difficult. In an attempt to reverse this, the division president, F. C. Webster, specifically requested that Brooks come to the territory and run an evangelistic series. If anyone could win someone to Christianity in the region, he reckoned C.D. could. It didn't take much for Neal Wilson to fulfill the request, since he himself had labored in Egypt for many years and had as great a burden as anyone for the people there.

Brooks would hold nightly services in the Cairo Center. Adventist ministers from across the region would help out in the evangelism, which would be an event of the field school. Eager to see Charles in action, many signed on.

The series got off to an impressive start. In February of 1967 Webster sent a cable to the world headquarters: "New day public evangelism in Middle East. 1,500 people attended Brooks's opening meeting in Cairo Center. . . . Attendance continues near 1,000 weeknights. We rejoice and ask your prayers."

The attendance was large, but C.D. was keenly aware of what it would mean for Muslims to become Christians. They would have to eliminate many cultural practices and beliefs and would most likely be alienated from their families, if not face outright persecution. So each night after the bustle and intensity of the meetings, he knelt by his bed and pleaded for the working of the Holy Spirit. Never before had the gospel demanded so much from a person as it did here, so he prayed with special fervor.

After nine weeks of preaching, Brooks conducted the largest baptism in the history of the Middle East Division: 38. Webster exclaimed to Brooks, "This is the greatest outpouring since Pentecost!" While not a big number in the United States, or even Africa to the south, this was unprecedented in an Arab land.

Before he had left for Egypt, C.D. had had a long conversation with H.M.S. Richards. Charles recalled that as a youngster in Greensboro he had heard the sure voice of this man of God adjuring his listeners to obey God's Word. Now they had developed a friendship in the form of long walks together. By then in his 70s with a half century of ministry under his belt, Richards gave C.D. wisdom that he couldn't get in a book. The young preacher told the old one that he was going to do a meeting in Egypt, then fly back.

"No, no, no, Charles," Richards said emphatically, shaking his head. "If you go that far, then it becomes a learning experience, and you must tour the world." He spoke grandly of the places where Jesus had walked, of the areas where Paul had preached. And then Brooks just had to see the millions in the metropolises of Asia.

"I'll speak to your president about it," Richards promised him.

The next time Brooks saw Wilson, his president informed him that he would go on an extended tour of the world after the meetings in Egypt.

As Charles went from place to place—the pyramids of Egypt to the Sea of Galilee to the Garden of Gethsemane to the Red Sea to Athens to the Great Wall of China to Bangkok—he did indeed marvel at the size and magnificence of God's creation. As a representative of the General Conference, he was pleasantly surprised at the warm reception he received, just the opposite of some places in Jim Crow America. More than ever, though, he grew in conviction of the great work that the church had to do in proclaiming the last warning message to the world.

***

A year later the man who had perhaps done the most to reverse the injustices of Jim Crow and racial oppression in America was gunned down in front of a motel room in Memphis, Tennessee. Martin Luther King, Jr., had the utmost respect for C. D. Brooks and other Black Adventist leaders such as C. E. Bradford, E. E. Cleveland, F. L. Peterson and Frank Hale. In fact, King had stopped by Cleveland's tent once to hear the young firebrand preach. Afterward the two pulpiteers engaged in a lively discussion of doctrine. They had a mutual respect for each other. Hale also knew the civil rights leader and had marched and toured with him on several occasions.

Brooks met Martin Luther King, Jr., twice. With others he was shocked when he heard of the assassination, and mourned the death of one of the greatest Americans of all time. In a sermon Brooks would later say this of King and the civil rights movement:

"God raised up a man to lead one of the most astonishing revolutions the world has ever witnessed. A revolution where the revolutionaries did the bleeding and the dying, a revolution where they refused to fight, placing their very lives, their very bodies, on the altar of sacrifice for principle and righteousness. I urge us never to forget it. Above the noise of snarling dogs and singing whips and crackling flames, above the dull thudding of clubs and chains, the shrill lunacy of haters, and the cackle of gunfire could be heard the patient voice of principle saying, 'Do not fight back. Our suffering will yet be creative and redemptive. Turn the other cheek. Love your enemies.' And as always, the will and Word of God were with power.

"That voice was heard by Black men and White men and all men, and the great surge of support swept toward the movement. Good men and good women of all races took the right side. Even a Southerner who became president listened and reflected and moved with God. I have lived on the other side of the revolution, and, with many of you, crossed over with joy into many civil rights that have long been denied. But alas, politicians arose and caused the pendulum to swing in the exact opposite direction, and the voice of righteousness fell silent, and the voice of frustration was heard in its stead."

The Teacher

While field secretary for the Columbia Union, C. D. Brooks trained hundreds of pastors and evangelists across the globe how to do evangelism. As he gave seminars, conducted field schools, and visited evangelistic series to provide hands-on direction, his ministry greatly expanded, because the scores of ministers he taught were using his methods to garner tremendous results. Baptisms in the union spiked during Brooks's tenure, and that was all the justification he needed for leaving the full-time pastorate.

The world church especially appreciated his preaching. No longer just a treasure of regional conferences and Black neighborhoods throughout America, the still-young Ministerial Association director had become renowned for laying out biblical truth in dynamic and pointed sermons. Wherever he preached, it would be standing room only. As cassette tapes came into circulation, people recorded his sermons and duplicated them by the thousands. They passed from person to person eager to hear the crisp, distinct voice that thundered from the speakers.

Inevitably, as with E. E. Cleveland, H.M.S. Richards, J. L. Shuler, and others, preachers young and old attempted to emulate C.D. Many requested copies of his sermon manuscripts and then repeated them word for word. Brooks discouraged that sort of thing, authenticity being important to him. God had made every individual unique, and the blessing that only they could give to the world would be lost in imitating another man. But it still happened frequently.

C.D.'s sermons were masterpieces. Because of his evangelistic orientation, the titles always grabbed the attention, for that was a must to get people under the tent. The arrangement and organizations of the messages were tightly woven and precisely packaged, everything purposely and seamlessly connecting to Christ by the end of the message. The illustrations he used were novel and engaging. His delivery was taut and crisp, his expansive vocabulary a sharp tool to drive home truth.

Brooks's service at the Columbia Union lasted from 1963 to 1971: he was field secretary 1963-1965, and ministerial secretary 1966-1971. Destined for higher things and a broader ministry, he was to move to the office next door and into the living rooms of homes across the world.

GENERAL CONFERENCE

"I didn't want to go to Antarctica, because there was no one to preach to."

I n 1971 C. D. Brooks received a long-distance call from Washington, D.C. On the line was none other than the president of the General Conference, Robert Pierson.

"Charles, we have met with the administrative committee, and we here at the General Conference are inviting you to join our staff." Pierson then asked Brooks to serve as one of the field secretaries of the world church. Praying simultaneously but sensing that it was God's will, C.D. accepted the job on the spot.

This would be the third in a series of increasingly broader spheres of ministry for Brooks, first on the regional level, then the union level, and now the General Conference level—the global level. Brooks's new responsibilities would be identical to those at the Columbia Union Conference, only now encompassing the entire church. One of seven general field secretaries, he was essentially a point man for the denomination, to be assigned to any type of field service or project in which the General Conference Committee felt he was needed. His new job didn't involve any moving or even change of workplace. However, the 41-year-old Charles was now a bona fide global leader. And he would replace his mentor, C. E. Moseley, as a field secretary of the church.

C.D. marveled at how far God had taken him. His parents were humble people, one generation removed from slavery. He had not been born a Seventh-day Adventist, just a country boy from North Carolina. Yet through God's power he had baptized thousands of individuals; he had preached to tens of thousands; he had overcome barriers of race and age; and in many ways he was a pioneer, first in the Columbia Union and now at the General Conference, being the first man of color to hold his position at the union level, and among the first at the GC.

Pierson and C.D.

Robert Howard Pierson was born January 3, 1911, in Brooklyn, Iowa. Although early-twentieth-century Iowa had few Blacks, Pierson would spend his career working among people of color. In fact, his birth as a preacher took place while ministering to African Americans as a young theology student at Southern Missionary College (now Southern Adventist University):

"Soon after school opened, the Ingathering campaign commenced; and with it doors opened for my preaching career to get under way early. My first Ingathering venture certainly did nothing to indicate that someday I would become a home missionary secretary. At the close of a lean day, as far as offerings were concerned, I knocked at the home of a Black lay preacher of a first-day church. When he did not respond affirmatively to my appeal for funds to assist our world mission program, I suggested that I would be glad to come and study the Bible with him.

"Perhaps he thought it would be a novel experience to have this beardless youth study the Scriptures with him. He promptly invited me to come back the following Tuesday evening to study the Word with him and his family.

"On my return journey to the college the fearful voice of inexperience began to taunt me for accepting such an appointment. But alas, alas, it was too late now! I had not only accepted his invitation, I had urged the lay preacher to invite all of his friends in for the cottage meeting. It was evident that I was perhaps prematurely launched on my preaching career. There was no turning back.

"Back home I turned to my one-book library—*Bible Readings for the Home Circle.* Thank the Lord for this book! I decided that I would speak on the second coming of Jesus. But when I scrutinized available texts on the subject, I instinctively knew it would be a meager offering. There was little I could contribute in addition to just reading the texts. This would take only about 15 minutes. What kind of preacher would they think I was if I spoke only such a short time? So I returned to the *Bible Readings* and found texts on the millennium and the home of the saved. I wanted to impress my expected 'congregation' with 45 minutes' worth of my ability as a Bible expositor.

"Well armed with Bible evidence but with no notes—only slips of paper placed where my Bible texts were and on which was noted the next scripture to be read—I set off the following Tuesday evening. Just what would happen if one of my paper slips with texts noted should inadvertently disappear, I had not considered. If an ill-fated wind had played this evil trick on me, my preaching career might well have been nipped in the bud.

"Driving my Model T Ford coupe to Silverdale (my stomach tied in knots), I secretly hoped no one would be at home. Surely I was bound for embarrassed disaster. Why had I been so brash as to let myself in for this appointment when I knew nothing—absolutely nothing—about preaching, or about the study of the Bible for that matter.

"Arriving at my destination, I found—to my despair—that the place was packed! For a few minutes I walked around that little house like Joshua around Jericho, endeavoring to generate enough courage to go in.

"There was no turning back now! Soon the boy preacher was in the midst of a friendly congregation for his dubious debut in the gospel ministry. How patiently and tenderly the Lord deals with ignorance and inexperience when His abiding place is a willing spirit! With what warm encouragement those Black saints responded to their youthful mentor. Their warm 'amens' and cordial fellowship saved the day. The truth triumphed. That night commenced a blessed spiritual relationship that resulted in a number of baptisms and a bustling Sabbath school in Silverdale. For some years the tiny flame was fanned by earnest ministerial students and others from the nearby college church. That night a preacher of sorts was born."

In the proceeding decades of ministry, Pierson served as a pastor in Georgia; seven years as a missionary in India; five years as president of the British West Indies Union; a year and a half as president of the Caribbean Union; four years as president of the Southern Asia Division; three years as Kentucky-Tennessee Conference president; a year as Texas Conference president; four years as president of Southern Africa Division; and four years as president of the Trans-Africa Division. It was in that final post that the General Conference session in Detroit in 1966 chose him as president of the world church.

With such a diverse background of ministry—a large majority of it working with Blacks—it was no surprise that Pierson entered the presidency with an agenda to improve race relations not only in the United States but wherever they were needed. Like Neal Wilson (who would follow him as GC president), Pierson would chip away at the wall of color prejudice in his own way, with well-placed, sure blows.

He also possessed a deep desire to reach the world with the three angels' messages. A pastoral orientation, with a call for revival and reformation, would characterize his leadership. E. E. Cleveland would become Pierson's most prolific spokesperson of this goal, spearheading the worldwide evangelistic campaigns "Mission '72," "Mission '73," "Mission '74," and "Mission '75." In C. D. Brooks, Pierson saw a sterling minister who completely jelled with his aims for the church: highly spiritual, evangelistically minded, and racially inclusive.

Because it would be hard to find two men who were more on the same page, Robert Pierson and C. D. Brooks maintained an exemplary and highly productive working relationship.

One time Pierson confided to him his ideas about race. "C.D., I've always known that God wasn't in support of that foolishness [racism]. It is Satan's masterpiece. He's not going to get most of us with liquor or women. No, he needed something more subtle and wrapped up in self-centeredness. In racism you have insecurity and ego and tradition—a combination of so many of the potent things he utilizes."

As with Wilson, Pierson began to believe that Brooks could do anything assigned him, however impossible it appeared. On one occasion Robert said to his field secretary, "Charles, I'm looking at your schedule and I see how busy you are, but please save some time for Europe. Europe is crying for Black ministry." The president then unfolded to Brooks a plan for rooting out racism in Europe, with C.D. as the main agent.

Robert Pierson resigned as General Conference president in 1978 because of health issues. Unwilling to retire from ministry, he stood in as interim pastor of the Kailua church on the island of Oahu in Hawaii at age 78. It was at that post that he died on January 21, 1989. When Pierson passed to his rest, Charles remained in the position to which his friend had hired him.

Travel
C.D. truly became a globetrotter, representing the Seventh-day Adventist Church from the most populous metropolises to the remotest areas. As he preached and conducted evangelistic campaigns the world over, Brooks realized that despite the endless diversity of people, each individual had the same fundamental desire: a longing for a relationship with Jesus and the freedom from sin that came with it. Although manifested in millions of different ways and behaviors, it all equaled the same thing.

On six continents ("I didn't want to go to Antarctica, because there was no one to preach to," Brooks quipped famously) Charles strengthened the faith of believers; learned of conditions and developing dynamics in various regions; dealt with doctrinal crises; mentored ministers; spoke for revival meetings and services; and led people to the watery grave—always baptizing. His trips could be lengthy, as seen in just the overseas part of his itinerary for the first three years of his job. One of the first assigned to him was a tour of South America from November 15, 1971, to January 16, 1972. Brooks's next extended trip involved the Inter-America Division from August 27 to October 21, 1972. All of April and May of 1974 Brooks traveled in the Far Eastern Division. In June he baptized 49 in Bermuda, and in August and September of 1974, he was in Lagos, Nigeria, baptizing 49 again. Dozens of domestic trips had Brooks speaking for Sabbath services, camp meetings, Weeks of Prayer, school graduations, seminars, etc.

Such extensive traveling was bound to affect the Brookses' marriage and home life. His initial trip to South America spanned continents and years, and Rene, Diedre, and Skip spent Thanksgiving, Christmas, and New Year's without their husband and father. Although the family had accepted the sacrifices that came with the ministry, it was not easy.

Such sacrifices were painful for Charles as well. He was an attentive husband and father, deeply in love with his wife and kids. Whenever possible, he would take them along with him on trips, but that was expensive. Sometimes Rene met him for a long weekend, but it was not as often as either of them would have wished. To be clear, C.D. traveled to advance God's cause, not because he didn't want to be at home or found exotic places so alluring. He was so sought after that his calendar was booked for years in advance—and such was the case for decades.

And so Brooks discreetly sought advice from a select few of his respected colleagues who had been clocking thousands of miles on the road for years. His longtime friend Maurice Battle—also a pioneering leader like Charles—gave him the simple but sage advice of writing intimate letters to Rene, Diedre, and Skip on his trips. That, of course, had been a sacred tradition that Charles and Rene had observed all throughout their courtship during his lonely days as a fledgling pastor in Delaware and Pennsylvania two decades before. It had worked then, and it would surely do so now.

Battle's suggestion was a godsend. Charles wrote to Rene every other day and to Diedre and Skip once a week. Because Walterene knew her husband's itinerary, she would often mail her and the kids' letters to his next stop, and C.D. would receive them as a most pleasant of surprises when he arrived. The family numbered the letters so they would know if they didn't receive one. As had been the case in Chester, the often-lonely Charles received a much-needed helping of love and affection from the words of the love of his life, Rene, and the pride of his life, Diedre and Skip, be he in New Delhi or New York.

In truth, the Brooks children learned geography from their correspondence with their father. Heretofore the subject had been only of passing interest to them, mostly concerned with locating places on flat paper maps and round plastic globes. But the subject sprang to life when they received letters in the mail postmarked Mogadishu or Honolulu. What a learning experience it was for them to become acquainted with the peoples and places of the world firsthand from their father!

When Diedre entered Oakwood College, she got so many requests to share her father's letters that she finally caved in (understandably, she was at first shy to share such personal correspondence between a father and daughter with her peers). The letters soon became like oracles in her dorm. By then C. D. Brooks was a household name, Diedre's generation having been raised on his preaching. As did the early church with the letters of the apostle Paul, she read her father's letters of spiritual advice and love aloud to her friends. Charles had no idea that she had done so until years later. When he found out, such fatherly pride filled his heart that he wept, thanking God for granting him an influence for good.

That is how the Brookses turned the oftentimes negatives of traveling into pluses. Walterene never complained about her husband's long absences, and the children learned ways to experience their father's love and presence as if he were right there with them. When the Brooks family was reunited after a long trip, their love for one another only grew, their time together being so much more precious.

1972: Jamaica

Not long after transferring to the GC, C.D. set his sights on the Caribbean island of Jamaica. By the beginning of the 1970s he had been all over the world, preaching and teaching. But as usual, he was itching to hit the sawdust trail and conduct a full-fledged tent revival. And so while on a tour of Adventist churches in the West Indies, God led Brooks to hammer his stakes into the fertile soil of Jamaica.

Just a few years before, E. E. Cleveland, at that time the GC Ministerial Association associate secretary, had swept through Jamaica to recruit as many budding pastors and evangelists as he could to come down to Trinidad for a field school. His field school was like that of Brooks: raw evangelism in action. It turned out to be an evangelistic extravaganza in itself, as more than 1,000 people came out each night to hear the visiting American. On Sabbath 1,500 flocked to the Adventist church in Spanish Town, where Cleveland was speaking, and the next day 6,000 packed the National Convention Hall in Kingston to do the same.

Despite his recruiting success, several factors seemed to militate against Cleveland's upcoming series in Trinidad's capital city, Port of Spain. First, previous evangelistic meetings in Trinidad had resulted in no more than 70 baptisms per campaign. Second, the meetings would take place at the height of the rainy season, October-November. But the groundwork done was extensive, the church collaboration impressive, the series well promoted, and, as always, Cleveland was indefatigable, determined to convert the whole island to Jesus.

The numbers speak for themselves. On the first four nights more than 10,000 people came to the meetings, with an average of around 2,500 to 3,000 a night at the two massive tents on the Prince's Buildings Grounds in Port of Spain. The second Sunday night saw 4,500 in attendance. Ministers from dozens of countries in the Inter-American Division were students in this real-time school of evangelism, noting the methods used to secure such impressive results. It was by far the largest evangelistic program ever held in Trinidad.

When Cleveland made his call to keep the seventh-day Sabbath, 1,329 non-Adventists responded. The first baptism saw 480 descend into the watery grave. The next Sabbath there were 135 baptisms, and the final Sabbath reported 135. In all, 820 baptisms were conducted while Cleveland was on the island. After he returned to the States, more than 400 more joined the Adventist Church under the able preaching of George H. Rainey, resulting in a total of more than 1,200 new members. From the close of the Trinidad campaign more than 20,000 believers had been baptized in a 12-month period in the Inter-American Division.

***

C. D. Brooks was the next big American evangelist to conduct an evangelistic series on a similar scale in the Caribbean. The president of the West Jamaica Conference, S. M. Reid, lobbied for Brooks to conduct a field school (i.e., tent meetings) in his territory. Realizing that it would be a prime educative endeavor, Andrews University permitted ministerial students to fly down and take part for course credits. The three conferences that covered Jamaica also put their ablest ministers to work to prepare the way for Brooks.

Adventists in the Caribbean love their church and love to go to church. And they love the ministry. When C. D. Brooks arrived, they treated him like a head of state. The Jamaican members would not even allow him to carry his own bags, deeming it an honor to assist the man of God. They always had a sumptuous meal ready for him, laundered his clothes, and drove him everywhere. He also had high-caliber assistants with him throughout the meetings, Tim Walters most prominent among them. Brooks was deeply humbled and appreciative for all they did.

Jamaicans came from all over the island to hear the powerful American speak. Brooks had rarely witnessed such a hunger for truth. One evening just hours before the meetings a typhoon blasted the island, leaving destruction and flooding it its wake. Then an hour before the meetings were to start he went to the tent to determine the damage. It was bad. The whole area was flooded about a foot deep for miles. Under the tent it was like a lake.

But Brooks was surprised to see an elderly woman seated in the middle of the flooded tent, her feet perched on the stabilizer of her folding chair, reading the Bible. He waded to her, his feet sloshing, his shoes as good as ruined.

"My sister," he said, a worried and confused tone in the words.

The woman looked up slowly, grit and strength in her worn face.

"Whopnin,' Pastah?"

Motioning to the water around them, Brooks asked, "What are you doing here?"

"Me waitin' fuh de meetin' ta staut," she replied, as if it were the most obvious thing in the world.

"But the water . . ." His voice trailed off as he swept his hand around the premises again.

Cracking a smile for the first time, she said, "Don' botha' me nun."

Brooks was catching on by now. These people meant business when it came to the Word.

"Should I cancel tonight?"

"Pastah, listen heayah. Don' cancel. Hab de meetin.' "

C.D. followed her advice, and sure enough, 10 minutes before the scheduled start, islanders descended from all over, pants rolled up, skirts pulled up, walking barefoot. To reward them for all their trouble coming out that night, Brooks gave them a sermon that they'd never forget.

***

We can best see the results of the evangelistic series from the perspective of the General Conference ministerial secretary, N. R. Dower. On baptism day thousands of people converged on a choice location in Montego Bay. As Dower flew into the island from Washington, D.C., from his plane window he saw an innumerable multitude on the beach, and squinting, thought, *I know beaches are popular here, but they can't be this popular.* Dower instructed the pilot to circle in and go low. He had no idea that a fellow Adventist preacher from the States was having a baptism that day.

Wealthy expats on sleek yachts had backed the vessels up to the perimeter of the area where the baptism was taking place and now sat on beach chairs on their decks in swimwear, entranced by the spectacle. C. D. Brooks and 10 other pastors were waist-deep in the blue water, the sun shining brightly on them while a cool breeze gently whistled about them. Ten deacons brought the people out to be baptized, while 10 more escorted them back to the sandy beach. Dower thrilled at the sight.

More than 500 were baptized that day in Montego Bay.

***

C.D. held campaigns on many other Caribbean islands. One of the most riveting experiences in all of Brooks's years of evangelism occurred in Antigua when he took his brother along as part of his staff. Elliott Brooks proved to be an efficient evangelist. One day he went to visit a woman whom he had invited to the meetings and who attended regularly, but seemingly as an observer, not one really moved by what she heard. As it was nearing decision time, Elliott knew that there was only a brief window before the opportunity to clinch a commitment would pass.

So he and another Bible instructor visited the woman's home. When they arrived, they saw a massive man in the yard wielding a machete, expertly slicing the high grass. Wearing work clothes, he had long dreadlocks and forearms like bundles of taut ropes.

Sensing the two men's approach, he slowly wheeled around, the long blade catching the sunbeams. "Whatchu wan?" he said, his voice low and malevolent. He had eyes that seemed to glow, so piercing that they evoked pure terror in the heart of Elliott Brooks.

"Is this the home of so and so?" Elliott asked shakily.

The man stared at him, ruthlessly taking his measure. "Yah, 'tis."

"We have come to talk to her about baptism."

The man snarled, "She ain't bein' baptized. I tol' huh if she get baptized I'll kill huh."

Knowing when to retreat, the Bible workers left, visibly shaken. But the woman continued to attend the meetings, and came up when Brooks made the appeal for baptism. Even on that day her expression was resigned.

On baptismal Sabbath she was at the beach with her white robe and towel, among the throng of thousands of people, some watching, others getting baptized. Charles Brooks was busy baptizing the seemingly endless queue of people lined up for dozens of yards along the shore, so he didn't witness what transpired. Elliott later related it to him.

As Elliott stood by the woman on the beach, encouraging her and making sure she had everything she needed, his fellow Bible instructor, who had visited the woman's home with him, appeared by his side with a simple but urgent message: "He's coming!"

Sure enough, the angry man was charging down the beach with the power and ferocity of a lion. The men in Brooks's team moved instinctively toward the cowering baptismal candidate, ready for a brutal tussle.

When he was within 10 feet of his wife, the husband roared, "Didn' I tell ya dat you are not goin' be baptized?"

"Yes," she said, head down, cowering.

"Didn' I tell ya dat if ya got baptized I was goin' kill ya?"

"Yes," she replied, nodding.

"Yah mean ta tell me dat you still gon' be baptized intah dis chuch?"

"I must," his wife said, a strange conviction in her voice that suddenly seemed more powerful than a whole army of men like her husband.

Suddenly the husband reached out, catching her by the shoulders. Elliott and the others tensed, ready to take the man's hands if need be. But no one was ready for what occurred next. The powerful man's hands slid gently down from her shoulders, and he sank to his knees before her.

"All me life I've wanted a religion wort' dyin' fah," he said, looking up at his wife, tears in his eyes.

That day she was baptized. And her husband was baptized not too much later, becoming a Bible instructor with Elliott Brooks.

***

On another island Brooks received an urgent request to pray for a woman possessed by a demon. Agreeing to it, he went to her home with two local elders. When they arrived, the woman was in what seemed to be a catatonic state, slouched in an unnatural position on the couch. C.D. had never seen a person in quite such a condition, and he could sense demons in the room. Nothing was right about any of it.

Charles opened his Bible and began reading the most powerful words that ever fell upon the ears of human beings. Then he and his elders knelt to pray, and he lifted his voice asking God explicitly for her deliverance. When they opened their eyes, the woman had sat up on the couch, intelligence in her eyes, an alert expression on her face. It reminded Brooks of the demoniac in the Bible "sitting, and clothed, and in his right mind." His team left, thanking God for the outcome. C.D. was sad to find out three weeks later that bats had flown into the woman's house, and she was hopelessly possessed again.

Demon possession was a consistent problem that Brooks faced while evangelizing the islands. Once a man who was excited about the upcoming baptism brought Brooks a fetish, two inches across, wrapped in tightly bound leather. The man had paid a princely sum for it, and explained that it kept him out of difficulty and protected his family. He asked C.D. what he should do with it.

"Burn it," Charles said.

The fetish went into the flames, and the man into the water.

Another individual told Brooks that one night he was walking down a dark lonely road when he heard voices unlike any he had ever heard before as clearly as if they were right next to him. Then he saw flames pass right above his head and streak down the road. Like the man with the fetish, this man's fate was to go under the water and come up in newness of life.

***

1973: Chicago

Working at the General Conference included many responsibilities that C.D., quite frankly, could have done without. In just his first year alone he served on the following committees: Bible Teaching Subcommittee of the Education Committee; Black Youth Problems Conference Planning Committee; Denominational Trends Standing Committee; General Conference Committee; Human Relations Committee; License and Credentials Committee; North American Regional Committee; Regional Department Advisory Committee; Regional Publishing Topics Commission Committee; Religious Liberty and Church/State Relations Committee; and several more standing and ad hoc committees. But he knew that God wanted him out in the field, on the sawdust, under a tent, and that's where he was going to be.

And so the 42-year-old field secretary set his sights on the great city of Chicago. At the time, Charles's brother-in-law, Jesse Wagner, was the president of the Lake Region Conference, while his roommate at Oakwood, Russell Bates, was lay activities secretary. C.D. had visited there several times and felt the place was ripe for an eight-week tent series in the summer of 1973. As with others, the Chicago campaign held a field school attended by 14 ministerial students from Andrews University and Oakwood College, among them Delbert Baker, later president of Oakwood University and a vice president of the General Conference.

Electricity shot through Seventh-day Adventism in Chicagoland when word got out that C. D. Brooks was coming to town. At this point he was among the most listened-to and sought-after speakers in the whole denomination. If a person hadn't heard his sermons in person, he or she had by cassette tape. Brooks always brought biblical truth in an irresistible way. A belief circulated among Adventists that if you had a relative or friend teetering on the edge of the church, a Brooks sermon would fix that, moving them safely back into the fold.

Charles spoke several times for rallies at Shiloh and other churches in the city to drum up support for the series, slated to begin on July 7. The members of the five churches in the immediate area of the prospective location responded, dozens going out into the communities of Chicago, visiting homes, giving Bible studies, passing out handbills, and spreading the word.

Legendary Bible instructor Beatrice Hamilton had chosen the location for the tent. The lot on 108th Street and Halsted Street on the South Side of Chicago in the midst of the endless Black ghetto had been selected for its central location, the tens of thousands of inhabitants within a square mile of it, the high amount of traffic that passed by daily, and the ability of church representatives to thoroughly cover the area. That was always C.D.'s modus operandi: to set up shop in the "worst" part of the city and let God bring roses from the concrete.

The canvas tent, christened "Pavilion of Hope," was Brooks's largest yet. The innovative evangelist would use the most cutting-edge technology of the day, preaching with the aid of a state-of-the-art projector and screen with color slides. High-quality recordings of the messages would be made for mass distribution later.

But all of these niceties should not give the impression that the series had smooth sailing. From the very beginning the devil tried to abort the whole affair before it even got on its feet. The local alderman forbade the lot being used for religious meetings. When his prohibitions were overruled by a Higher Authority, the upset man showed up hours before the kickoff, insisting that there would be no parking on unpaved areas (half of the space assigned for parking was unpaved). Opening night saw Lake Region president Wagner running up and down the boulevard to the stores and businesses, requesting permission to use their parking lots. They said yes. But then the alderman informed them that the tent had to be approved by the fire marshal or closed immediately.

C.D. calmly spoke to the alderman, trying to reason with him. When he announced that the tent had too many chairs, Brooks promised that they would remove some.

"I mean before I leave," the city official replied, a smug smirk on his face.

So Brooks and his staff began stacking the 200 surplus chairs behind the piano (only to unstack them and set them up later during the meeting when the overflow crowd called for it).

More "issues" surfaced with the pavilion, all addressed on the spot by Brooks's team.

The very next night the troublesome alderman showed up again. This time, however, Charles had simply had enough. When he again threatened to shut everything down unless Brooks jumped through more hoops, C.D. informed him, "We are not going to obey this order, and you are not going to dispossess us without the court saying so." Brooks and the alderman stood facing each other, resolute expressions on each face. The alderman was the first to look away, storming off muttering into the Chicago night.

No sooner had the series begun than the defamation began—as it always did. Adventist evangelists had to deal with perpetual slander of their church, their meetings, and their characters. One night as Brooks preached, a woman listened from across the boulevard. A Bible instructor spotted her and walked over, trying to talk her into coming inside.

"They lied to us, they lied to us," she kept saying to the instructor, who figured she must be insane. Then the woman began speaking sensibly: "The pastors at my church told us that it would be a money-grabbing thing. That the pastor would get up and beg for money, dupe the people, grab the money, then get outta Dodge!"

Brooks baptized her in the first ceremony.

One young man regularly attended the meetings but would never take a seat. Yet it was obvious that he was interested. The night for the presentation of the change of the Sabbath arrived, and C.D. preached it in so clear a manner that even the children in the audience understood it. (One kindergartner would ask his mother after the service, "Mommy, why do we go to church on Sunday, since God says Saturday?")

The meeting ended, and although it was late, the young man hurried to see his priest.

"Father," he breathed, out of breath in the confessional, "there's a man out here preaching, and he told us tonight that our church changed God's Sabbath from Saturday to Sunday."

"We did," the priest replied without a moment's pause.

Taken aback, the young man rejoined, "Wait, you must not have understood me."

"We did change the day of the Sabbath. Now, my son, I want you to stay away from those meetings and don't ever go back."

Baptized by C. D. Brooks, the man studied at Oakwood and became a Seventh-day Adventist minister.

***

Another remarkable story from the Chicago series of 1973 concerns a man and his wife who came to the meetings every night. The man was dapper, always dressed to a tee, hair perfect, smelling good. The wife was stylish and elegant, always by her man's side. Together they strolled into the tent, cool and confident, the royalty of Black Chicago.

One day the couple pulled up to the tent as the last rays of the sun were sinking in the west, touching the man's gold Cadillac before disappearing out of sight. The man's suit matched the colors of his ride: gold and burnished brown. His wife wore a black dress that clearly did not come from any low-end department store.

C.D. made an appeal for sinners to come home that night. The husband and wife stayed seated—always cool—looking on. When Brooks was through shaking hands and visiting with attendees, the man approached him, his wife staying seated.

"Pastor, I need to speak with you." The men took seats near the pulpit, out of earshot of the visitors still milling about.

Once situated, the man began, "I have some good liquor in my house, fine and expensive. Also got some vintage wine. . . . Now, I have respect for you, your church, and the Lord. So if I'd become a part of your church, I couldn't keep that liquor. Do I sell it or give it away?"

Brooks, who had been studying the sophisticated individual the whole time, decided that he was sincere. He paused a thoughtful beat, then said, "My brother, I need to clear something up with you right from the start. There is no such thing as 'good' liquor, so what you probably mean is expensive liquor or liquor with a high reputation.

"Now, about your question. The Bible says, 'Woe unto him that giveth his neighbour drink.' Let's say a man whom you give or sell the alcohol to gets good and drunk. Then he beats his wife and his kids, or he gets in his car and takes off down the street and winds up in a wreck and kills himself or someone else. Don't imagine that God will ignore that. Record will be made against you in the books of heaven."

Taking Brooks's measure, the man returned, "Then what should I do with the liquor?"

"Here's what I'd do with it. I'd collect every bottle and stack it on the back of the toilet. Then I'd shut the door and kneel before the toilet. Let's call it an altar. I'd offer a prayer to God, asking Him to accept my humble sacrifice. Then I'd uncork each bottle and pour them down the toilet one by one. When I had emptied every one, I'd vow to God, 'By Your grace I will never drink another drop of that stuff.' "

Charles would never forget the man's response.

"Pastor, if you would have given me any other answer, I would have walked out of here, and you would have never seen me again."

That man became a head elder in the new church that resulted from the evangelistic series. He and his wife are now asleep in Jesus.

***

A woman named Mabel Green also had a compelling experience in that Chicago series. Mrs. Green's neighbor was Arsie Childress, a member of the Shiloh church. One day Sister Childress saw Mrs. Green leaning against her fence, obviously faint from the scorching August heat.

"Sure is hot, isn't it?" she said to Mabel.

"Child . . ." Mabel responded, conveying everything in one word.

"I know where it's cool," Arsie said.

That night Mabel accompanied her to the Pavilion of Hope, only two weeks before the close of the meetings. Mabel Green had been a lifelong member of a first-day church in the neighborhood, her passion singing in the choir. Yet she was so engrossed by what she heard under the tent that evening that she began to miss choir practice, a thing she had never done before.

The week she visited the tent the choir members were being fitted for new robes. Mabel Green felt herself torn. Should she remain a member of her church, which she had attended since childhood, and get fitted for a new choir robe, or should she respond to the Holy Spirit and follow the new truths that she found so thrilling?

Mrs. Green decided to attend choir rehearsal that Thursday night and be fitted for a robe. Yet she asked her children (who had by then begun attending the revival themselves) to save her a seat. After being measured for a gown, she sped to the Pavilion of Hope, arriving just as Brooks stood to speak. The message was so convincing, and the Holy Spirit's power so infused the tent, that Mabel decided that very night to be baptized into the Seventh-day Adventist Church on Sabbath. The next morning she called the choir director and requested a refund.

***

"It won't happen."

Delbert Baker was a freshman theology major at Oakwood College when he sent a letter to C. D. Brooks requesting to work with him in Chicago the upcoming summer. When he told some of his fellow theologs about the letter, they replied with the above comment.

When Brooks came to Oakwood's campus, a palpable buzz spread among the ministerial students. Already one could hear his sermons blasting from dorm rooms morning and night. Many of the students knew them word for word, able to reproduce them with Brookslike pitch, rhythm, and cadence. Not a few theology majors wanted to be like C.D., and already during the early seventies a plethora of Brooks mimics had emerged.

When C.D. walked the campus, it was as if the school had a prophet in its midst, his aura that of a Samuel or Elijah. "The man of God is here! Brooks is here!" students whispered to each other. When he spoke anywhere on campus, the place would be packed, veritably humming with electricity. After he left, his visit was the theme of conversation for weeks to come.

Baker also admired Brooks. In the summer of 1972 he worked as a ministerial intern for E. E. Cleveland in Houston. Wanting to round out his evangelistic training under another expert, he felt he couldn't go wrong by asking, so he wrote Brooks a letter.

To his surprise, and that of his naysaying fellow theology majors, Brooks replied that he would indeed be pleased for Baker to be his ministerial intern that summer. Baker looked forward to two months of watching a master at his craft, absorbing as much as he could from him while winning souls.

In Chicago he immediately saw that Brooks ran a tight ship. Everything was a system with him. The team was unquestioning of Brooks, always acting immediately on his instructions. The Bible instructors thoroughly canvassed the neighborhoods of the city. The tent was always neat and orderly. The nightly programs ran like clockwork, everyone fulfilling their assigned duties. Above all, Baker marveled that even before Brooks entered the city, everyone involved knew that success was certain. That's just how it happened with C.D. As with Napoleon, opposing forces would often surrender at the mere tidings of his approach.

The young ministerial intern also noted that C.D. constantly sought to better himself. He was always reading. Always studying the Bible. Always learning new words. Always watching the news for current events to illuminate his sermons on prophecy. Always gathering anecdotes to enrich sermon points. And always studying his audience to determine if the truth was sinking in, and if not, what he could do differently to get it to hit home.

Undergirding all of this was a profound and abiding belief that God had called him to his service. He was God's man. Brooks saw himself as prophetic. His preaching was the Lord communicating to people. On this, Baker never sensed any wavering from Charles.

C.D. sometimes assigned Baker the Scripture reading, offering, or announcements, so that the young ministerial intern periodically occupied the pulpit with Brooks. After a time it dawned on Baker what some of the principles that made Charles's preaching so potent were. First, there was the conviction that he was called of God and that the Lord was speaking to His people through him. Next, Brooks prayed over his messages and put time into preparing them. He thoroughly exegeted the passages he would use, then entered into the mind of the Bible character he was preaching about. A rich imagination lent texture and human interest to his sermons. He always brought out some little-known fact or a tidbit of information that was intriguing, all the while tying it into his message. The man was also a wordsmith, able to masterfully manipulate the English language to serve his purposes.

Charles preached with the power of a man who believes something with his whole heart. Because he did so, he wanted more than anything for the people listening to him to also believe. It was a life-or-death matter, and he spoke with urgency and intensity. From this came a nearly irresistible charisma: people wanted to follow Brooks into biblical truth. And then there was the undefinable X factor that God used so well.

"Thank you for the privilege of working with you," Delbert Baker told him as he shook his hand at the end of the summer.

***

The Lord richly blessed the Chicago series. More than 600 people attended each night, with almost 1,500 on Sundays. A total of 243 new believers resulted, and the Stratford Memorial church resulted. The testimony of the man for whom the new church was named in honor of is as touching as any story from the series itself.

Harry Stratford was one of C.D.'s finest assistants in the Chicago series. A superb Bible instructor, warm people person, and humble worker willing to help out wherever needed, Stratford was best known as the "question man," proctoring the quizzes covering the message from the night before with prizes for those who answered correctly. His love for the Lord and people was so evident that just seeing him in action was a strong witness for what he believed.

Toward the end of the series Stratford became ill. Seeing him in this condition and knowing how hot it was, C.D. gently suggested, "Why don't you take some days off and relax and enjoy your family?"

"No, Pastor!" he replied. "If I'm going to die, I'll go with my boots on!" And so he put in a day of Bible work in the relentless sun.

Elder Stratford's efforts paid off. He saw the baptisms, taking part in them by doing all the little things that needed to be done. Just five days after the series' end, though, he lay in the hospital, near death. His wife and child were there standing at his bedside, tears streaming down their cheeks. Just minutes before he breathed his last, Stratford suddenly asked his wife, "Are you holding my hand?"

"No, I'm not holding your hand."

"Somebody is holding my hand," he insisted.

The Stratford Memorial Seventh-day Adventist Church is alive and well today, a testimony to the living faith of its namesake.

On the Front Line

C. D. Brooks's tenure as a General Conference general field secretary would last an amazing 24 years, among the longest in denominational history, spanning three GC presidencies and six United States presidencies. When he began in 1971, the membership of the Seventh-day Adventist Church was 2,145,061. When he retired in 1995, it had grown to 8,812,555.

Brooks helped guide the church through some of its toughest times. During the Ron Numbers and Walter Rea controversies of the late 1970s and 1980s over the inspiration of Ellen White, C.D. was an unwavering advocate of her writings and prophetic gift. The Desmond Ford fallout over the sanctuary did not affect him, he attended Glacier View only because the church had asked him to do so. Later he would remark that he "honestly didn't know what all the fuss was about. My daddy had a third-grade education and grasped this truth."

He also partook in the church's triumphs. At the 1980 GC session in Dallas, Texas, it adopted the 27 fundamental beliefs that articulated the basic doctrines of Seventh-day Adventists. In the 1980s Brooks was partly responsible for the growth explosion in Latin America and Africa, when many thousands of believers were baptized in one day. This golden age of evangelism was the beginning of the present demographic of the overwhelming majority of Adventists being people of color, a third residing on continental Africa. In Indianapolis, Indiana, at the 1990 GC session, C.D. was present when delegates from around the world nominated a man of color, his friend George Brown, to be the president of the world church (Brown would decline because of several factors beyond his control). This silent triumph in race relations was a clear indicator that the denomination had come a long way since the stormy 1962 session.

Yet C. D. Brooks is part of a rare breed that made their mark in dual arenas. His legacy rightly includes his impressive tenure at the General Conference—but it is his other responsibility, performed along with his GC position, that he will be most remembered for, a ministry that his name was to be synonymous with.

BREATH OF LIFE

"People became addicted to Breath of Life."

Walter Arties III was born in Pittsburgh, Pennsylvania, in 1941 to Walter Arties II and Catherine Arties. Walter II was a Seventh-day Adventist pastor in Greenville, Mississippi, but because of the poor caliber of the region's hospitals, the couple thought it best to go north to the Steel City and stay with extended family until their child was born. The family of five moved around a lot, as was usual for ministers' families in those days: Mississippi to Tennessee to Alabama, then later north to Connecticut and New York City.

By the time he was 19 Walter knew he had to get out of the Big Apple. Too many of the guys he grew up with were getting into trouble with the law or, worse, ending up dead. The day he left, his mother saw him packing and knew he wasn't coming back. Walter was going west to the city of dreams: Los Angeles.

In southern California Walter roomed with several friends in a decent part of L.A. One of his friends, Glenn Howell, owned a housecleaning business, and the guys cleaned houses and barbershops around the Los Angeles area well into the night. Life was good. Walter was young, living in the entertainment capital of the world with a roof over his head, and a job that put some spending money in his pocket.

But his natural gifts spurred him to greater ambitions. Always an Adventist and loyal to his faith, he became involved in music ministry. On one occasion a group of young adults from the University church in Los Angeles, where Walter was a member, received an invitation to present a program at another church. At its conclusion the young people decided to sing together and asked Walter to teach them a song. The "Walter Arties Chorale" was born. The Christian Talent Agency (CTA) caught wind of the young musician and his choir and began to represent him. Before long they suggested sending Walter out as a soloist as well. He and the chorale presented concerts across the region, singing for various churches and then with musicians such as Andrae Crouch and Billy Preston while making cross-country tours.

Dr. Byron Spears, son of evangelist Byron Spears, Sr. (known as the "Walking Bible" because of the vast amount of scriptures he could quote from memory), was executive producer for Walter's first album, *Peace*. CTA, realizing its potential, heavily promoted it, and it sold a respectable amount of units. Around that time NASA was making a series of tapes for astronauts to listen to while in space. It selected Arties' title song, "Peace," as one of the tracks for the astronaut's playlist in space. "His music is out of this world" was the slogan CTA used to sell Arties' records.

In music Walter found his love and true calling in life. His touring and performing of sacred music gave him a sense of fulfillment like nothing else, not only because he was using his talents but also spreading the word of Jesus' love. So he honed and perfected his craft, establishing a name for himself in southern California.

That is not to say that other prospects never tempted him. A major record store in Hollywood called Wallich's Music City had his album as the pick hit for more than two weeks. In those days you could walk into a booth and listen to records to decide if you wanted to purchase them. Walter spent hours listening to music in those booths. One day Clyde Wallich, the store's owner, approached him with a proposition: "If you are willing to sing a different type of music, I have a brother at Capitol Records. We will produce and market it, and you can make some real money." Arties declined.

One event changed Walter's life forever, infusing him with a greater purpose and a dream that he would work doggedly in the future to bring to pass. In August 1965 rioting broke out in Watts, a low-income, predominately Black community in the south central section of Los Angeles. The spark that incited the riots was the arrest on suspicion of drunk driving of a young African American motorist named Marquette Frye. A crowd of onlookers witnessed the scene, and a violent altercation erupted between certain residents and law enforcement. What ensued was a six-day rampage of burning, looting, and violence. In a desperate attempt to restore order, authorities deployed some 14,000 National Guard troops and enforced a curfew across a 45-mile radius. When the rioting ended after six days, it left a staggering 34 dead, more than 1,000 injured, almost 4,000 arrests, and property damage upward of $40 million.

Watching this mere miles away, Walter Arties was first shocked and bewildered, then deeply saddened about what was happening to his people. Never one to be passive, he resolved to do something about it. Black America needed the gospel of Christ now more than ever. The only question was how to reach them. Just a kernel at first, the idea began to form in his mind of a gospel program for the Black demographic with singing and preaching. As the years went by, his dream became more of a plan, then a proposal he came to push wherever he went and to whomever he spoke.

At the dawn of the 1970s Arties found himself on the staff of KHOF Radio and Television Network. As a consequence of his new position, the name of the young Black musician began circulating in more and more circles. Walter met with Bill Bright, the president of Campus Crusade for Christ International, at a fund-raiser banquet in which he was invited to sing. Bright was so impressed with Arties that he asked him to sing at Expo '72 in Dallas, Texas, to be held in the Cotton Bowl that year. Walter quickly accepted.

More than 100,000 young people on fire for Christ packed the Dallas stadium. Arties sang for opening night. Unbeknownst to him after he finished, Billy Graham rose to give the keynote address. The evangelist and the crowd were so impressed by Walter's singing that Cliff Barrows, the Billy Graham Association music coordinator, invited him to sing for several more evangelistic series.

Although Walter Arties and Billy Graham never became close friends, the two had mutual respect for each other. Shortly after Walter had begun singing on a part-time basis he was walking out of a hotel as Graham was going in.

"Hello," Arties called.

"Hello, young man," Graham replied. "What brings you here?"

"I came to sing for you."

Known to be jovial and warm, Graham laughed. "Then I'll see you at the team meeting."

After the meeting the two got a chance to talk.

"What do you do when you're not singing?" Graham inquired.

Arties explained that he was a Seventh-day Adventist and was trying to start a gospel program for African Americans.

Graham smiled. "Wherever I go, I see your hospitals, schools, and churches. Your church does a great work throughout the world."

The famed preacher knew about Walter's denomination, for earlier

Graham had stated publicly at a congress on evangelism, "No matter how devoutly we keep Sunday we are not keeping the Sabbath. Our Seventh-day Adventist friends keep the Sabbath."

Once, before Graham spoke, Walter sang "In This Very Room," and Graham requested him to present that song at every event that he was available. Walter traveled around the world for the Billy Graham Association, and his voice became recognized globally.

But Arties knew that working with Graham was not what God ultimately wanted him to do. He sensed that everything he had done so far was preparation for something greater. With Graham's organization he learned how to sing before large crowds and how to produce a television program. There he met people, established contacts, and learned the ins and outs of the business.

At one meeting Walter had finished singing to 40,000 in a baseball stadium when the host, Cliff Barrows, hurried onstage and asked the crowd, "We are trying to get this man to sing full time for us! Do you think that's a good idea?" The crowd roared its approval. But Walter heard a distinct voice in his head: "This is not where I want you."

By then it had become known that Arties was a Seventh-day Adventist, and he started running into problems with the Minneapolis office of Graham's association. They weren't too favorable toward Adventists, and were starting to make that fact clear. Meanwhile, Adventists didn't appreciate Arties performing for the evangelical Billy Graham, and they also indicated their disapproval.

Selling the Dream

Around this time Arties branched out into radio and television production, accepting a full-time position as director of public affairs at KHOF in Glendale, California. KHOF ran evangelical Christian programming, and Arties was the ideal PR man for the station—young, articulate, and well connected. Among other things, he distributed KHOF materials at his concerts, sold programming spots, generated funding, and generally increased the exposure of the station. Working with the founders of Trinity Broadcasting Network, Paul and Jan Crouch, and other titans of religious programming, as he had with the Graham group, Walter again made important connections at KHOF.

Arties pitched the idea that had been percolating in his mind since the Watts riots of a Christian television program for African Americans to the manager of KHOF. By that time he even knew what he wanted to call the show: "Breath of Life." During his devotional one morning he had come upon Genesis 2:7: "And the Lord God formed man of the dust of the ground, and breathed into his nostrils the breath of life; and man became a living soul." All that day Walter couldn't get the words "breath of life" out of his head—their simplicity, power, and vitality. In order to live, human beings needed the breath of life. It was so apt, because with all that was happening in the tumultuous civil rights era, Blacks needed that breath more urgently than ever.

The manager was supportive, but not overly so. Arties would later realize that it was providential, because Adventist support and backing was what he needed. When he kept getting tepid responses from the non-Adventist Christians whom he pitched the idea to in California, Arties decided to approach Adventist church leaders. He first went to the ministers and administrators in the regional conferences, the obvious choice because they were Black, so the program should immediately appeal to them. Arties also spoke with Black ministers at the General Conference, E. E. Cleveland and C. D. Henri among them.

The Black leadership did not need much convincing at all. Arties' dream had long been theirs. Cleveland told Neal Wilson about the idea, and the NAD president was immediately enthusiastic. Wilson requested that Arties create a pilot so that he could have something tangible to use to drum up support and make the plan a reality.

***

Walter set to work on the pilot. The manager of KHOF graciously provided him equipment for the show and the television crew to produce it. As a member of University, the large Black church in South Central Los Angeles, Walter asked his pastor, Samuel Meyers, to give a sermonette for the program. Meyers agreed. Walter had the music part covered: a superb quartet he had formed earlier would sing for the telecast, along with the chorale.

The pilot aired in 1973 on KHOF television in southern California. The broadcast was an admirable start, simple yet professional, infused with plenty of gospel. The program included a call-in number for prayer requests and feedback, a receptionist at the Southern California Conference office routing the calls to an office where several volunteers fielded them. Fortunately, the pilot did not cost Arties anything, which was a good thing, because he had no money.

Immediately church leaders expressed their support for the telecast.

First among them was the president of the Southern California Conference, Harold Calkins, who came to the station with the conference committee, which in turn agreed to recommend it to the Pacific Union. Breath of Life had clinched the support of its home conference.

Now Walter had to sell his dream to the rest of Adventism. Neal Wilson had advised him to approach the regional conference presidents first, so that's what he did, hitting the road with his quartet, who put on concerts at churches with a showing of the pilot as the main event. The people loved it. Walter's quartet performed to packed churches, halls, auditoriums, gymnasiums, and camp meetings across the nation.

At the invitation of C. D. Henri, vice president of the General Conference, Arties made his pitch for Breath of Life to a committee comprised of all seven regional conference presidents. In those days he had no funding whatsoever and was incurring considerable expenses traveling from place to place. After a dynamic presentation to the administrators, Jesse Wagner, president of Lake Region Conference, and C. D. Brooks's brother-in- law, stood and proclaimed, "This young man came on his own dime. I'm going to cover his expenses, and you all are going to cover me." Walter knew that he had accomplished his purpose.

The regional presidents, a tight-knit group in those days, unanimously offered their support to Breath of Life. The Black leaders assembled that day wrote letters to Neal Wilson and Robert Pierson stating in effect that the Black Adventist church backed Breath of Life. Now it would seek even wider support.

At Neal Wilson's behest the North American Division invited Arties to a communications advisory held in Hinsdale, Illinois. By now Walter was a pro at selling the idea, his spiel refined and polished. The committee was duly impressed, but hesitated because of financial considerations.

At the point when it seemed Breath of Life might get rejected, William Loveless spoke up. Loveless, a highly respected minister, at the time pastored the 7,000-member Loma Linda University Church, the largest Seventh-day Adventist congregation in the world. He was known for being outspoken on controversial issues, for taking courageous but unpopular stands. In 1957, while pastoring the General Conference's unofficial church, Sligo, in Takoma Park, Maryland, Loveless defied the church board's policy on not permitting Blacks to become members. Despite resistance from powerful and wealthy members, he insisted on an inclusive membership policy, and eventually won out.

"People are rioting in the streets," Loveless said before the advisory committee. "Breath of Life needs to be done, and I support it fully."

The North America Division voted to endorse Breath of Life.

***

Walter Arties and his Breath of Life program had one more hurdle: the General Conference. Getting the backing of the GC was essential, because the Adventist Media Center (AMC), a GC-run Seventh-day Adventist radio, television, and film center, had just opened in Thousand Oaks, California. It was Arties' plan to run Breath of Life from the new operation, under the aegis of the church. Already It Is Written and Faith for Today had moved to AMC, and in Arties' mind it would be the ideal spot for Breath of Life.

The Communication Department there had already shown interest. Black leaders at the GC—C. D. Henri, E. E. Cleveland, and Charles Bradford—had talked about the project to Robert Pierson, urging him to put the GC's full support behind it. When Pierson's secretary called Arties and told him that the president requested a meeting with him, the young musician knew that God had brought his dream to pass.

So Walter flew across the country to the GC's offices in Washington, D.C. Once in the building, he visited with several people, telling them of the latest developments and getting reports of their efforts on behalf of the broadcast. To others he pitched the plan for the one hundredth time, knowing that the more people that were behind it, the greater a success it would be. When it was time to meet with Pierson, Arties offered up a prayer as he stepped into his office.

After so many people had spoken in favor of it to Pierson, it did not require much selling on Walter's part at all. In the middle of the conversation Pierson asked Arties, "Whom do you have in mind for a speaker?"

"C. D. Brooks," Arties replied without a moment's hesitation.

Robert Pierson broke out into a wide smile. "There's no one we'd rather have than Charles Brooks as a speaker for this program. We would love to see his ministry expanded in this way."

With that the two men shook hands. Walter Arties walked out of the office with the full support of the General Conference of Seventh-day Adventists for Breath of Life.

***

In the spring of 1973 C. D. Brooks attended ministerial meetings at Oakwood College. Alabama is beautiful in early spring, the temperature perfect, the trees and flowers in full bloom. An endless variety of colors charm the eye, while the song of birds delights the ear. Juniors and seniors have outdoor weddings during the season.

But Brooks was oblivious to the spring beauty. Walter Arties, Neal Wilson, Robert Pierson, E. E. Cleveland, and others had approached him about being the Breath of Life speaker-director. Each believed that God was leading him to media, but C.D. just didn't see it. Yet everywhere he went people were urging him to do it.

One morning toward the close of the meetings he walked from his guest room on the second floor of Edwards Hall and stood at the balcony. The view overlooked the Eva B. Dykes Library and the administration building. The grass was a rich green, swaying in the wind in line with the flags lining the sidewalk leading to the library entrance. Students picnicked on the lawn, some threw baseballs or kicked soccer balls, while others stood around engaged in conversation.

As Delbert Baker, Brooks's ministerial intern the summer before in Chicago and a sophomore theology major, was leaving his dorm room he saw his mentor pensively staring out from the balcony. Since it was the first time he had seen him since Chicago, he strode over to greet him.

Baker asked Brooks about the new believers in Chicago and other general questions about his welfare and ministry. The whole time they were talking it seemed as though Brooks wasn't quite there, as though he was thinking about something else.

"Elder, I understand that you've been asked to be the speaker for Breath of Life."

C.D.'s eyes came alive, and his body straightened. He was now alert and focused.

"Yes, they've asked me."

"Which way are you leaning?"

"Delbert, it's something new. I don't know anything about television. I know evangelism."

Pausing, Baker considered Brooks's words.

"But Elder, wouldn't this be a great opportunity to expand your ministry, branch out, and reach more people? You can take your skills and blend them into this new avenue."

Shaking his head, C.D. replied, "Maybe. I'm hearing that from a lot of the brethren. I just don't know, though . . ."

Baker had never seen him in such a state of ambivalence. The man was usually assured and unwavering. Brooks sensed that he was on the cusp of a decision, one that would be a turning point in his life. But there was a struggle going on in his mind.

"I'm praying about it, laying it before God," he said, staring into the distance once again.

***

"It's a great idea—but I don't want to do it," C. D. Brooks declared.

When the preacher and singer met once again to discuss Brooks being the speaker-director of Breath of Life, it dawned on Arties that his biggest challenge yet lay in convincing Charles to get on board with Breath of Life. In truth, he had thought long and hard about who the speaker should be. Counseling with others, he had weighed the pros and cons of name after name. In the end, no one even remotely matched up to C. D. Brooks.

By the early 1970s Brooks was one of the premier preachers not only in Black Adventism but in North America and beyond, a reality acknowledged when the church asked him to deliver the Friday night sermon on June 13 at the 1975 General Conference session held in Vienna, Austria, the first one outside of North America. C.D.'s sermons were powerful—biblical, Spirit-filled, and strikingly memorable. The man himself had an impeccable reputation, considerable gravitas, a commanding yet kindly manner, and was handsome, dapperly dressed, and supremely articulate. But he was not amenable to the idea, despite others whom he highly respected urging him to do it.

"But Elder Brooks," Walter Arties countered, "this is a prime opportunity to reach people with the gospel. Television is a medium that reaches millions of people."

"Maybe. But I'm a contact preacher. I need to see the people, be near them. I don't know anything about TV. It's a great idea, but I'm not your man." Brooks shook his head as he spoke.

Praying as he reasoned with C.D., Walter repeatedly stressed how many people television could reach. One could never tell who would hear the gospel through the medium. Brooks could be in only one place preaching from a tent, but with television he could be in living rooms, bedrooms, stores—everywhere.

Television sets had entered American homes in modest numbers during the late 1940s. At that early date it was primarily a luxury and novel entertainment piece affordable only to well-off urbanites. Many Christians were suspicious of the animated box, denouncing it as of the devil. Adventist thought leaders were also leery of television in its earliest days, seeing it as another wicked invention to desensitize minds with pleasure-seeking while the signs of the times played out around them unheeded. However, as time went on and televisions became more mainstream and then ubiquitous, Adventists grew much less hostile toward the new media.

In fact, among Christian denominations, Seventh-day Adventists were the undisputed trailblazers in television programming. Evangelistically minded Adventists, always in search of new ways to reach people, quickly saw the potential of television in reaching the masses. In 1950, as televisions were increasing in sales but the TV boom was still in its infancy, William Fagal, an Adventist pastor, aired the program *Faith for Today* on WJZ-TV (now WABC-TV) in New York City on May 21. *Faith for Today*, sponsored by the church with its full backing, was the first national religious telecast in North America.

Faith for Today was one of the most innovative ministries in Christian history. It started a Bible school in 1952. Ultimately more than a half million completed the correspondence courses, and more than 30,000 joined the church. When the ministry relocated to the Adventist Media Center in California in 1972, it debuted the award-winning show *Westbrook Hospital*. Three years later Faith for Today produced a successful film on John Huss. The TV drama special *The Harvest* appeared in 1979, also garnering acclaim and awards.

George Vandeman, another Adventist evangelist, was a visionary of the first order, once again not only in Adventism but larger Christianity. In the spring of 1956, when televisions were becoming accessible to every American and color TV had become more widespread, Vandeman began *It Is Written* on 13 stations. The show was the first Christian television program to broadcast in color. Millions have viewed it through the years.

Faith for Today and *It Is Written* were commanding large viewing audiences by the time Arties hit upon his idea for a television program. It is certainly true that he got much of his inspiration from those two pioneering ministries, and church leaders supported the idea based partly on the impressive track records of Vandeman and Fagal. But Arties and others also recognized that *Faith for Today* and *It Is Written* were not appealing to or reaching the Black demographic of the nation. Therefore, the need for Breath of Life.

"You can reach so many people," Walter again said to Brooks, real passion in his voice. "Hundreds of thousands will hear the truth—people that would never step foot in a tent."

The potential to reach so many began to move the seasoned evangelist, someone who lived for that very thing. "I will do it for a while and see what happens," C.D. finally said. That day neither man could have predicted that "a while" would be more than two decades.

Launch

Just as Faith for Today and It Is Written were trailblazing ministries, so Breath of Life was destined to be. At the time, America had little or no Black religious programming, so Walter Arties was spot-on in his assessment that it would fill a much-needed market niche. Further, in 1974 when Arties entered the new Adventist Media Center in Thousand Oaks to make plans for the first Breath of Life telecast, little did he know that his program would be the very first ministry to produce a series out of the facility. That first telecast was called "Has God Forgotten Us?"

The plan was for C. D. Brooks, still holding the full-time job of General Conference field secretary, to fly out to California several times throughout the year, tape as many episodes as possible during his stay, then return to Washington. His title would be speaker-director of Breath of Life. Walter had the full support of Robert Pierson and Neal Wilson for the plan, for the General Conference now officially owned and operated Breath of Life Ministries. So in July of 1974 C.D. arrived at Los Angeles International Airport to an excited Walter Arties, and the two made the short drive to the Adventist Media Center.

Earlier that week Arties had picked up another essential team member from the airport. Louis B. Reynolds had been born 13 years before C. D. Brooks in his neighbor state of South Carolina. He had completed a two-year ministerial course at Oakwood College in 1936 and pastored in Kansas and Missouri for six years. Then in 1938 the young minister married Bernice Johnson, and the couple had two daughters shortly after. Reynolds was ordained to the gospel ministry in 1941, the year his second daughter was born.

Louis made history in 1945 by becoming the first Black editor of the oldest Black religious periodical in America, *Message*. It occurred during the inauguration of regional conferences and was a signal of the assumption of Black Adventists to positions of leadership in a church that had hitherto largely denied them the right. Reynolds was editor of *Message* for the next 15 years, working from the magazine's offices at the Southern Publishing Association in Nashville, Tennessee.

While editor, Reynolds for a number of years was simultaneously the chaplain of Riverside Sanitarium, the first Adventist-run hospital for African Americans. During this period he also earned a B.A. at Fisk University, the historically Black college a short drive from the *Message* office. A prolific author, he published numerous books: *Dawn of a Brighter Day* (1946), *Little Journeys Into Storyland* with C. L. Paddock (1947), *Look to the Hills* (1960), *Great Texts From Romans* (1972), *Bible Answers* with Robert Pierson* (1973), and *We Have Tomorrow* (1984).

After *Message* Reynolds was the district leader for the Northeastern Conference for three years. The talented Black minister and writer went to the General Conference in 1962 as the associate director of the Sabbath School Department. In Washington he earned a master's from Howard University in 1968, and was awarded an honorary doctorate from Union Baptist Seminary in Birmingham, Alabama, in 1970. Interestingly, Reynolds and Brooks shared the latter honor, C.D. being awarded an honorary doctorate the same year from the same school.

It was at his General Conference post that Arties first approached Reynolds about being the scriptwriter for Breath of Life. He was something of an obvious choice, at the time being the premier writer in Black Adventism along with E. E. Cleveland, and possessing the rare gift of writing simply and accessibly for a wide audience. Furthermore, as the longest serving editor of the oldest Black religious magazine in America, Reynolds knew how to appeal to a Black audience with the pen. Because Brooks wouldn't have time to write scripts with his busy schedule, Reynolds would prepare them for him.

At the brand-new facility in Thousand Oaks, the three Breath of Life team members sat together at lunch brainstorming about the first program. Walter Arties soon found himself listening raptly as Brooks and Reynolds fired off ideas, building off of each other. It was a marvelous thing: two Black Adventist titans brainstorming for a television series that could potentially reach millions. Arties had to pinch himself to make sure he wasn't dreaming.

They decided on a series highlighting Black people in the Bible. Reynolds, who had a keen eye for art, commissioned a series of paintings of the queen of Sheba, Philip and the Ethiopian eunuch, Rahab, Simon of Cyrene, and other Africans in Scripture. He in turn asked several Adventist Washingtonians—Elvira Arties, Selena Kirby, Jacqueline McDonald, and Sarah Willis—to raise money for the artwork. The women didn't disappoint.

The paintings were displayed behind the Breath of Life Quartet as they sang and C.D. as he spoke.

Walter Arties and his team did whatever they could to fulfill Reynolds' vision for what became known as the Heritage Series. Arties counseled with dozens of his contacts and former colleagues, doing all he could to make the series as professional as possible, knowing that the initial broadcast would to a great degree set the tone for the ones to follow.

Meanwhile, Reynolds was busy with the script, thinking as he wrote of the millions of Blacks across the nation, and what would appeal to them. How could he best communicate the gospel? How could he show that they had a part in God's plan? How could he write in a way that would match Brooks's personality, words that would flow from him easily and authentically? The two men consulted into the wee hours of the morning.

The finished product was a script that was potent and crisp, appropriate for Brooks's dynamic personality, and one that would successfully reach the hearts and minds of not only Black America, but Americans of all colors, ages, and walks of life. Brooks's short, poignant messages aligned neatly with the large paintings behind him, creating a coordinated and sophisticated effect.

Although C.D. turned out to be a natural on-screen, he himself did not anticipate that he would be. He craved live preaching in a tent or church, not in front of a camera. In fact, up to that point he had not been on television. The Heritage Series shoots were nerve-racking for him, but he knew that he just had to get used to it. Although they were staged (in the most literal sense of the word), he tried to be authentic and genuine, but it was tough at first, especially if one had to go through several takes and say the same lines again. The technical director, Bruce Braun, would tell C.D. that he had 19 or so minutes. If Brooks went over or under that allotted time by just seconds, they had to do the whole thing once more. Worse, if he coughed or split a verb, it would be caught on camera and could not be redone, because the broadcast had no money to redo such mistakes. They'd just be immortalized on tape. Brooks found himself praying for precision.

To top that off, instead of preaching to a crowd of actual people, C.D. spoke to a red light on the camera. That little red light could downright irk a speaker.

However, Walter and the rest of the crew were amazed at Brooks's poise and presence on the screen. Always prepared, he was never rattled or nervous. His delivery was polished and crisp, yet warm and genuine. Later if he came to the end of his lines on the teleprompter and he still had time to fill, he could ad-lib for minutes on end with script-worthy delivery. Arties realized that his selection of Brooks as a speaker couldn't have been better.

When George Vandeman heard about Breath of Life, he was delighted. He was also pleased that his friend and fellow evangelist C. D. Brooks would serve as the speaker. In Los Angeles the *It Is Written* speaker pulled C.D. aside and said sotto voce, "Charles, I want to give you one important piece of advice: don't let them force you to do more than one program a day." Smiling, Brooks thanked Vandeman. He knew he meant well, but also recognized that *It Is Written* had a very healthy budget. The fledgling Breath of Life, however, did not as yet have such funding, and as a Black-run program probably never would. So in four or five days' time, Breath of Life usually produced more than a dozen programs.

***

In Walter Arties' original vision for the program, music played an integral part. But he had no idea that the show would launch the careers of several internationally renowned artists and bring worldwide fame to his Breath of Life Quartet. The show's first musical director was Shelton Kilby III. Born in Washington, D.C., Kilby studied music at Columbia Union College (now Washington Adventist University), the Preparatory School of Music, Howard University, Los Angeles City College, and in Idar-Oberstein, Germany, where the renowned pianist Inga Murdoch privately tutored him. He earned a B.A. in religion with an emphasis in Old and New Testament from Atlantic Union College. Insatiable for education, Kilby would acquire more degrees and certificates throughout his life.

A fine baritone singer, Kilby most excelled in piano and musical composition. His textured and layered scores could transport listeners to the very gates of heaven. No sooner had the telecast gotten off the ground than Kilby's name was on the list of credits along with C. D. Brooks and Walter Arties.

Also on the Breath of Life crew was manager Philip Moores, treasurer G. G. Steward, and technical director Bruce Braun. The Hollywood-based Video Tape Enterprises, an outfit Walter had worked with before during his days at KHOF, taped the program with multimillion-dollar equipment. At least one of the television crew was converted as a result of listening to the Spirit-filled programming while he recorded.

Promotion

With the Heritage Series completed, Walter Arties knew that he had to promote the ministry more than ever. The price tag to produce a single *Breath of Life* episode could be as high as $25,000. The Heritage Series, with all the other added expenses, cost the ministry a quarter million dollars. The General Conference gave only partial financial support. The rest the ministry had to raise itself. At such an early date the tithe and offerings from new members that Breath of Life brought in did not yet justify such large expense. So when he was not planning and producing, Arties was out fund-raising.

The founder of Breath of Life had many things going for him. First, Breath of Life was a General Conference ministry. He carried the full weight of the church's imprimatur when soliciting funds from members. Next, since his was one of only three Adventist television programs, he did not yet have to compete with many other entities for donations. Also, C. D. Brooks was by now a household name in Adventism. With him as speaker—the public face of the ministry—it was much easier to get support than if the speaker had been a lesser known figure.

***

In 1975, for the first time, a General Conference session convened outside of the United States. At the convocation in Vienna, Austria, Breath of Life was well represented. C. D. Brooks gave a moving devotional on July 9 entitled "New Life." The organizers had requested Walter Arties to sing during the session. Four days later at the evening business session on Sunday, July 13, GC vice president W. D. Eva asked Brooks to speak about the ministry to the seated delegates.

"Through the providence of God a new television series called *Breath of Life* is ready for viewing wherever the English language is understood," C.D. told them. "Thirteen segments are completed. Ours is a full message series.

"We are committed to go now into Detroit, Michigan, northern California, and Memphis, Tennessee. After about the eighth segment is viewed, we plan to begin evangelistic meetings which will run concurrently with the TV series. We expect much fruit under God. We feel that the Lord has given us a fresh approach that will interest thousands who wouldn't normally attend our churches. We believe these programs will appeal to men and women of all ethnic backgrounds who are hungering for truth.

"We therefore have great expectations for Breath of Life. We have some

of the finest music available, with marvelous visual effects. It is my privilege to be the speaker for the series. The program is taped at the Adventist
Radio, TV, and Film Center in Thousand Oaks, California.

"How did it all begin? In our midst is a gifted young man, Walter Arties.
We have already been blessed with his music. There are many calls for his
gifts and expertise. Lucrative offers have been put before him. But he is
determined to serve God and His church with his talents. He understands
the potential and the advantage offered to us through the visual media.
The dream was his. God gave him the vision. Now, through the excellent
cooperation of our leaders, through generous appropriations and support,
Breath of Life is a reality. Our team is small but enthusiastic. I would like
you to meet Louis B. Reynolds of the Sabbath School Department, who is
our special researcher, and Walter Arties, producer of our program."

Arties followed with brief remarks. Now the world leaders knew about
Breath of Life.

Evangelistic Onslaught: Detroit

When the Heritage Series was complete and ready for television in 1975,
superstations and networks did not yet exist. Those who wanted to air a
program had to purchase a slot from a station in a specific location through
a time-buying agency. Each time the program ran again it had to pay an
additional fee.

C.D. and Walter Arties had developed a systematic plan of evangelism
for Breath of Life Ministries, not unlike what Brooks used in his own evangelistic campaigns. First, the *Breath of Life* series would air on television for
a month or so in the target city. Advertisements for the program would appear in newspapers. Then church members would flood the city with flyers and handbills advertising an evangelistic campaign with Breath of Life
speaker C. D. Brooks. Walter Arties, soloist, accompanied by Clyde Allen,
second tenor; Shelton Kilby III, baritone; and James Kyle, bass; all forming
the Breath of Life Quartet, would provide the music. Those who responded
to the program's invitation for viewers to enroll in a Bible correspondence
course were visited and tutored (as needed) through the course. Then it
was time for the evangelistic meetings, which took place in some venue in
the city (an auditorium, theater, large hall, or a good old-fashioned tent).

The TV programs would still be running on the air during the series,
and even a little while afterward. When the baptism had taken place and
the meetings concluded, the evangelists assigned the new Adventists to lo-

cal churches and to members who would nurture them in the faith. Then the Breath of Life team would pack up and do the same thing in another city.

The Lake Union Conference was the first to invite Breath of Life Ministries to its territory to run an evangelistic series. President L. L. Bock and the executive committee pledged the help of the churches to assist in whatever way they could. Jesse Wagner, C.D.'s brother-in-law and a member of the union conference executive committee, served as the liaison between Breath of Life and the Lake Union, as well as the Lake Region Conference, of which he was president. The huge metropolis of Detroit was to be the ministry's first proving ground.

Black Detroit in 1975 had a population of almost 700,000, itself equivalent to the size of a large city. Having migrated to the northern city in unprecedented numbers during World War I, often at the rate of 1,000 per month, they had come in search of better jobs, a better racial climate, and a better life. Although they often faced difficulties, employment was plentiful, the city being a major producer of automobiles as well as wartime and industrial products.

In 1959 a young entrepreneur named Berry Gordy began a record label called Motown. On the strength of star acts such as Smokey Robinson, Stevie Wonder, Marvin Gaye, the Temptations, the Supremes, and later the Jackson 5, Motown became one of the most successful music labels in history, putting Detroit on the map as the capital not only of Black music but American music as a whole.

Sadly, however, as in Watts, a devastating riot erupted in Detroit in 1967. Once again, it resulted from police activity, this time as a result of officers raiding a bar in a predominately Black neighborhood in the northwest section of the city and making a mass arrest. African American residents, fed up with economic inequality, unemployment, police abuse, and unjust housing policies, and emboldened by the Black militant movement, committed extensive acts of vandalism. Authorities deployed the National Guard, and by the time the riots ended five days later, 43 people were dead, almost 1,200 injured, and some 7,000 arrested.

Things were not all bad for Black Detroit, though. In November of 1973 the city elected Coleman Young as mayor, the first African American to occupy the office. A year later Erma Henderson was the first Black woman elected to the city council. In 1974 and 1975, respectively, the First Independence National Bank, an African American institution, opened, and WGPR-TV (channel 62), the first African American-owned television station in the nation, aired its initial telecast.

Walter Arties was the first of the Breath of Life team members on the ground in the Motor City. After researching the television stations best suited to carry the Heritage Series, he visited their offices, providing them demo tapes. Once their executives had screened the footage to judge the caliber of the recordings and determined if the program was suitable for their stations, Arties negotiated prices.

Arties paid for all 13 episodes of the Heritage Series to air in continuous rotation on WXON-20 for 26 weeks—half the year. After the airing of eight episodes, the ministry worked the neighborhoods of Detroit in several different ways. First, church members visited those who had called in for Bible correspondence lessons or prayer. Second, they canvassed the neighborhoods of Detroit, capitalizing on the name recognition generated by the program. (Often Arties, soloist for the program and a member of the Breath of Life Quartet, showed up at a resident's doorstep and was excitedly recognized as "the man who sings on TV." Brooks was also known to appear at front doors, always needing to reach out and touch the people. They often asked for his autograph.) Finally, members distributed handbills at businesses, stores, recreation centers, churches, on the streets, and anywhere else people gathered.

The church members of the Lake Region Conference showed up in great numbers to assist with the series. Everyone did their part. Kids accompanied their parents door to door and in front of stores. Some became adept at handing out flyers themselves, and it was an impressive witness when a 6-year-old excitedly invited a person to a religious meeting. Teenagers and young adults gave Bible studies, distributed flyers, and helped out at the Better Living center, the site of the meetings. Some members used their special talents to assist the outreach, be it technical expertise, knowledge of the city, financial management, secretarial skills, etc. Those mature in the faith or too elderly to go out prayed and donated money to the cause. All of them were in reality Breath of Life representatives.

The pastors, of course, were integral. Samuel Flagg was exemplary. T. Marshall Kelly did whatever he could to assist, often raising his strong baritone voice during the meetings in the ministry of song. Norman Miles mobilized support. E. S. Dillett, George Bryant, and R. L. Smith were indispensable.

The evangelistic series lasted three weeks, the meetings taking place every night but Thursday. The venue was the Better Living center, a large auditorium owned by the Lake Region Conference.

C. D. Brooks was on fire in Detroit. Night after night his preaching cut through to his hearers. His clipped voice seemed to pierce the inky abyss of Detroit's ghettos, where those for whom Christ had died now struggled to survive, his words shining bright beams of light into every corner. All who heard his preaching left with one overriding impression: there is hope, great hope. Jesus had not forsaken them. In fact, He was very close, beckoning them to eternal life with Him.

The birthplace of Motown was no stranger to stellar music. But the secular musical acts could not hold a candle to the musicians of the Breath of Life ministry. The Breath of Life Quartet harmonized. Shelton Kilby played. T. Marshall Kelly sang. Brenda Spraggins serenaded.

In truth, African Americans had never witnessed such an evangelistic blitz. A Black religious television program was an entirely new thing—it being well before the appearance of such televangelists as Frederick Price, T. D. Jakes, Juanita Bynum, and Creflo Dollar. *Breath of Life* was also on the radio simultaneously, so people could watch it at home on their couch, then leave and listen to *Breath of Life* on the radio in their cars. Further, the live evangelistic campaign follow-up was also unprecedented. Detroit came face to face with the voice of the three angels of Revelation, crafted to speak to the frustrated situation of Blacks in America.

The baptism, the climax of every evangelistic series, took place before a standing-room-only crowd, hundreds clamoring to watch people make good on the most important decision of their lives. A large pool sat on the stage, and while the candidates were led up, rousing music reflected the joy in heaven. Fifty-eight souls were baptized that day, but responses from the television program and meetings kept flowing in, and the total number reached more than 200.

Memphis

The next campaign began with a miracle. In May 1976 channel 13 in Memphis, Tennessee, gave the Breath of Life telecast a free half-hour slot. Stations in Nashville; Columbus, Mississippi; and Tuscaloosa, Alabama, followed suit. The first program aired on June 6. The evangelistic series began on June 13. No one anticipated that it would be a landmark in Breath of Life history.

The programs that aired that summer were new. Instead of featuring artwork of people of color in the Bible, they now displayed as a backdrop portraits of prominent Blacks in American history. Brooks drew from their lives spiritual lessons. C.D. used Frederick Douglass, who had witnessed the falling stars in 1833, as a springboard to the subject of the second coming of Christ. Charles Drew's pioneering work with blood plasma illustrated the blood of Christ spilled to save humanity. Martin Luther King had a dream, but another king in the Bible also had a dream—an entrée into Daniel 2 and Bible prophecy. The series was an ingenious way to preach the gospel, all the while instilling racial pride through recounting the dignified history of Blacks.

After two weeks of the Breath of Life series airing in the Memphis area, the evangelistic series began. The meetings took place in a high school auditorium. C. D. Brooks, a native Southerner, admitted that it was the hottest summer he had ever experienced. The sweltering heat and thick humidity were so relentless that many days he told his Bible workers to go home to air-conditioning.

When during the nine-week Memphis series of 1976 two ministers who loved to debate challenged him to a televised showdown, Brooks declined. In his younger days he would have taken them up on their offer. Now that he was more mature it held no appeal, and he regarded it as a big waste of time.

Upset by C.D.'s refusal, the two ministers spread word that they were going to have their debate whether Brooks was amenable or not. They would go to the auditorium during a nightly meeting and stand up in the middle of his message and have the debate right then and there. The Adventist pastor hosting the Breath of Life campaign, Robert Willis, Jr., heard about the threat and told Charles that he would handle it.

The night of the planned interruption Willis assigned two of his members who were former boxers, big men the size of linebackers, to accompany the two contentious ministers throughout the proceedings. When the ministers showed up, the boxers ushered them to seats right on the front row, sitting on either side of them. They whispered to the now-intimidated debaters, "With sincerity we welcome you. We want you to feel at home. But we will not permit you to disrupt this meeting. If you try to, we will haul your carcasses out of here. Make no mistake about that." The ministers did not make a peep the entire time.

The initial baptism netted 116, with scores more to follow. When it became obvious that the existing congregation could not handle the influx of new members, the conference president, Charles Dudley, an outspoken supporter of the ministry when it was just an idea in Arties' mind, declared, "Folks, we need a new church that's called Breath of Life." Pointing to the parking lot, the shrewd Dudley announced that everyone should get in the vans. Twenty minutes later the motorcade arrived at a beautiful edifice in Memphis's Hickory Hill and Fox Meadows area. When all had gathered inside, Dudley announced that the building had been purchased and that it was their new church.

And so, the Breath of Life Seventh-day Adventist Church in Memphis, Tennessee, was the first, but certainly not the last, congregation to bear the TV ministry's name. In no time the membership skyrocketed, and the church was among the top in the conference in terms of tithing, ministries, and attendance.

Quitting

The year 1977 was unprecedented in terms of evangelistic scope and success. Breath of Life swept through the capital of the South, Atlanta, Georgia, from March 26 to April 16, baptizing 141. Just months later the ministry went international, answering a request to come to the island of Trinidad. Three weeks of evangelistic meetings took place in Arima, where two large canvas pavilions seating 2,500 could still not accommodate the masses that pressed in each night, despite it being the height of carnival season. The series resulted in 131 baptisms. After the Breath of Life team departed, an evangelist named Stephen Purcell continued the meetings and baptized 154 more. In just 18 months Breath of Life was responsible for nearly 1,000 baptisms.

Shortly after the Trinidad campaign C. D. Brooks received a letter at his home in Washington, D.C., from Alvin Munson, president of the Seventh-day Adventist Radio, Television and Film Center (now the Adventist Media Center). The gist of its contents was "Dear Pastor Brooks: We are glad you are joining the SDA Radio, Television and Film Center family. We will be glad to assist you in moving to this area. We will need you to do this and that . . ." C.D. chuckled to himself. The truth was that he was quitting.

Brooks mailed off his own letter a few days later—resigning. He reminded Walter that he had told him that he was going to just help Breath of Life get started, then, once it was securely on its feet, continue his duties as field secretary full-time. To be honest, the trips to California and the tedium of taping for days on end were nerve-racking and exhausting. And so Walter Arties found himself trying to convince C.D. to stay, just as he had had to talk him into coming.

Arties flew to Washington to see Brooks. One day Charles opened his office door to find Walter standing in front of him.

"Elder Brooks, the ministry needs you," Arties said with fervor, as the two sat across from each other. "We are just getting started. Can you stay on, stay with us?"

"You all cannot afford me," C.D. said with a chuckle. "Each episode costs roughly $25,000. If my family moves to Los Angeles, there is no way Breath of Life can pay for my housing and salary. I wouldn't even feel right asking for it. But I would need it to live." Brooks didn't mention that the General Conference would be loath to lose their dynamic field secretary.

"How about we work out a schedule in which you come to California less frequently?" Walter proposed.

"To be honest, Walt, it tires me out. All the things I do as field secretary—the traveling, speaking, and all that. It's wearing me thin."

Their back-and-forth went on for a while. After the two had reached a standstill, neither giving in, Arties pulled out his trump card.

"C.D., in the past 18 months we have brought 1,000 to Christ. One thousand!"

Brooks was quiet.

"Who knows how many more have heard the truth that we don't even know about?" Walter pressed.

Pensive, Charles pursed his lips, and his brow furrowed.

"The gospel going out, on the airwaves . . . Incalculable," Arties said in a loud whisper.

C.D. looked over at him. "OK. I'm in."

Renown

During the same period that Brooks thought of calling it quits, Louis Reynolds' time was wrapping up at Breath of Life. Like C.D., he was on staff just to help the television ministry get started. Having accomplished that admirably, he acknowledged that it was time for him to bow out.

Serendipitously, C.D. had concluded at this juncture that he ought to write his own scripts. "It's like wearing someone else's armor," he told Arties, speaking about reading words on a teleprompter that he did not pen. Brooks had always taken pride in crafting his own messages in his own distinct style. From now on he would write his own.

By this time those on the team took to calling the speaker-director "Chief," something that bothered Brooks at first but that he soon got used to. His face and preaching were now known not only in the Adventist Church worldwide, but by the public in the United States. The 1975-1976 edition of *Who's Who in Religion* contained an entry on C. D. Brooks. The next year he was featured in *Notable Americans*. Much to his chagrin and embarrassment, he was something of a celebrity. Now when he went from place to place, people frequently asked for his autograph.

But unlikely as it seems, he may have gotten more acclaim from his sermon cassette tapes than his television appearances. In the late 1970s his sermons with such titles as "We Can Take Jericho," "Amen," and "Flesh, Iron-fisted Tyrant" were purchased and then replicated and distributed by the thousands. The rumor began to spread that Brooks's tapes were the most circulated among Adventist preachers and evangelists, and it was certainly not far from the truth.

Music

The speaker-director was by no means the only member of Breath of Life Ministries who had gained renown. The Breath of Life Quartet had become one of the most sought-after groups in the denomination, and also received countless invitations to perform from wider Christendom. The group released an album in 1975 called *Plenty Good Room. Spirituals* came out in 1977, followed by *Ghetto Child* two years later. The records sold well.

Another performer on Breath of Life destined for fame was a young Wintley Phipps. Born in Trinidad and raised in Montreal, Phipps studied for the ministry at Oakwood College and Andrews University. His rich baritone voice and winning manner made his ascent in the music world almost inevitable. He first sang for the Breath of Life telecast in 1975 when he was just 20. That same year his debut album, *I Give You My Life,* appeared, produced by Walter Arties and featuring arrangements by Shelton Kilby. Phipps went on to worldwide recognition, singing for five United States presidents at National Prayer Breakfasts; national political conventions; Nelson Mandela, Mother Teresa, and Pope John Paul II; and for numerous television shows, including *Soul Train, Saturday Night Live,* and the *Oprah Winfrey Show.* Producing dozens of albums, Phipps received nominations for several Grammy awards.

The Oakwood chorale, Aeolians, also performed for the show several times in those early years. The professor whom Brooks had looked up to and had such a bond with, Eva B. Dykes, had founded the group the year before he enrolled at Oakwood. Although the student choir had already performed at large venues such as the Kennedy Center, it wasn't until Alma Blackmon became the director in 1973 that it gained international renown. In the 1970s the Aeolians toured extensively, both in the United States and abroad. During Blackmon's tenure they appeared on *Breath of Life*.

Other prominent music performers on *Breath of Life* as the ministry was getting off the ground were Brenda Spraggins, Ullanda Innocent-Palmer, Edwina Humphrey Flynn, Eleanor Wright, and T. Marshall Kelly. Walter Arties always tried to get top-notch musicians for the program, because he knew that anything geared toward Blacks had to have superb music, and it was one of the best ways to reach people with the gospel. In this he succeeded remarkably.

News

As the Breath of Life telecast developed, it added a news segment featuring current items of interest to the program's target audience. One of the first announcers was Brenda Blackmon Wood, daughter of Aeolians director and Oakwood professor Alma Blackmon. Brenda attended Oakwood, Loma Linda University, and La Sierra University, earning a B.A. in speech communication and mass media from the latter. While at Loma Linda she interned at Breath of Life. Wood was yet another member of the team who achieved fame in their respective fields, she as a news anchor for an NBC affiliate in Atlanta, Georgia.

So, although low on money, Breath of Life was in no way short on talented people, individuals whom the wider world would come to acknowledge as exceptional in their fields. With God's blessing, all of this translated to high-caliber evangelism.

The Warner Theatre

One of the largest and most extensive evangelistic efforts in Breath of Life history occurred in the nation's capital during the final months of 1978.

That year was a momentous one for Washington, D.C. The second mayoral election under D.C. Home Rule took place, with the controversial Marion Barry clinching the election for the first time of many. The civil rights movement had accomplished many of its aims and seemed to be receding, although racial unrest and clamor continued among the large Black population of Washington, some 70 percent of the city's inhabitants. African Americans were somewhat bipolar there, some of the nation's wealthiest and most powerful Blacks mere miles from its poorest and most destitute. Drugs were already devastating the population, and the 1980s would usher in the era of crack cocaine and AIDS.

Walter Arties negotiated a good price with local station WDCA-20, and *Breath of Life* began airing in early 1978. After months of programming, some 200 specially trained laypersons from area churches flooded the city with more than 60,000 full-color handbills. The response was so enthusiastic that the Allegheny East president, Luther Palmer, figured a large venue would be needed to hold the meetings. One spot stayed riveted in his mind: Warner Theatre.

The Earle Theatre opened in 1924, famous not only for its magnificent auditorium, but as a world-renowned rooftop garden and tony ballroom and restaurant. The hot spot in D.C. for vaudeville and popular music acts throughout the 1930s, it had by 1945 transitioned solely to movies. Two years later the Earle was renamed the Warner, for its owner, Harry Warner, one of Hollywood's Warner Brothers.

In the 1950s and 1960s the theater showed popular movies such as *Ben-Hur* and *Doctor Zhivago*. But as was the case with much of downtown D.C. in the 1970s, the Warner suffered a decline. It experienced a resurgence in the midseventies as a popular convert venue, however. Just months before Breath of Life ran a four-week campaign there, the Rolling Stones sold out the spot.

A coup—or better a miracle—took place. After much prayer and negotiating, Luther Palmer and Edward Richardson, pastor of First church and coordinator of the evangelistic series, were able to book the Warner Theatre for four weeks. If Adventists were supposed to be the head and not the tail, they certainly did so now, for the Warner was once again the most coveted entertainment venue, as it had been in the 1940s.

Additionally, Palmer put forth extensive effort to train Bible instructors and rally conference membership around the effort. The conference appointed Dupont Park pastor Robert Willis as Brooks's associate evangelist. Meanwhile, Shelton Kilby was placed in charge of music, with a little help from Arties.

Approaching his fiftieth birthday, C.D. had never felt more excited and primed to hit the sawdust trail, although now it was marble and carpet. Plus, the series would be a special one for him. For even though he had lived in the Washington area for almost 20 years, he had been so preoccupied with conducting evangelism elsewhere around the globe that he had not done anything in his own backyard. This would change all of that in grand fashion.

The night of October 20 witnessed a traffic jam on the streets around the Warner Theatre, and a dearth of parking spaces. Some had to walk miles just to enter a theater in which they could not find a place in the 2,000-seat auditorium. Some nights the doors were closed because so many people were inside that fire marshals considered the place an imminent fire hazard. During the day a mobile health clinic parked at the curb in front of the theater, run by Dr. Lennox Westney and a staff of doctors and nurses. High-powered lawyers, businessmen, bankers, and politicians drove by wondering what act was performing at the Warner.

But it was no act. The electricity in that auditorium could have powered a large city. Often when Brooks finished a response in the Q&A segment, the crowd broke into spontaneous applause at his frankness and audacity. As C.D. preached, all eyes were fixed on him as he unfolded the mysteries of God's Word as if for the first time. From the opening song to the closing prayer the Holy Spirit moved from seat to seat, person to person.

Everyone within earshot was liable to get converted. The woman operating the spotlight was riveted by the messages night after night. She stopped eating pork when she learned that the Bible forbade it. Her cigarette packs got tossed in the trash after she heard about the dangers of smoking. When she saw the seventh-day Sabbath in the Bible, she couldn't wait for Saturday to roll around. All the while she had requested Bible studies and faithfully completed the lessons. As a result, she was the first to respond when C.D. made the appeal for baptism.

***

A prominent Presbyterian minister in the community received a Breath of Life handbill one day in the mail. The titles piqued his interest. The first night he ventured to the Warner alone. The second night he brought his wife. It wasn't easy to get her to come, for long ago she had rejected organized religion because of the glaring hypocrisy of many of those who claimed to follow it.

When C. D. Brooks preached that God required conversion and baptism to be saved, the man felt convicted that he needed to be converted and baptized, despite years in the Christian ministry. Engaging in a little deflection, he suggested to his wife one evening that she should be baptized.

"You know how I feel about organized religion" was her reply. Bow-ing her head, she thought, *I just don't want to have my expectations dashed again.*

Husband and wife decided to leave all organized churches and began an independent ministry to Washington's castaways—those who were indigent, especially those without homes and crack addicts. But they kept attending those meetings at the Warner.

One night the preacher's wife confided to C.D., her husband beside her, "I'm thoroughly convinced of the truth I've heard, but what shall I do?" Quiet distress creased her face. "I don't believe in organized religion. Can't I just pay my tithe to you and let it go at that?"

"No," Brooks replied, smiling. "It isn't your money that God wants. He wants you. And regarding organization: the Lord's true church has a global assignment. How do you suppose we could carry the gospel of the soon-coming Savior to every corner of the globe without some type of organization?"

"We couldn't. It would be impossible," she declared, realizing too late that she was convincing herself with her own words.

Still smiling, C.D. waited.

In a moment she broke out into a wide smile too, a weight seeming to lift from her. "I'm ready to be baptized."

The next Sabbath the couple was baptized together.

***

Ministers from other denominations were baptized. One night four preachers representing four churches responded. Thinking of his flock, one of them purchased each sermon on cassette tape. When he played them for his congregation, many of them also became Seventh-day Adventists.

***

One day a man who cleaned buses was going through the motions of another day on the job. In any given bus he'd find dozens of pieces of paper and toss them in his trash bag. But this time as he bent down to grab a crumbled sheet his eye caught the face of C. D. Brooks. Unraveling the paper, he was intrigued by the titles as his eyes scrolled down the crinkled page: "What Is Love?" "The Unpardonable Sin." "Surviving in Sodom." "Hell in the Home." "When Men Plead With Mountains." "A King From Outer Space." "A Horn That Talked and Balked and Stalked." "Seven Women for One Man!" "The Question That Stumps Even God." The man showed up at Warner that night, and every night after. The evangelist he first saw on that flyer baptized him. God was so good to the bus cleaner that he even found an Adventist woman shortly after he joined the church.

***

Although he had worked with C.D. for four years and knew as well as anyone the exceptionality of the man, it wasn't until the Warner meetings that Walter Arties grew from highly respecting Brooks to being in awe of him.

One night at the Warner Arties filled in for the sound man, who was ill. C.D. had just started his sermon for the night on the state of the dead. Suddenly, with no warning, the Volume Unit meter stilled, and the amplifier shut off. Just a word before, Brooks's voice had been amplified across the vast theater; now silence.

Immediately realizing what had happened, C.D. stepped away from the lectern and walked to the edge of the stage.

"I know what this is," he fearlessly told the audience, his jaw tight.

Then, without notes or a microphone, the man preached an entire sermon with extraordinary clarity and force, his distinct voice filling the auditorium. No one missed a word. Arties had never seen anything like it, even when he sang for Billy Graham. When Brooks said "Amen" at the closing prayer, the power came back on. Later Arties would marvel that the devil's plan had backfired: instead of not hearing him because of the power failure, the audience hung on Brooks's every word *because* of it.

On another night Arties sang the appeal song after a particularly impassioned message by Brooks. Walter was familiar with evangelists putting it all on the line—he once had witnessed E. E. Cleveland preaching while bleeding profusely—but he had never experienced what he felt that night. When C.D. began making his appeal, calling people to Jesus, and he moved near Arties, Walter could literally feel energy radiating from the man. It was a divine force so strong that he almost had to stop singing. No doubt feeling the same thing, hundreds responded to the Holy Spirit, leaving their seats and crowding to the front.

***

Initially, the series resulted in 267 baptisms. The follow-up meetings added dozens more. A new Breath of Life congregation consisting of the new converts organized on December 9, 1978. North American Division president Neal Wilson and General Conference president Robert Pierson attended the opening ceremonies. Today the Breath of Life Seventh-day Adventist Church is a banner congregation in the Allegheny East Conference, worshipping in a spacious, state-of-the-art sanctuary in Fort Washington, Maryland. The Warner series was so wildly successful that the next year Breath of Life held another one there.

About six weeks before the dedication of the new Breath of Life church, Robert Pierson announced his retirement, because of health issues. C.D.'s good friend Neal Wilson replaced him, becoming president of the world church of Seventh-day Adventists on October 17, 1978. At the General Conference session in Dallas, Texas, the delegates officially reelected him as president on April 18, 1980.

The Inauguration
The dawn of the 1980s brought more triumphs for C.D. in D.C. On January 20, 1981, Ronald Reagan was inaugurated the fortieth president of the United States of America. The nation was hopeful that the charismatic former actor would lead America to a future much brighter than its recent past of assassinations, civil unrest, wars, and governmental scandal. The inauguration ceremony on a chilly but bright winter morning articulated those hopes.

When the inauguration planners asked the Seventh-day Adventist Church to do a segment at the religious inaugural celebration, the denomination chose C. D. Brooks as speaker and the Heritage Singers as musical accompaniment. Thompson U. Kay of the Christian Record Braille Foundation served as the sign-language translator for the entire event. Brooks spoke for 15 minutes to 8,000 people on the Tuesday evening at the Starplex Armory. At the close of his message the Heritage Singers sang "Gentle Shepherd," "Rise Again," and "God Bless America."

Love and Grandchildren
By the new decade Charles and Walterene had been in love for more than 30 years, though it seemed but a day to them. And as the years went by, their love for each other grew deeper and still deeper. Their secret? They prayed together and read the Bible together. They talked for hours every day and did thoughtful deeds for each other. They stayed young with each other. They took interest in the things the other liked. They cultivated trust and affection. They compromised. They gave each other all of themselves. Although they rarely had disagreements, when they did they resolved them in a short time. They helped each other with their jobs. And all of it kept the romance alive.

Throughout all their years together, Rene never had to open or close a car door when she was with Charles. When he was off preaching on the other side of the world, Rene wrote on his mirror in fragrant soap how much she missed him and loved him, all for him to read when he got home. If he knew that she wanted something, she would find a gift box on her pillow. He even knew her favorite chewing gum, and suffice it to say, she was never without it.

The lovers often returned to Niagara Falls, their honeymoon destination. There above the cascading waters they reaffirmed their love and commitment to each other. Both saved every letter they ever wrote to each other, placing it in an elegant treasure chest that they had chosen together. Husband and wife had a golden key for it. On special occasions one of them would invite the other to take the key and unlock the memories, which they enjoyed together.

Charles liked to shop with Rene, and she liked him to shop with her. The two always held hands in the mall. One didn't even have to reach for the other—the hand was already there in place. When they were in the women's section of the department store, Charles often strayed off. When she located him, he would have three or four dresses in his arm that he had picked out for her. Brown was his favorite color on her. He had immaculate taste.

Rene called Charles "honey." He must've heard that word a million times from her lips, but every time it sent a jolt up his spine. She said it to him not only when they were alone, but even when they were around others. At the schools where she taught, Rene's fellow teachers frequently asked her, "When is honey coming?"

Charles and Rene celebrated two anniversaries: the day he proposed (and she said yes) and the day of their wedding. But really, in truth, the lovers found any and every excuse to have a special evening together. When their children were still at home, some nights Charles and Rene put them to bed early. Then it was all candlelight, exquisite cuisine, soft music, and crackling fireplace. After the kids went off to college and later lived with their own families, the special nights happened more frequently.

On March 23, 1980, Bradley Tramel was born, son of their daughter, Diedre, and her husband, Samuel Tramel. Charles and Walterene were grandparents! It was a special and unforgettable time for them. The excitement, the anticipation, the fussing, the worry, then the pure joy of a baby—their grandson—born into the world. Brandon Tramel was born in 1984, then Skip's daughter, Courtney Danielle Brooks (her initials the same as her grandfather's), in 1991.

The Principal

Walterene Brooks's career mirrored her husband's in terms of ground-breaking accomplishments. After teaching at Sligo Elementary for five years (and almost 20 years in Adventist schools), she believed that God was leading her to the public schools. Already she was a member of the Educational Standards Commission of the State of Maryland. Getting a taste of leadership in that post, Walterene set her sights on administration at a local public school.

By this time the Brookses were living in Silver Spring, Maryland, in an Adventist community of townhouses named for the street which they lined: Pitcairn Place. One morning after a prayer session for guidance, a determined Walterene Brooks drove to Upper Marlboro to the main office of the Prince George's County Public Schools. When a receptionist greeted her, she replied, "May I see someone about employment opportunities with P.G. County Schools?"

Rene got an appointment with a director within the hour. The woman asked about her education, experience, etc., but Rene couldn't shake the impression that it was all just pro forma. She knew she had the job, whatever it might be. Sure enough, the official offered her a position as vice principal of Kentland Elementary School in Landover, Maryland. Rene had 10 days to accept.

"Honey, I got a job," she told Charles that evening.

"That's wonderful, Rene," he said with a big smile, taking his wife in his arms.

The two discussed it for an hour. Then they took to their knees and asked the Lord's guidance. Walterene Brooks accepted the job, the second Black teacher to ever work in the school.

As at Sligo, Rene was a trailblazer for race in the Prince George's County school system. Most of the schools in the county at that time were predominately White. Race didn't matter one bit to Rene, though—she loved all kids the same. She developed a reputation as being tough but fair, holding the students to the highest standards but with compassion.

Rene certainly had the help of her husband. Whenever he was in town, he dutifully dropped her off and picked her up from work each day. And as he did in the other schools Walterene had taught at, Charles put on student plays, writing the scripts and building the stage props. He was careful to involve every child, always encouraging and supporting them. At times Rene wondered if the kids at Kentland loved her or her husband more.

Walterene was such a remarkable vice principal that the County School Board asked her to be principal of John Carroll Elementary. Once again she was one of the few Blacks on the staff, but throughout her more than 25 years there that would reverse itself, while educational standards and student performance skyrocketed. The recipient of many honors and awards, she retired with her husband in 1996, a legend among Maryland educators. Her daughter, Diedre Tramel, now follows in her footsteps.

Into the 1980s

In the first years of the 1980s C.D. flew to California several times a year to tape for Breath of Life. The staff was still small, yet one year it produced a record 52 programs. By 1984 the ministry had completed a total of 105 episodes. The segments had expanded to news, a health corner, question-and-answer, and preaching, with music interspersed throughout. Also, the telecast was increasingly interactive. The question-and-answer segment might feature students from Loma Linda putting questions to the speaker in real time. Or the programs might be taped in Adventist churches or other TV-friendly venues. No longer was C.D. preaching to the inhuman red light—he had live audiences now.

With the era of superstations dawning, Breath of Life took advantage of the developing market. Establishing syndication with the Black Entertainment Television network, the ministry reached a potential audience of 8 million households each week. The network's satellite reached more than 1,200 U.S. cities, as well as the islands of Bermuda, the Bahamas, and the U.S. Virgin Islands. Brooks admitted to Arties one day that Walter had been correct: television enabled one to reach more people at one time than ever before in history.

Other ministers were now holding evangelistic meetings under the Breath of Life name. Utilizing the same modus operandi, men such as Charles Bradford and J. Malcolm Phipps added to the church. The brand was growing, and was becoming synonymous with soul winning.

Yet Breath of Life struggled financially, a reality that would hang over the ministry for the whole of the 1980s. Still depending heavily on General Conference appropriations, Walter Arties, C. D. Brooks, James Kyle (then director of field services), and others tried to raise funds and develop the donor base. But it was tough going, for the recession of 1981-1982 hit African Americans hard. Further, as much success as it had experienced, Breath of Life was not yet a ministry to which the membership felt comfortable donating large amounts of money. In 1983, when the other SDA television ministries were receiving scores of millions annually, Breath of Life got just $170,000. "There is no shortage of ideas for programs," Brooks quipped. "Our only holdup is more consecrated finances to work with."

No one could have guessed that, despite its financial struggle, Breath of Life would go international.

Palau

As Dr. Howard Baker intently watched *Breath of Life* on a small television set on the tropical island of Palau, his excitement grew. The powerful program put on by brown-skinned people would be a perfect fit for reaching the English-speaking, brown-skinned people of Palau with the gospel of Jesus. When the closing credits appeared, he formulated a plan to get the ministry to the island and people that he had been doing medical missionary work among for so long.

The physician wrote a letter to Breath of Life requesting that they place the telecast on the air in as much of Micronesia as possible. Next he contacted G. Ray James, president of Guam-Micronesia Mission, who in turn forwarded the request to the division office. Request granted, the TV program took the island by storm, confirming Baker's judgment. Soon the Breath of Life team received a formal invitation to conduct an evangelistic series on the island.

When the Breath of Life entourage consisting of C. D. Brooks, Walter Arties, James Kyle, Adrian Westney, and Ron Murphy stepped from the small prop plane and onto the tarmac near the capital city of Koror in March of 1981, they met hundreds of Adventist Palauan young people singing the praises of God. Arties thought to himself that he had never seen a sight so beautiful in all of his life.

Palauan pastors Mokokil Solomon and Willy Nobuo, neither of whom could contain their excitement at the arrival of these American celebrities of the gospel, drove the team to Koror.

"We are glad you have come, because you look so much like us," Solomon remarked.

And it was true. Brooks and Arties could have passed for Palauan. How important was establishing commonalities to win people to Christ!

And win people they did.

Three weeks of nightly evangelistic meetings resulted in 203 baptisms, one of the largest in the island's history, and most impressive when considering the population was only 14,000. Tua Tmetuchi, the wife of the governor, was baptized, along with many of the island's highest-ranking professionals. Scores of young people also became Adventists, 50 percent of the island's population being under 14 years old. C.D.'s interpreter was the main judge on the island and an ardent Seventh-day Adventist. Having a burden for those on the other side of the law, he arranged for 18 prisoners to come to the meetings every night, three rows reserved for them. Ten accepted baptism. All told, the series converted 1.5 percent of the population of Palau to Adventism.

After the meetings in Micronesia the Breath of Life Quartet flew to Japan to perform. C.D. returned to the States. Shortly afterward Kyle announced to the team that he believed God was calling him to be a physician and that he would step down as director of field services to attend medical school. As with Brooks and Arties, the man who replaced Kyle would become synonymous with Breath of Life.

Baby Brooks

"Is this Elder Brooks?" one theology major asked another, listening intently to the powerful words coming from the tape recorder.

"Nah, prophet," the other replied. "It's Baby Brooks."

***

Reginald Orealus Baker was born in Washington, D.C., on October 20, 1942, to Temple Robinson (father) and Verdell Baker (mother). Reggie was primarily raised by his grandmother, Fannie Baker, first in the nation's capital and later around Oakwood. By the time he was 8 he had found his calling, preaching to his second-grade classmates during recess. One day while in his early teens he was cleaning his grandmother's bathroom and sensed the Holy Spirit say to him that as he was now cleaning the tiles and making them sparkle, God could do the same for him. Reggie lived for the Lord from that point on.

The Smithsonian Museum turned out to be a pivotal place in Reggie's life, for it was there that he met his future wife. He suavely asked Patricia Rice in front of a particularly uninteresting exhibit to accompany him to lunch one summer day in early 1964. She accepted. The two had many more lunches, marrying on November 22, 1964. Prior to taking nuptials, Reggie changed his surname to Robinson in order to carry on his father's name.

Reggie attended Columbia Union College, and upon graduation began his ministry as youth pastor at the historic First Seventh-day Adventist Church off Georgia Avenue in the District. Able both to speak and sing well, Robinson had successful pastorates in Maryland and New Jersey. His sermons were dynamic and Bible-based, and his singing voice was a rich tenor. Often he would preach a sermon and then sing for the appeal. Above all else, Robinson had a shepherd's heart, full of love and compassion.

In 1981, just after the close of the Palau meetings and the resignation of James Kyle, Breath of Life invited Robinson to serve as director of field services, public relations, development, and the Bible school. After four years of superb work resulting in hundreds of baptisms and tens of thousands of dollars raised, the ministry made Robinson the associate director/speaker and evangelistic series coordinator in 1985. He was a perfect fit for Breath of Life Ministries, because like his mentor, C. D. Brooks, Robinson's sole focus was saving others.

Breath of Life satisfied the young man's evangelistic hunger. He conducted revivals across the globe, leaving new churches in his wake. Often he would preach alternate nights in the same meetings with C.D., in a different location in the same city, or in a nearby town. Other times they would be on the opposite sides of the world, preaching the same gospel. Once in Barbados in 1989 C.D. and Reggie baptized 520 and established the first Breath of Life church outside the United States.

By the mideighties Reginald Robinson had established himself as the third member of the Breath of Life trio. The ministry's advertisements featured him and Walter Arties on either side of C.D. And like Brooks and Arties, Robinson's name will be forever linked with Breath of Life.

People affectionately referred to him as "Baby Brooks" because of the amazing similarities between his preaching style—the voice, the cadence, the inflection, the mannerisms—and that of his mentor, C. D. Brooks. When people closed their eyes while Robinson was speaking, they would most likely think that they were listening to Brooks. Yet the mark Reginald Robinson left on the world for Christ was all his own.

Australia

C.D. and Breath of Life had amazing experiences in Australia, as well. As with the Palauans, the team had instant rapport with the Aboriginals on the continent, because like African Americans, their hue was darker than the ruling race, and they were oppressed as a result. In fact, as in the United States with Blacks during slavery (and after), the Aborigines were considered subhuman. Yet the cultures of the Americans and the Australian Aborigines were vastly different, and the Breath of Life team faced the challenge of preaching the gospel in a relevant and compelling way.

One White family traveled halfway across the country to hear Brooks preach to the Aborigines. The wife and mother of the family was active in prison ministries. His preaching so affected her that she began distributing his tapes to the prisoners. One time she gave some cassettes to a man named Jeffrey sentenced to life for first-degree murder. Intrigued, he listened to the sermons and gave his heart to Christ. To the woman and the rest of the prison band his conversion appeared genuine. In fact, the prison administration and the prisoners marveled at his "getting religion." When any kind of uprising, disturbance, or disagreement occurred, the warden sought the advice of the born-again convict or asked him to act as mediator.

Jeffrey desired to be baptized, and he wanted C.D. to do it. By this time Brooks and his team had wrapped up the series and returned to the States, however. So Jeffrey petitioned the warden for a temporary release so he could be baptized at a Seventh-day Adventist church close to the prison. The response was negative. Although upset, Jeffrey did not lose his faith.

After being back in Washington for a while, Brooks received a phone call all the way from a prison in Australia. It was Jeffrey. He told C.D. of his predicament, distraught that he couldn't be baptized, as the Bible instructed. "My friend, what has happened to you is the providence of God," Brooks calmly told him. "If you were baptized in a church, how would your fellow inmates know? The people in church would see you, but that's it. If you are baptized in prison, it will be a witness to thousands." When the minister in charge of the prayer band held a baptismal ceremony in the prison, six were baptized, Jeffrey and five others that he had led to Christ. Other prisoners became interested after witnessing their fellow inmates' courage and the solemn joy of the ceremony.

After baptism Jeffrey continued to gain respect in the prison and was entrusted with increased responsibility. The prison authorities assigned him to work in the library and later as a welder. Eventually he again decided to petition the warden to give him temporary leave from the prison so that he could visit the Adventist church nearby. He asked simply for one Sabbath to worship with fellow believers.

After hearing him out, the warden pushed his chair back, opened his drawer, and pulled out a wallet-sized picture. He handed it to Jeffrey across his desk.

"Know this man?" he inquired.

"Yes," Jeffrey replied, puzzled.

The warden's jaw tightened. "Let me tell you something. This man ruined my family, and I want him taken care of. You do that for me, and I will let you out to go to your church."

"Sir, I can't do that. I am a Seventh-day Adventist Christian. This would be against my Lord and Savior."

"That's what I thought," the warden said angrily. "Get out of here. Think about it. If you change your mind, come talk to me."

All night Jeffrey tossed and turned in his bed. He had no conflict about his refusal, but the incident had upset him.

The next day when Jeffrey reported for work at the welding shop, his supervisor told him, "You don't have work here anymore. Get out!"

Jeffrey got the same response at the library. With no job he would have no money for commissary or basic supplies. Finally he went to the warden's office to find out what was going on.

"Have you changed your mind?" the official demanded.

"No, I have not, sir."

"Then from now on your job is to clean toilets," the warden spat.

As Jeffrey performed the foul task on his knees, a strange, beautiful thing happened. He told C.D. later on the phone that it was as if angels were right next to him as he cleaned. He had never had such a joyful time in his life! The hours went by like seconds.

That night he slept peacefully. The next morning he woke up excited and reported to work 10 minutes early. His supervisor told him that he was to go to the warden's office. Ready for anything, Jeffrey knocked on the warden's door. Inside, the warden motioned for him to be seated.

"Jeffrey, you don't have to clean toilets. This was all a test, and you passed with flying colors. You can go to your church. We now know that you are really a changed man."

For years afterward C.D. continued to receive phone calls all the way from Australia. Jeffrey was regularly baptizing fellow prisoners.

Church Matters

Speaker-director of Breath of Life was only Brooks's secondary job title. He was first of all a field secretary for the General Conference, and throughout the 1980s he was at the forefront of momentous developments that transformed the Seventh-day Adventist Church.

As mentioned previously, he was a delegate to the 1980 General Conference session in Dallas, Texas, and there voted in favor of the adoption of the 27 fundamental beliefs. Earlier the same year he attended the Glacier View Conference and served as a member of the Sanctuary Review Committee.

Many wanted Brooks to take a higher post in the church. At the 1985 General Conference session in New Orleans, Louisiana, Wilson asked him to be a General Conference vice president. Although honored, C.D. declined, stating that God had called him to evangelism, not the bureaucracy of governance. As important as such things were, they just weren't what he was born to do. At the same session, he delivered the Friday night devotional message called "The Hands of the Trinity."

Months after the GC session, C.D. received another honorary doctorate in divinity, this time from Andrews University. The program for the ceremony read: "In recognition of his great service to the Seventh-day Adventist Church as an outstanding religious broadcaster, writer, preacher and consummate evangelist, the faculty of Andrews University presents Charles D. Brooks as a candidate for the degree Doctor of Divinity, honoris causa."

C.D. had indeed established himself as a thought leader in the church through the pen. In the 1980s and 1990s he had an advice column in *Message* called Dear Pastor, in which he fielded tough questions such as "I know my husband is cheating on me. How can I stop him?" "My dead husband appears to me during the night. Is this truth?" "What type of music is best in church?" and "A close relative sexually molested me when I was much younger. I still feel dirty. How do I make these feelings go away?" The column was popular because of its frank but compassionate answers based on Scripture. Besides this, he wrote dozens of articles for church periodicals, and his sermons were so polished that they were frequently published without any alteration for flow or readability. Brooks was the prototypical versatile evangelist, winning souls through every available medium, be it television, radio, cassette, or print.

He was at the forefront of the evangelistic thrust of the church during the 1980s. Africa was the continent on which the Adventist Church experienced the most growth in that decade. The Inter-American Division (comprising the Caribbean and Latin America) came in a close second. In those storied years, sometimes a single day yielded thousands of baptisms. Today the denominational membership is overwhelmingly people of color, with about a third residing on continental Africa. The 1980s phenomenon of day-of-Pentecost-like soul winning was the real starting point for the demographic shift.

C.D. ran evangelistic meetings throughout the span of the decade in Africa, Central America, and the Caribbean. In one series in Barbados in 1989 he baptized 500 people. Often he found himself called to conduct revivals in countries or particular cities where growth was stagnant. In each place the field secretary taught by example his hard-won knowledge of the most effective evangelistic methods. People so beloved and revered him in those places that many newborns were christened "Charles Brooks."

During the early years of the 1980s the Breath of Life telecast began airing throughout Africa and the Caribbean, the local pastors fielding the requests for Bible studies as well as putting on the follow-up meetings. It was an expansion of Arties' original vision of the broadcast primarily reaching African Americans, for the program and ministry had now transcended the limits of nationality, race, and location.

That decade a total of five Breath of Life churches organized: Culver City, California (1982); Rochester, New York (1986); Jacksonville, Florida (1987); Columbia, Missouri (1988); and Barbados (1989).

BET

When Breath of Life Ministries began in 1974, television superstations did not exist, so Walter Arties had to purchase time slots on individual stations. All of this changed in the 1980s with the inauguration of a new era in television. The first superstation that *Breath of Life* appeared on was the Christian network PTL. But in the late 1980s the program would air on a secular superstation, reaching a greater number of people than ever before.

Entrepreneur Robert Johnson got his start in television as an industry lobbyist in the 1970s. He quickly noticed a lack of programming for Black people, and with something like a secular version of Walter Arties' dream of religious programming for that demographic, he made plans to start a channel just for them. In 1979 he and his wife, Sheila, founded Black Entertainment Television. The cable network began broadcasting two hours a week in large East Coast cities on January 25, 1980. BET, as it came to be known, was the first of its kind whose target audience was African Americans. By the end of the year its now-24-hour-a-day programming had spread across North America and throughout the Caribbean.

But like Breath of Life, BET had financial struggles in its early years.

Only the shrewd maneuvering of the Johnsons saved it from folding. As they became more attuned to their viewers, sitcom reruns and music videos became a lesser part of the programming. By the mid-1980s a more diverse lineup emerged, including news, sports, comedy, and talk shows. The last years of the decade found the BET viewership in the millions.

In 1988 Walter Arties attended a National Religious Broadcasters meeting at which he heard Robert Johnson make a presentation about BET. As he listened he became more and more excited about the possibility of the station reaching *Breath of Life's* target audience. After the program Arties approached Johnson and spoke with him about airing *Breath of Life* on BET. Johnson was enthusiastic about the prospect, and the two exchanged information. Just months later TRANSDA, the time-buying agency at the Adventist Media Center, purchased time slots on BET for *Breath of Life*. In early 1989 one could hear C. D. Brooks's clarion voice for the first time on the Black Entertainment Television channel, potentially reaching 90 million people a week.

The Final Years
C. D. Brooks didn't know it, but when the clock struck midnight on December 31, 1989, his time with Breath of Life was nearing a climactic end. The 60-year-old preacher would go out with an evangelistic blitz. During the first half of the 1990s he and Breath of Life would reach their peak in terms of baptisms, churches established, viewing audience, and international recognition.

Indeed, the start of the 1990s bode well for Black Adventism. The church had come a long way since the General Conference session of 1962 in terms of Black leadership. In 1966 Frank Bland became the second Black to serve as a general vice president. C. D. Henri and G. Ralph Thompson followed in 1975. Charles Bradford was elected president of the North American Division in 1979, the first Black to hold the position. The next year G. Ralph Thompson became the first Black secretary of the General Conference, effectively the second in command of the world church. People of color now simultaneously held two of the most powerful offices in the denomination.

That same year (1980) Robert Carter became president of the Lake Union Conference, the first Black elected to the top spot of a union. The General Conference session of 1985 named Calvin Rock a vice president of the world church. Most significantly, at the 1990 GC session in Indianapolis, Indiana, George W. Brown, a Black man born in the Dominican Republic, was nominated president of the world church. Brown declined because of considerations of his age and his wife's health. At the same session Matthew Bediako became the first Black African to hold the position of vice president of the General Conference.

The Black membership in the North American Division was nearing the 200,000 mark in 1990, with an annual tithe of some $70 million. Impressively, that was 26 percent of NAD membership and a tithe income of more than any other division outside of the NAD.

Although he wouldn't admit it, C. D. Brooks had done much to bring such things to pass. His evangelism, along with that of others such as G. E. Peters, J. H. Laurence, E. E. Cleveland, G. H. Rainey, and W. D. Scales, was essential to the huge increases in membership. On the leadership side, Neal Wilson and Robert Pierson's strategy to put C.D. on the front line in order to break down racial barriers among ministers and laypersons was an important factor in Blacks obtaining leadership positions in the denomination.

But the advance was to not stop until Jesus came, and as he entered his sixtieth year Brooks was more determined than ever to rescue as many as he could from the devil's grasp.

1991: Brooklyn

On August 10, 1991, Breath of Life embarked on its largest evangelistic meeting to date. Sponsored by the Northeastern Conference, in whose territory the ministry had already established a church in Rochester, New York, the preparations were extensive. After months of laying the foundation with Amazing Facts courses (almost 1,000 completed), Bible instruction, literature evangelism, flyer distribution, and prayer, the evangelistic series commenced at the Walt Whitman Theater on the campus of Brooklyn College. The main auditorium seated 2,500, while overflow seats accommodated 500. They were easily filled, with an additional 2,000 clamoring to enter. Still many more thousands viewed the meetings on a local TV station and BET.

The Breath of Life team was at its finest and most mature. C.D. preached. Arties coordinated. Reggie Robinson assisted Brooks on the pulpit. The musical lineup was extraordinary: T. Marshall Kelly, Ullanda Innocent, the Breath of Life Quartet, Myrna Matthews Haynes, along with a number of local musicians. Clifford and Freddie Harris of the Drug Alternative Program (DAP) held free addiction recovery and support seminars.

For four weeks the fervor never let up. Those who attended remember well the many thousands leaning forward in their seats to hear the unvarnished truth . . . the buzz of holy excitement . . . the anticipation of the outpouring of the Holy Spirit as at Pentecost . . . the marvel of so many surrendering to Jesus Christ and accepting Him as their personal Savior. Those who had any part in the Brooklyn evangelistic series of 1991 will never forget it.

After four weeks 308 went to the watery grave, in this instance two gigantic portable pools just outside of the theater. The conference established the Kingsboro Temple Seventh-day Adventist Church for the new members, now one of its premier congregations. Today it has more than 1,000 members.

Additional new churches followed. The year after Kingsboro a Breath of Life congregation started in Newark, New Jersey, on the other side of the Hudson River. Across the nation in Seattle, Washington, another church comprised of the newly baptized came into being. In 1993 the Bahamas became home to a Breath of Life church. The same year, a half globe away, Moree, New South Wales, Australia, gained a church.

Honors: Christ of the Narrow Way

The 1990s bestowed signal honors on C. D. Brooks. In September of 1989 the Ellen G. White Estate commissioned the largest painting in the history of the Seventh-day Adventist Church as it moved with the denomination's world headquarters to its new location in Silver Spring, Maryland. The mural would be 30' x 8', occupying an entire wall in the White Estate reception area, where thousands of tourists every year would begin their tour of the premises. Adventist artist Elfred Lee depicted Ellen White's first vision in December 1844, recorded in *Early Writings*:

"While I was praying at the family altar, the Holy Ghost fell upon me, and I seemed to be rising higher and higher, far above the dark world. I turned to look for the Advent people in the world, but could not find them, when a voice said to me, 'Look again, and look a little higher.' At this I raised my eyes, and saw a straight and narrow path, cast up high above the world. On this path the Advent people were traveling to the city, which was at the farther end of the path. They had a bright light set up behind them at the beginning of the path, which an angel told me was the midnight cry. This light shone all along the path and gave light for their feet so that they might not stumble. If they kept their eyes fixed on Jesus, who was just before them, leading them to the city, they were safe. But soon some grew weary, and said the city was a great way off, and they expected to have entered it before. Then Jesus would encourage them by raising His glorious right arm, and from His arm came a light which waved over the Advent band, and they shouted, 'Alleluia!' Others rashly denied the light behind them and said that it was not God that had led them out so far. The light behind them went out, leaving their feet in perfect darkness, and they stumbled and lost sight of the mark and of Jesus, and fell off the path down into the dark and wicked world below" (pp. 14, 15).

A little more than two years later Lee completed the painting. Stunning in its color and detail, *The Christ of the Narrow Way* was a tour de force of Adventist theology and history. A narrow trail on a steep cliff leads to a shining light representing glory. Hundreds walk the narrow way, some having fallen off the precipice into the darkness below. Jesus is the center of the painting, His glory radiating in beams throughout its length. Behind Him to the left is His law, and to His right the three angels of Revelation 14.

Near the beginning of the path, a young Ellen White kneeling in vision receives light emanating from Jesus. Above those walking up the narrow way are the great historical figures of Adventism, each in characteristic poses: William Miller, Joseph Bates, Rachel Oakes Preston, Uriah Smith, John Loughborough, James White, Kate Lindsay, John Harvey Kellogg, Jones and Waggoner, A. G. Daniells, Anna Knight, Charles Kinney, Marcial Serna, William Spicer, Eva B. Dykes, Harry Miller, the Stahls, H.M.S. Richards, and others. The painting also features some of the church's great institutions, such as Battle Creek College and Sanitarium, the Dime Tabernacle, Avondale, Oakwood, Loma Linda Hospital, and the General Conference headquarters.

At the painting's commissioning, leadership agreed that the historical figures depicted had to be deceased, lest politics get in the way. But the artist did include some of the living at the head of the narrow path. Just a few strides from glory is a determined C. D. Brooks.

***

In 1991 C.D. was the divine worship speaker on Sabbath at the Oakwood College Homecoming, one of many times he was so honored at the annual event.

Nineteen ninety-four saw the 64-year-old inducted into the Martin Luther King, Jr., Board of Preachers and Collegium of Scholars at Morehouse

College in Atlanta, Georgia. C.D. shared the honor with Charles Bradford. The two would be honored together again years later.

Also in 1994 Christian Resources International (CRI) began remastering C.D.'s sermons for radio broadcast and mass distribution. Already dozens of stations across the world featured them, but it was yet another platform for increased exposure. In 1996 his sermons ran on the program *Reach for Life,* and scores more stations purchased CRI's package.

C.D.'s unofficial tape ministry continued to flourish. American Cassette Ministries (ACM), audiovisual departments in churches, and other tape distributors had sold C.D. sermons en masse for years. Consistently their best seller, ACM alone had several hundred of Brooks's sermons for sale. Meanwhile, members and ministers alike copied and circulated his tapes themselves. The great evangelist allowed such businesses, and all others, to reproduce his sermons without asking for any royalties. He just wanted to get biblical truth out. Many believe that his sermon cassettes are the most numerous and widely circulated of any Adventist preacher.

Church leadership also held the veteran minister in the highest regard. On a sweltering Sabbath morning (the temperature was more than 100°F) in September of 1994, General Conference president Robert Folkenberg rose to speak. C.D. happened to be sitting in the audience. In his opening remarks, Folkenberg motioned to Brooks and quipped, "When the sun comes out, the stars don't shine."

Months later, on December 3, 1994, Breath of Life celebrated its twentieth anniversary at Takoma Academy. More than 2,000 people attended. The convocation highlighted the ministry's astounding accomplishments: 12,000 baptized; 13 Breath of Life churches established; and 200 shows aired. During the Sabbath service church leaders, family, friends, and colleagues shared what C.D. and the ministry meant to them. They presented gifts and plaques to a slightly embarrassed Brooks. Although they honored him, he knew it wasn't about him. All praise went to God.

NET '95

The next year the church gave a nod to C. D. Brooks's 40 years of prolific evangelism by his participation in the largest and most extensive evangelistic program in Seventh-day Adventist history up to that time.

By the 1990s the North American membership's growth was lagging significantly behind South and Central America, the Caribbean, and Africa. In response, early in 1993 the North American Division commissioned a task force to devise a more effective evangelistic plan. What developed was something unprecedented in scope: NET '95.

Mark Finley, speaker/director of *It Is Written*, would preach for 24 nights to a live audience at the Chattanooga Convention Center in Chattanooga, Tennessee, from February 18 to March 25. Titled *Discoveries in Prophecy*, the broadcast would be linked via satellite to the newly established Adventist Communication Network (ACN), then rebroadcast on the Three Angels Broadcasting Network (3ABN) and dozens of other television and radio stations. Leadership encouraged all 4,706 Seventh-day Adventist churches in the North American Division to present the nightly meetings in their churches and invite non-Adventists to attend. The approach extended to schools, organizations, businesses, and homes—wherever any place had the capability to act as a downlink.

To prepare for the event the church mailed 7 million handbills to homes across America, along with advertisements featured on billboards, buses, television, radio, newspapers, periodicals, and posters. Thousands of members descended on cities and suburbs, towns and villages, to spread literature, give Bible studies, and invite people. In all, NAD spent two years in preparation and almost $1 million, not to mention the time and financial expenditures of local congregations.

Many of the flyers advertised both Mark Finley and C. D. Brooks, causing some confusion as to who was the main speaker. But C.D. had chosen the role that he had grown to love throughout the years at Breath of Life and in church periodicals: question-and-answer man. Each night the veteran evangelist read tough questions submitted from the audience and answered them in his profoundly simple way. The people loved him, and many reported that it was their favorite part of the program. He was so popular, in fact, that the church asked him to do the same thing the next year and for several other NETs. Brooks was happy with doing whatever he could to lead others to Jesus.

On opening night 653 sites presented the meeting, with 66,165 viewing from those locations, 22,601 being non-Adventist. The average attendance was 40,243. At its close, some 5,000 people were baptized. Such results were simply staggering for North America. A new era of evangelism had arrived, and the NETs continued every year into the next millennium.

C. D. Brooks, who started out in a tent with Praeger slides, was on the vanguard of the new technological revolution of evangelism 45 years later.

I Want My Church Back
But as much as he was pleased with the technological innovations that allowed more people to hear the gospel, he felt that in many areas in which his church seemed to be progressing it was really retrogressing. From the start of his ministry in 1951 he had witnessed Adventism undergo (inevitably) myriad changes, some good and others not.

When Mervyn Warren invited Brooks to challenge fellow ministers at the Annual Pastoral and Evangelism Council Board at Oakwood College, C.D. decided to unburden his heart. In the Moseley Complex Chapel on Wednesday evening, December 7, 1994, Charles preached a message to a standing-room-only crowd that became the most controversial and the most celebrated of his ministry. The title: "I Want My Church Back."

The veteran evangelist began by explaining what prompted his message in words confided to him by a friend:

"A brilliant professional friend of mine called me long distance. In an almost desperate tone he said, 'Charles, I want my church back!' Then with anguish in his voice, he said, 'I don't know if I can ever get it back!' "

To illustrate his sermon, C.D. had hung two sticks wide apart on either side above the pulpit. He explained:

"In the writings of Ellen G. White, the Lord's servant draws a line over here against this extreme [indicating the stick to the right], and then she draws a line over there against this extreme [indicating the stick to the left]. . . . Notice she leaves a broad swath down the middle. And I can walk here, and you can walk there, and we're still within the safety zone. We don't have to think alike. We don't have to wear a uniform. You can be you, and I can be me. But let's stay in the safety zone, and we're better off near the middle of the road . . . avoid the extreme."

With that preface C.D. laid out his concerns:

"We are now facing an unusual time in which those on the inside of our church are questioning our distinctive teachings and doctrines more than those who despise us. And many of us are walking away from the mandate that God gave to us.

"My dear fellow workers, I want to tell us today that one of the powerful keys to success and power in our churches and our pulpits and in evangelism is resolute faithfulness to the Word of God, and to the message God has given to us to preach! We must preach our message—all of it!

"There are forces that seem to be assiduously dismantling what was so laboriously put together under the indispensable aid of the Holy Ghost.

There is this tincture of erudition that we carelessly call scholarship, but that is more scholasticism. Ellen White says, 'It is as certain that we have the truth as that God lives.' She spoke of a platform of truth. . . . She said, Don't get 'off the platform.' "

Brooks spoke emphatically about the growing tendency to water down the message to "reach the youth" and to "grow the church":

"Among us there are those who appear to be tired of our message—bored with it. There is a swelling cry for something different, unique. Some are saying, 'We want a modern message that is designed for young people.' That doesn't go along with the awesome prophecy of Malachi 4. For when the Elijah message comes, just before the great and dreadful day of the Lord, the Bible says, 'The hearts of the fathers and the children will be turned toward each other.' We are not to be divided by age and generation.

"The media uses a term 'simulcast,' meaning that they are broadcasting in English and Spanish and other languages at the same time. But to us the gospel is coming down from glory simulcast. I've preached to little children, and they've come up and said, 'I enjoyed your sermon,' and I thought it was too heavy for them.

"My beloved fellow workers, loose liberalism does not accomplish what we think it will accomplish. George Whital, writing in *Washingtonian Magazine*, says, 'The churches that make the greatest doctrinal and moral demands on their members'—he mentions the evangelical and fundamentalist Protestants—'are growing. Their churches are booming. In contrast,' he says, 'the churches that have a hard time telling you why you ought to be a Christian, the churches of the old main line, like the Episcopalians, the Methodists, the Presbyterians, and the United Church of Christ, have been hemorrhaging congregants since the midsixties. It is vanilla Protestantism that is dying.' And then he says, 'Theological friendliness, avant-garde worship, and political correctness are a prescription for ecclesiastical catastrophe. Millions are leaving because they have no good reason to stay.' "

Then Brooks used an illustration from his ministry to debunk the notion that not preaching standards was a more loving approach:

"A blond girl came into my office at one of our colleges where I was preaching, and she burst into tears, sobbing uncontrollably. When I asked her problem, she said, 'Pastor, my parents don't love me.'

"I said, 'How can you say that? They're sacrificing to keep you here, and you are dressed very well. They've taken good care of you. Why do you say that?'

"She said, 'Because they don't care what I do.'"

C.D. indicated that some of the church's biggest problems came from the lowering of standards and abandonment of biblical preaching:

"Young and old need the discipline of the Word of God. When people feel as though they can do as they please, then the church loses its premium value. They figure we don't care. But 'feel-goodism' is pervading our congregations, creeping in, and our churches and our schools are foundering. Our income is being depleted. We have our biggest budget crisis this year. . . .

"The devil is pleading every device. He is pleading culture and pluralism and scholarship. And he is impressing many of us to try to modernize God by humanizing Him. God already answered that: 'I am the Lord, I change not! I am the same yesterday, and today, and forever!'

"I hear a lot about 'Oh, we need someone now to make Scripture relevant.' . . . Fellow workers, if God said it, it's relevant! It's our extraneous ideas about what He says that are irrelevant!"

Providing an antidote to the poison seeping into the church, Brooks cited the examples of those he looked up to in his ministry:

"The preaching of the Word, even with love and tact and diplomacy, will inevitably cause confrontation with our sinful, carnal natures. And we are not called to make the Word popular, but to preach it with power! And I'm one of those transition preachers. Pastor Peay and I and others, we came along and became a connecting link between the old and the new. Those old warhorses preached it straight. Peters, Peterson, W.W., Walt Starks, J. H. Laurence, Rowe, Robert Bradford—they stood up with a burden under the aegis of the Holy Ghost, and it poured out of them! These men made and built Black Seventh-day Adventism!

"In 1946 a skinny preacher named E. E. Cleveland came to my hometown. Never heard anything like it. There was one thing I knew when I looked at that preacher: he believed everything he preached! And he made me believe it! These are the men to emulate."

Charles then divulged his method of sermon preparation:

"You know that our laymen today are too caught up and preoccupied to study, and with little substance coming from the pulpit. . . . I've got two libraries: one at my home and one at the General Conference, and they are rather extensive. And I like to read the hardbacks and the softbacks. But when I go into my study, the bookshelves immediately behind my chair have the Spirit of Prophecy, several versions of the Bible, and *The Seventh-day Adventist Bible Commentary*. And when I get ready to read the other books [names non-Adventist commentaries], I've got to get up out of my chair and walk over to get them. But if I get through with the Review and Herald and the one out in Idaho [Pacific Press], then all this other becomes simply a skeleton on which I can hang the meat of Seventh-day Adventism. And verily my people can be fed.

"*We've* got to confront our people for their sake. Not pamper them—you're not helping them. We've got to dare to guide them. Some of what they're doing is because they don't know any better. We've got to guide them concerning where they ought to go, what they ought to do, what they ought to wear, what they ought to think. And we ought to do it with the Word of God and the Spirit of Prophecy!"

Then he went on to explain what happens during a sermon:

"When we talk to our people, it's not a purely human-to-human encounter. There is a person called the Holy Ghost. It's our privilege to have Him standing by us and moving out there in the congregation. He will take a difficult truth and apply it to the heart. You think I didn't have to give up things I liked?

"I'd rather save one person with the truth and with the Holy Ghost than comfort 10,000 in their self-deception. And we fail our people when we water down and compromise and undermine and repudiate the message that God has given us to bear and to live!"

One of the reasons for the coldness of some Adventist churches, he believed, was their failure to preach standards:

"Not only that, we embolden them to defy our standards. We embolden them to follow their own whims and offend fellow church members and even their parents. And many of them have chips on their shoulders. They are so self-confident they dare you to say anything.

"A young woman that had always been friendly came to church loaded down with jewelry. And when I approached her ready to speak, she wouldn't even look at me. She avoided me. She couldn't be friendly as usual. No wonder our churches are turning cold! It's because they remain guilt-ridden and insecure and not sure of what they really stand for. They hear of easy divorce, moral falls even in the ministry, Sabbaths on the golf course, or on the bicycle trail, or at the beach, theatergoing, attacks on the Spirit of Prophecy. What's happening among us?

"Ellen White says, 'Of all the sins that God will punish, none are more grievous in His sight than those that encourage others to do evil.' And of all the groups of people on the topside of the earth, none has such an awesome responsibility resting upon it, as well as privilege, as the Seventh-day Adventist ministry."

Next C.D. addressed the emotionalism that sometimes characterized divine worship:

"Many who feel a lack of the Spirit are trying to compensate with a shaking, rocking, rollicking religion. They want to feel good. But that good feeling will replace their faith, and it will be wiped out in a crisis. . . . The Bible says, 'There is no peace, saith my God, to the wicked.' Many of our people are getting caught up in the subjective, ecstatic experience, and the 11:00 service is like cocaine—a temporary fix! And before the sun sets they are right back to where they were: unhappy, critical, not doing so well. And what do I want now? A loud, thumping, bumping religion. And it will cause me to delight in making the old saints uncomfortable. And we are being divided. . . . We're not supposed to set our churches on fire; that's the work of the Holy Ghost."

With the sticks still hanging above the pulpit on either side, Brooks continued to stress balance, even in preaching the gospel:

"I said to a congregation on Sabbath, 'Gospel is good news, but it's not just the cross. Thank God for the cross! But the gospel is more than that. Gospel is health reform—that's good news! Gospel is social reform—that's good news!

"I was invited to preach for the sixty-fifth anniversary of the high school I graduated from some 40 years ago. I walked in there, and what a crowd! The head table was longer than this auditorium. I had given word that I couldn't arrive there until after sunset. They said, 'We understand that. We'll take care of the preliminaries, and you just come right in.' And I did. I sat right in the middle. These tables were loaded, many of them with former classmates. I looked out, and they kept waving and winking and carrying on. Finally it dawned on me, Oh, they looked awful! You think I look old! You should have seen them! Our message is good news! I tried to figure it out; I looked back, and I said to myself, 'I've been keeping the Sabbath for 54 years. That's seven years of Sabbathkeeping, which means I got seven years of rest that they never got!"

Brooks confided that some attitudes in the ministry especially hurt him:

"And it hurts me today. Some of you have heard a rumor that I'm getting ready to retire. It hurts me today to see that among us many, rather than kneeling in humility, are standing up like the Pharisee in the narrative of Christ with jaw set and shoulders squared to debate with God, and the pulpit is losing its nerve. I'm not suggesting that you browbeat anybody. I don't do that! Ellen White says that rationalism exalts human reason above the Word of God. And many of our beloved people are making dangerous decisions based on how they feel rather than on the explicit revelations from the Bible and the Spirit of Prophecy. Error is always appended to this: How I feel. They love to talk about theater now and evolution, and even the mark of the beast is getting a dressing-down in our own journals. What are we doing?"

Black Adventism was especially facing a challenge:

"Harold Lee was addressing a convention not long ago when he said, 'Neo-Pentecostalism will be the death of Black Adventism.' And I wrote that down. Our people are especially vulnerable, because we are such an emotional people. We've been here too long. Divided and separated by racism, by advantage, education, money, and privilege, we've been forced into being reactive, but we've come too close. Don't let us be cheated now and miss heaven after all we've gone through."

Brooks made it clear that he was not attacking any one culture. Every culture had elements to be proud of. But there were also elements in every culture that went against the Word of God. Although C.D. culturally identified with Blacks and was proud to be a Black man, he refused to be defined by race, ethnicity, or nationality. Instead, he would be identified only with Jesus. He shared an experience from his youth to illustrate:

"A long time ago I was adopted. There is a Seventh-day Adventist culture, and I was born into this Adventist culture by adoption, which is a legal compact. My daddy and mother adopted a boy before I was born. I never saw him. As he grew older he got into trouble with the law and spent time in jail. Finally he said, 'I want to leave this family.' He was adopted. No person born of Brooks blood in my large family has ever spent a night in jail! What's the difference? He was adopted. He came in from another nature. The rest of us were born with Brooks blood. So I have been adopted, but I have been born again! Adoption makes me His; new birth makes me like Him. There is the commonality of the blood."

Next Brooks leveled his aim at ornamentation, sharing an experience he had to illustrate Seventh-day Adventists' special uniqueness.

"I loved it when you could look at a young woman and know she was an Adventist. I got invited to a camp meeting, went into a town, and didn't know where to go. My wife said, 'Honey, stop and phone.' Then it dawned on me that no one answers the phone at a campground on the Sabbath, at least they used to not answer it. And I was desperate, and I looked at a car easing by and I saw some women, their faces clean. They looked like something. I pulled my car into that lane and followed them. My wife said, 'Honey, what are you doing?'

"I said, 'I'm following those people!'

"'You know who they are?'

"'No! I just know how they look!'

"And I ended up at my destination."

C.D. expressed his misgivings that gospel music had become tainted with worldly elements. Not wanting to be misunderstood, he spoke of his appreciation for sacred music done right:

"I like gospel music! I probably like it more than many sitting out here. . . . And I can prove it. For 35 of the past 37 years I have gone every November to Germantown, Ohio, a mecca of gospel music. Twenty-eight of those trips were over the Thanksgiving weekend, giving up my family holiday to be inspired with those people. Our precious Eleanor Wright, the late Eleanor Wright, wrote most of the music. They were message songs. They rebuked sin! They encouraged the discouraged! That's one reason she did not die a millionaire, because she stayed faithful to this message. . . . Eleanor Wright wrote 'Naaman' the weekend after I preached it in Cincinnati, Ohio. And when my father-in-law died, she wrote one for our family called 'I Don't Plan to Stay Here.' "

Holy music had also blessed him while a student at Oakwood:

"When I came to Oakwood, I had never heard the *Messiah*. One day, going at 3:00 a.m to the dairy where I worked, I heard music over in the chapel. Lights were on. Then when I came back I heard a *thump, thump, thump*. Eva Dykes was beating out the time with a staff. I said to somebody, 'What's going on over there?'

"They said, 'They're getting ready for the *Messiah*.'

"I admit I didn't know what it was. But I'm too cool to let people know I was that naive. I said, 'Oh, yes!'

"On the night it was presented, it felt as if the top of my head would blow off. When they got to the "Hallelujah Chorus" I didn't need a royal example to get me to my feet as the choir sang, 'He shall reign for ever and ever, for ever and ever, for ever and ever. Hallelujah! Hallelujah!' "

But seeing how powerful music was in conveying the gospel, the enemy sought to corrupt it.

"I don't believe the drum is a bigger sin than the trumpet or the psaltery or the harp. It's what we do with it! So Satan had a huddle, and he said to his imps, 'Let's develop crossover.' Why would a saint want to cross over?

" 'Let's develop crossover!' said the devil. 'Let's blend some of ours with some of theirs. Let's start off with a balance, and then let's gradually move off center. And then let's talk about Christian jazz and religious gospel rock. They are contradictions of terms, you see. Let's get them moving and grooving like our crowd in our places when they are getting down. Then, after we get them moving so that their senses cannot be trusted [as Ellen White says], let's pull out all the stops.'

"Satan starts out small. No one comes to sudden ruin. It takes time to corrupt the soul. Gradually the devil perverts. One departure from principle begins the journey. . . . Whom do we think we're dealing with? He's called a wily foe. He's no friend of ours. He names these coffin nails called cigarettes 'Salem (peace),' 'Kool,' 'True,' 'Joy.' Whom do we think we're dealing with when he names the poison of alcohol 'Southern Comfort'?

"Movies—if you say anything about them, you're old-fashioned! I don't mind that opprobrium. Call me old if you want to; God is older than I am. And when God tells us something, He gets it right the first time! He doesn't have to edit or adjust.

"We serve a timeless God. And time, as we know it, is about to experience a cataclysmic collision with eternity. We are about to enter His realm of time and space. But when we do, the truth will still be the truth. Sabbath will still be Sabbath, because truth never dies."

After C.D. shared more experiences from his youth, he thundered:

"Fifty-four years ago I joined this church. I've been somewhat educated, illuminated, experienced. I'm getting ready to retire. But I want to tell you, nothing's changed. We've matured, and we've been enlightened. People are meaner, more immoral. But nothing's changed. God's law is still a transcript of His character. It's too high for us, so He gave us a ladder called grace that we might climb up.

"The sanctuary is still in heaven. It is not going anywhere because Ford said so. Judgment is still going on. God still hates pride. Men are still born in sin. Men must be born again. Dead folk are still dead. Christ is still our only Savior. None but the righteous shall see God. We've got to be without spot or wrinkle or any such thing. We've got to be covered with His righteousness alone. He still sends the Holy Ghost. And He is still seeking the lost. He is still saving sinners. And it is possible to delight ourselves in the Lord and the truth! Our message is still valid! And if we stand around waiting for our truth to change, we're exactly like the Protestants who want the Sabbath to change."

Knowing that he was nearing retirement, Brooks conveyed his concern about shoddy evangelistic practices:

"Oh, please, get what I'm saying. I do evangelism. Brethren and sisters, we are not in competition with one another. When you run a church meeting and baptize 60, you've done what some eight-week campaigns under a tent do when they baptize 200. We're not in competition. Let us glory when the Lord does it. . . . If I ever hear a man bragging about how many he baptizes, I worry about him.

"But I tell you something, and I mean it with all my heart: If you don't like what I say, at least give me credit for being honest and sincere. When I work as hard as I do to run an effort, I want somebody to stay at least until after the snow falls. Don't let me hear that you baptized 250 and nobody can find them! When Earl Cleveland and Bill Scales and George Rainey and Eric Ward and all of those along with many pastors who have not made it their specialty, when they do it, the church is enlarged, and the folk know what they believe."

Brooks concluded his message with the story of the man in Chicago who came to him wondering what he should do with his valuable wine collection. When Brooks held up the standard of truth based on God's Word without watering it down, the man was converted. He ended his message with these words:

"Brethren, this truth will win souls. You don't need to play games and fool people. This truth, with its dignity and its power, this truth attended by the Holy Ghost, will win souls—the best kind.

"I want my church back!"

The Last Meeting

As C.D. alluded to in his landmark message, his storied tenure with Breath of Life was drawing to a close. But it would end as it began: bringing people to Christ on a grand scale.

In late 1994 Walter Arties flew to Canada to meet with church officials about a Breath of Life campaign there. The leaders and members both wanted Brooks and his team to come north and do in their territory what they had done all over the world. But unfortunately the details couldn't be worked out. Arties boarded a plane back to California.

Providentially, he had a layover in Phoenix, Arizona. Soon, discovering that his flight to Los Angeles was late, he decided to phone Hubert Cisneros, the health, ministerial, and youth director for the Arizona Conference. After exchanging pleasantries, Cisneros asked Arties where he had been. Walter explained that he had gone to Canada to arrange for Breath of Life evangelistic meetings there, but they had fallen through.

"We'd love for you to come to Phoenix," Cisneros said in a no-nonsense tone of voice.

He then asked Arties to contact him after he arrived in California, which would give him time to determine if the Arizona Conference administration was amenable. They talked for a while longer, then said their goodbyes. Soon after, Arties boarded a flight to Los Angeles.

Back in California, when Walter checked his voice mail later that day, he had a message from Hubert Cisneros. While Arties was still above the clouds Cisneros had spoken to Arizona Conference president Herman Bauman. It so happened that recently a longtime member of one of the conference churches had died and left $40,000 to the Arizona Conference earmarked for evangelism. You couldn't get more evangelistic than Breath of Life! The president wanted the ministry to come to Phoenix.

And so the groundwork was laid. For three weeks the Phoenix-area churches prepared the way for Breath of Life, distributing flyers and advertisements and doing Bible work. As always, the excitement of the members was palpable. Together Adventists of various ethnicities worked in concert to build up the kingdom of God. What C. D. Brooks and Alvin Stewart had accomplished so long ago in Newark was now commonplace.

The meetings took place in March and April of 1995 in downtown Phoenix at the Central Seventh-day Adventist Church. Every night there was an overflow crowd. The Arizonans had never experienced a campaign of such magnitude. In full support of his field secretary, General Conference president Robert Folkenberg made provision for a television crew to videotape the entire campaign—all four weeks—a first for C.D. and Breath of Life. Later the ministry sold the videos as sets, then made them into DVDs, and finally posted them on the Internet. The sermons were played endlessly in small groups, prayer meetings, Weeks of Prayer, and church services the world over.

The 64-year-old Brooks was as much a preaching powerhouse as ever, speaking every night but Thursday, and, after introducing the Sabbath, twice on Saturday. When the series began winding to a close, conference president Bauman asked the audience if they'd like C.D. to stay for an additional week. There was thunderous applause. The meetings resulted in 50 baptisms.

The Arizonans didn't realize that they would be the last ones to hear C. D. Brooks as speaker for Breath of Life.

RETIREMENT

"The Lord has been so good to me. Even in my 80s
I get too many calls to speak to accept them all."

On a breezy morning in Miami, Florida, on October 21, 1995, more than 4,000 Adventists descended on the James L. Knight Center for the Sabbath service. The occasion: a rally for what was billed "the greatest evangelistic thrust ever witnessed in the city of Miami." Although the Breath of Life campaign was to begin on July 6 of the next year, the members representing almost 30 churches in the city were raring to go.

During the service Malcolm Gordon, president of the Southern Union Conference, and R. R. Brown, Southeastern Conference president, expressed their full support for the Breath of Life initiative. Ira Harrell educated the members on the best ways to attract people to the meetings. The legendary evangelist T. A. McNealy, the local pastor-coordinator, informed the vast audience of the strategy to reach the millions in the Greater Miami area, an area popularly known as the unofficial capital of Latin America. The flyers, handbills, lead cards, and Bible correspondence materials would be made available in English, Spanish, and French to reach the diverse population. Reginald Robinson delivered a rousing sermon. In the afternoon Sony Roy of the Synergistic Evangelism Institute explained how the series would use the most recent evangelistic techniques.

The only person missing was the evangelist who would preach for the meetings.

The Heart Attack
On Sabbath, June 10, 1995, C. D. Brooks had just concluded a powerful sermon on the Godhead at the South Central Conference camp meeting on the campus of Oakwood College. Dozens had responded to the appeal for baptism, and after the benediction, South Central Conference presi-

dent Joseph McCoy asked C.D. to stay with those who had come forward while he greeted those filing out the back of the sanctuary. When McCoy strode away and Brooks began talking with the people seated in the pews in front of him, a peculiar sensation in his chest grabbed his attention. It had been slight all morning, even while he was preaching, but now it was throbbing.

After a half hour the sanctuary had emptied. McCoy, Walter Arties, and some other leaders escorted C.D. to Wade Hall, about 150 yards from the church, where lunch was waiting. In fact, there would be a ceremony in Brooks's honor. But Charles felt worse and worse as the program went on, and when it was time for him to say a word he whispered to McCoy that he did not feel up to speaking. At this the conference president grew worried.

"Elder Brooks, are you OK?" he asked with concern.

"I should go back to my hotel."

McCoy offered to walk him to his car, but C.D. waved him off, saying he would be fine. Passing a seated Arties, he squeezed his shoulder and said he would see him a little later. Walter wasn't too worried, considering his longtime associate to be in robust health; he thought it was just a passing pain. Brooks graciously waved goodbye and thanked everyone for the occasion. Exiting Wade Hall into the sauna that was Alabama in the summer, he started what soon felt like a cross-country trek to his car in the church parking lot.

When he was within a few steps of his car, an unbearable pressure seized his chest, and he fell to the ground, his hands clawing at the side of the vehicle for support. As he lay on the red Alabama soil, his heart thumped double time, and in the back of his mind he believed he was going to die. He thought of Walterene. At this he felt a jolt of strength, and he stood, though his legs wobbled. Although the yellow ball in the blue sky was far away, it felt as if it were hanging right over his head. He had been to Africa many times, and it had never felt this hot. Sweat poured down his face, his suit dusty from his spill.

Step by step, C.D. stumbled back to the entrance of Wade Hall. Amazingly, at the height of camp meeting no one saw the famous minister staggering along the sidewalk. After much stopping and starting, he made it to the double doors. Inside, it felt like the inside of a refrigerator. He collapsed onto a couch in the lobby.

A college student coming from the elevator was the first to spot him. She hurried over to him, and he told her that he needed a doctor.

"I know where one is," she said. And although wearing heels, she sprinted away at full speed.

Walterene, he thought as he slouched on the couch.

The student returned with a man dressed in a suit. He was there for camp meeting, had heard Brooks's sermon, and was dining in the campus cafeteria when the young woman had burst through the cafeteria doors. After a brief examination the physician stated that C.D. had suffered a heart attack. The student and doctor helped Brooks to the doctor's car just outside the entrance. With C.D. safely inside, the physician peeled away, breaking every traffic law to get his passenger to Huntsville Hospital. At one stretch they actually drove on the sidewalk. Brooks remembered thinking, *If this heart attack doesn't do me in, this ride will . . .*

Walterene, he again thought as the car careened around turns.

When they pulled up to the emergency entrance of the hospital, a group of hospital staff were already outside with a wheelchair and other medical equipment. After they had Brooks securely in the wheelchair, they stripped off his shirt, and a couple started plunging needles into his arm, another held a stethoscope to his heart, while someone else checked his blood pressure.

Once C.D. was in a room, an internist who happened to be working that Sabbath immediately took charge, ordering a cardiograph. After studying it, he looked at Brooks and said gravely, "Sir, you are having a major heart attack—now." Then he broke out into a whirl of instructions. Attendants scurried around Brooks like ants. Once Brooks heard one plucky orderly ask, "You want me to give him this?" and the doctor's reply, "Yes, and now!" Later C.D. discovered that the procedure under question was a "clot-buster," which had to be used within an hour of the initial problem or it would do no good.

Walterene, he kept thinking amid the melee.

After he had stabilized and was feeling better, the hospital transferred him to intensive care and allowed him visitors. Walter Arties was the first through the door. No sooner had Brooks seen him than he demanded, "Does Walterene know?"

"No, she doesn't."

"You must be the one to tell her! She must not hear it from anyone else! Only you must tell her!" C.D. was adamant.

He was concerned about his wife, because she had a tragic history of the men closest to her dying from heart attacks on Sabbath. Her beloved father, John H. Wagner, had succumbed to a heart attack on Sabbath, August 11, 1962, at age 60. Her younger brother, Jesse, had died from a heart attack on Sabbath, June 11, 1977. Thus it was imperative to C.D. that the tactful and reassuring voice of his longtime friend Walter Arties tell Rene what had happened, that her husband was fine, and that he was not going to die.

Walter hurried from the room and sequestered himself in a quiet area of the hospital with a phone. As his finger pressed the numbers to the Brookses' Maryland home, he breathed a prayer.

What followed was the hardest conversation that Arties had ever had in his life. Walterene was hysterical. As had happened to her father and her brother, she was sure her "honey" was going to die from a heart attack on Sabbath. After Arties' assurances that C.D. was alive and OK, he requested her son-in-law, Samuel Tramel, to arrange to fly her and Diedre to Nashville, Tennessee, or Birmingham, Alabama. Walter would then pick them up from either airport and drive them to Huntsville.

When Walter returned the phone to its cradle, he felt completely drained. He whispered a prayer that all would be well with his dear friends, the Brookses. Hours later he received a call from Samuel Tramel: Walterene and Diedre would fly into Birmingham. True to his word, Arties picked them up and saw them to the hospital.

Once through the sliding glass doors Walterene rushed to her husband's room, refusing to leave his side the whole time he was there. Neither doctor nor nurse nor orderly nor intern could pry her from her husband.

The show of love and support while C. D. Brooks was in the hospital was heartwarming. Several times a day musical groups from Oakwood came to sing to him. Scores of fellow church leaders and ministers made appearances. A never-ending parade of well-wishers appeared at his door.

After a few days the hospital moved him to a spacious suite equipped with an extra bed and stationed a guard at the door. He and Walterene were served the finest food, and their every need was attended to. Nonplussed by the special treatment, C.D. inquired about it, and discovered that two vice presidents of the hospital were Seventh-day Adventists. They had given orders that the evangelist should receive the full VIP treatment.

Brooks next went to the nuclear medicine department for testing. The results revealed a blockage approximately two inches long in otherwise healthy arteries. He underwent an angioplasty and stent placement. The procedures were successful, and after extensive instructions on what to do in emergency situations, what medication to take, and the need for regular checkups, the hospital discharged him. He had spent one week in Huntsville Hospital.

Even while in the hospital, Brooks had been pining to get back to evangelism. Just days after returning to his home in Maryland he made plans to do a television series for Breath of Life on the seven churches of Asia Minor. But once at the Adventist Media Center in front of the camera, he realized that he didn't have the strength he'd had before the heart attack. When he'd lose energy or begin perspiring, the camera caught it all on tape.

Undaunted, he began planning for the series to end all series in the metropolis that was Miami. Impressed by Ellen White's statements on evangelizing the cities, Brooks felt a burden as never before to tell everyone he could about Jesus. With Arties and other leaders he strategized for taking over the city the next summer. That fall ministers in Miami began motivating their members, distributed literature, purchased advertisements, and gave Bible studies.

With all the activity, however, C.D. began to feel even more drained. When he spoke to his old friend Neal Wilson, now 75, 10 years Brooks's senior, Neal warned him that he should take it easy on himself. "Don't do Miami," he warned. "It's way too soon after the heart attack."

As the months passed, this advice proved prescient. C.D. was at first upset, then disappointed, then resigned to the reality of his diminished strength. Yet he still pushed on. The problem (if someone chose to call it that) was that C.D. put every ounce of himself into a sermon when he preached. He held nothing back. For one hour he stretched every fiber of his being. But as 1995 drew to a close, his body was making it clear that it could not bear the strain any longer. Because C.D. recognized that the zeal of the Lord's house consumed him, that God's Word was in his heart as a burning fire shut up in his bones, he knew he could never give less than every ounce of himself. So after consulting with his bride of nearly 45 years, C. D. Brooks decided to retire.

Retiring

For the past 20 years he had held two jobs simultaneously. When he announced to the General Conference family that he was retiring, it produced a huge outpouring of love and appreciation for the beloved man of God that had been with them for 25 years. On October 28, 1995, church headquarters held a retirement program for him in the main auditorium at the General Conference. Almost 1,000 church leaders, GC employees, retirees, and friends gathered to honor a ministry that had spanned 44 years. Although someone figured up that C.D. had baptized 12,000, the number of people that those thousands brought to Christ; the number brought to Christ through his guidance of hundreds of ministers; the inspirational, encouraging, and sanctifying power of his messages that spurred those who listened to win others; and the countless numbers who heard him on tape, video, television and radio and who came to Christ as a result—it was in reality truly incalculable. The words spoken that day only partly conveyed the reality of the global and eternal reach of a ministry blessed by God. As the unwavering goal of C.D.'s life unfolded in those testimonials, more than one person present renewed their commitment to bring others to Christ. The majesty, grandness, and profundity of a life lived for Jesus shone brightly.

Brooks's retirement as general field secretary of the world church would be effective January 1, 1996. However, C.D. never really left the General Conference, for after his official retirement, leadership invited him to keep an office on the top floor of the building. Throughout the years in his honorary office church leaders would stop by to consult with C.D., ask him to serve on committees, fill his calendar with speaking engagements, interview him, solicit his prayers, get premarital and marital counseling, express their gratitude for his ministry, and countless other things.

***

Brooks's retirement from Breath of Life was a little longer in coming. The tapings from the Phoenix campaign filled the 30-minute television spots for months. Although the much-anticipated Miami series did not materialize because of Brooks's health, C.D. agreed to be the question-and-answer man for NET '96, lasting from October 5 to November 9, 1996. This time the event would be worldwide.

Held in Orlando, Florida, each meeting was translated into 13 languages, shown in 45 countries, and viewed by more than a half million people. Secretary of the General Conference G. Ralph Thompson reported that "NET '96 was the most successful global outreach of evangelism this church had ever undertaken." In North America alone "it resulted in the largest annual report of baptisms ever." Estimates vary as to the baptism total from NET '96, because of rebroadcasting and follow-up programs, but it was in the tens of thousands. C.D. was once again on the forefront of an epic soul-winning event.

***

In early 1997 C.D. finally broke it to Walter Arties, his right-hand man for almost a quarter of a century, that he was retiring as Breath of Life's speaker-director. After the heart attack Arties knew that it was only a matter of time before he would hear those words, but they still strongly affected him. During 24 years of ministry the two had started one of the first television ministries by Black people for Black people; produced some 200 programs; baptized 12,000 people; established 13 churches; exposed millions to biblical truth; appeared on some 1,300 cable stations; traveled the world several times as ambassadors for Christ; mentored and trained countless ministers in evangelism; and revolutionized Seventh-day Adventists' and wider Christendom's outreach and media presence.

C. D. Brooks would occupy a unique place in Seventh-day Adventist history. The public face of Adventism at the dawn of the media revolution that was to forever change the world consisted of four evangelists who had vision, courage, the Holy Spirit, and a thirst to reach others that only mass media could begin to quench. These men grace the 152-square-foot mural entitled *Founder's Wall* at the Adventist Media Center: C. D. Brooks, H.M.S. Richards, George Vandeman, and William Fagal.

A second wave of Adventist televangelists followed in their footsteps, legends in their own right: Mark Finley, Lonnie Melashenko, Walter Pearson, and Dan Matthews. With NET '95 inaugurating the era of satellite evangelism, followed by NET '96, NET '98, Pentecost '98, NET New York '99 and others into the new millennium, gifted evangelists such as Dwight Nelson and Doug Batchelor soon emerged.

Seventh-day Adventist television networks began to form. On November 23, 1986, Three Angels Broadcasting Network (3ABN) started to broadcast on satellite, eventually providing 24-hour programming with several sister stations. Hope Channel debuted in 2003, the official channel of the Seventh-day Adventist Church. Today it also broadcasts 24 hours, with 14 channels worldwide.

It is impossible to measure the influence that the original four Adventist electronic evangelists have had on Adventist media.

***

In the spring of 1997 the Breath of Life Ministries board convened at the Oakwood Elementary School in Huntsville, Alabama. C. D. Brooks asked the chair for permission to address the board. Once it was granted, he announced to those present that he was tendering his retirement. He had barely spoken the words when the board members stood as one, applauding the man who had made the ministry all it was. The session voted that he be speaker emeritus for life.

A Successor

The similarities between C.D. and his successor were numerous. Brooks was born in the South; Walter Leonard Pearson, Jr., was born in Mobile, Alabama, in 1945. Charles studied for the ministry at Oakwood; Pearson graduated from there with a degree in theology in 1967. C.D. had a daughter and son; the year Pearson graduated he married Sandra Holland, and the couple had a daughter and a son, Ericca and Walter III.

Brooks started his ministry pastoring in Allegheny; Pearson pastored churches in the Allegheny territory, being ordained in Mount Vernon, Ohio, in 1973. Brooks was a power preacher who used stories like tools; Pearson was a gifted preacher, driving his point home through expertly crafted and delivered stories. Charles was youth-oriented; Pearson was appointed director of Youth and Urban Ministry programs for the Allegheny West Conference.

C.D. pastored the largest churches in the conference; in the 1980s and early 1990s Pearson held pastorates for five years at North Philadelphia Church and eight at Atlanta Berean. Brooks spoke on all corners of the globe; Pearson preached in numerous countries, his influence growing internationally. Like C.D., Pearson left pastoring for work at the General Conference, first as associate director for evangelism and church growth at the Ministerial Department and then as associate director of the Ellen G. White Estate. And as with Brooks, it was while holding a position at the GC that Pearson received an invitation to be speaker-director of Breath of Life. Walter Pearson began his tenure in the summer of 1997.

On December 18, 1997, GC president Robert Folkenberg and NAD president Al McClure honored C. D. Brooks for his 25 years at Breath of Life in a special ceremony at the General Conference. At the occasion Walter Pearson presented Charles and Walterene Brooks with a beautiful portrait of the couple. The transition was complete.

At the Head of Another Media Revolution

Although C.D. had retired from Breath of Life, his presence would live on as never before in the media. Brooks never distributed one cassette, videotape, CD, or DVD of his sermons. He simply did what God told him to do: "Preach the Word." But throughout the past half century his sermons have been recorded, then distributed, then distributed again and again and again. On television his messages were played endlessly on reruns. Later they had second and third lives on VHS, CD, and DVD players in homes, schools, churches, and cars. With the Internet revolution in the late 1990s, Brooks inevitably appeared on the Web. And then, with the advent of a juggernaut of a Web site, Brooks's messages became ubiquitous on PCs, laptops, notebooks, tablets, iPads, iPods, cells, smartphones, and every other device able to "connect."

In February 2005 three young employees of the e-commerce transfer company PayPal named Steve Chen, Chad Hurley, and Jawed Karim created a video-sharing Web site appropriately called YouTube. Their first post was a few months later on the night of Saturday, April 23: a 20-second clip of Karim narrating in front of an elephant exhibit at the San Diego Zoo. A year and a half later YouTube garnered nearly 700,000 views a week, and Google purchased the site from the trio for $1.65 billion in stocks.

Nothing has yet challenged YouTube's standing as the most popular video uploading and viewing site. As of late 2013 YouTube reported that its viewers watch more than 6 billion hours of video each month, more than 1 billion users visit every month, 100 hours of video get uploaded every minute, and videos stream in 61 languages. The site's red-and-white logo displayed in a gray background is becoming as iconic as those of McDonalds and Apple.

The same may be said of YouTube as of cassette tapes: that Brooks is the most widely circulated Adventist minister on the medium. People have uploaded hundreds of his sermons. And so the old, old story that Brooks loves to tell is being retold tens of thousands of times. And it will be related still more times when the next all-consuming technology debuts.

The Bradford-Cleveland-Brooks Leadership Center
The three elderly African-Americans stood at the red cordon, their advanced years arrived at after sweltering summers under tents behind pulpits in front of people at the foot of the cross. On the right was a slightly stooped E. E. Cleveland, diminished in figure but taller than ever in stature. He had led 15,000 to the waters of baptism. To his left was Charles Bradford, seemingly as robust as ever, a dynamo of innovation and administrative virtuosity as the first Black president of the North American Division. And finally the third of the trio, the trim and elegant C. D. Brooks,

upright and stately in his bearing. The great pioneer of Black Adventist media, he was one of the most prolific soul winners in the history of Adventism. The date was October 22, 2007; the occasion: the dedication of the Bradford-Cleveland-Brooks Leadership Center on the campus of Oakwood University.

The idea for the facility had been long in coming. In the 1950s and 1960s E. E. Cleveland held evangelism seminars under the auspices of the General Conference for ministers and theology students. Beginning in the 1960s Brooks also conducted such field schools. Conducted under tents and in halls, sometimes in rooms and auditoriums, such seminars were the model for the Annual Pastoral and Evangelism Council convened each year in late autumn on the campus of Oakwood University starting in 1979. A high point of the year for both ministers and other church employees, the councils were a time for fellowship, updates, and seminars by the innovators and experienced ministers at the forefront of evangelism.

In the 1980s, at the urging of NAD president Charles Bradford, Oakwood College administrators directed by President Benjamin Reaves collaborated with the regional presidents' Black Caucus (comprised of such individuals as Stennett Brooks, Willie Lewis, Meade Van Putten, J. Paul Monk, Luther Palmer, Jr., Charles Dudley, and Jackson Doggette) to sketch out plans for a facility named in honor of E. E. Cleveland that would house a department dedicated to pastoral evangelism and enrichment. However, at the time the plans did not come to fruition.

When an old student of Cleveland's and Brooks's field evangelism seminars, Delbert Baker, became president of Oakwood in 1996, the plans were dusted off and restudied. After considerable editing, updating, and refiguring, Baker presented the regional conference presidents and the Oakwood board of trustees with the revised plans. The result was an entity founded in 1999 as the Bradford-Cleveland-Brooks Institute for Continuing Education in Ministry (BCBI), later renamed Bradford-Cleveland-Brooks Leadership Center (BCBLC).

Plans were made for a building, but money had to be raised first. After some negotiations, it was decided that Oakwood would provide most of the funding, with the regional conferences, North American Division, and General Conference assisting with varying amounts. The construction of a 10,000-square-foot, $2.5 million addition to the C. E. Moseley Religion Complex began in 2005. The space consisted of six classrooms, eight offices, a boardroom, a library/computer center, and a 200-seat auditorium. Construction concluded in October 2007.

The church's top leaders attended the inauguration and opening of the BCBLC: Jan Paulsen, GC president; Matthew Bediako, GC secretary; Bob Lemon, GC treasurer; Ella Simmons, GC vice president; Don Schneider, NAD president and Oakwood board chair; Alvin Kibble, NAD vice president; Roscoe Howard, NAD secretary; Charles Cheatham, GC presidents' board chair; Gordon Retzer, Southern Union president; Ron Smith, Southern Union secretary; Benjamin Browne, South Central Conference president; Harold Lee, recently appointed director of the BCBLC; the officers of Oakwood College, as well as distinguished Oakwood donors. And of course the three giants for whom the edifice and center were named were present.

Harold Lee later summarized the purpose of the center: "The building will facilitate the training of pastors and lay workers for the church, along with providing workshops, conferences, and seminars on ministry and lifestyle development. The main focus of the center is the provision of faith-based, relevant, lifelong learning opportunities for clergy and nonclergy in ministry. Participants in these studies will be offered Christ-centered strategies to address church and societal issues, evangelism and church growth, and community service and disaster relief training. The center's aim is to become a think tank for church and community members of all faiths working together to develop resources for excellence in ministry. These resources will be available worldwide. The facility also provides instructional space for the first master's degree offered on Oakwood's campus—the Master of Arts in Pastoral Studies. The primary objective of the BCBLC is to support the new master's program."

The proceedings at the inauguration of the new center honored C. D. Brooks. But throughout the ceremonies, and later as he escorted his wife away, he couldn't stop praying: "Lord, let this center point people to Jesus, His truth, the blessed teachings that You have entrusted to this church. Let its influence tell for good, instructing men and women on how to win souls and lead Your church. More than just an edifice with state-of-the-art facilities and men's names chiseled on it, may it lead to the finishing of the work."

The Death of Two Friends
The man whose name appeared next to that of C.D. on the new edifice

at Oakwood University, the one who was responsible for a 15-year-old Southern teenager entering the ministry, died on August 30, 2009. E. E. Cleveland's funeral services took place at the Oakwood University church on September 9, 2009. Those who gave tribute to the great evangelist at the service read like a *Who's Who of Adventism:* Winnie Rivers, Charles Bradford, T. Marshal Kelly, Walter Pearson, Rosa Banks, Calvin Rock, Harold Lee, Merlin Burt, Benjamin Browne, Mervyn Warren, Delbert Baker, Leslie Pollard, Varnard Mendinghall, Gordon Retzer, James Cress, Barry Black, Jan Paulsen, Wintley Phipps, Craig Newborn, and Steven Norman. But only one man was asked to do the eulogy: C. D. Brooks.

After nearly three and a half hours Brooks finally stood to speak. "By every calculation, E. E. Cleveland qualifies as a great man," he began. Nearing his eightieth year, the seasoned old preacher related the old story of sitting under Cleveland's tent and hearing the voice of God call him by name. "Cleveland was a mighty warrior. He stomped the enemy with purpose. He swung the scythe of truth both ways—a double-edged blade. And error was cut down on the right hand and the left hand. And the voice said to me, 'This is what I want you to do.' " After telling how Cleveland had guided him again and again in his ministry, C.D. expressed surprise that Cleveland, who always spoke of how he so wanted to live to see Christ come, was now asleep. "It has come to this. I'm a boy that he helped so much, inspired so much. I stand above him to eulogize him. But I tell you confidently that at this very moment angels are discussing Earl Cleveland." Christ would return soon and raise up His sleeping servant, as well as all of those who loved and lived the truth.

***

On December 14, 2010, Neal C. Wilson breathed his last in his home in Dayton, Maryland. At his funeral at the General Conference headquarters on January 19, 2011, C. D. Brooks told those gathered that Wilson "stood as a tower of righteousness in a desert of despair, and he brought hope to our hearts." Besides friend, mentor, colleague, fellow minister, confidant, and brother in Christ, C.D. summed it up when he stated, "Neal Wilson was the greatest man I have ever met."

Holding Hands in Glory

C.D. retired from his official positions, not from evangelism. As he approached his seventieth, seventh-fifth, then eightieth year of life, the fire inside of him to bring others to the truth still roared. From his office in the

General Conference, his longtime and trusted personal assistant, Denyce Follette, carefully managed appointments and speaking engagements, just as she had during the 1970s and 1980s. And there were still more speaking requests than he could meet. Charles took as many as his health permitted, doing Sabbath services, Weeks of Prayer, camp meetings, and television spots.

He was constantly amazed at the reach of influence God had blessed his ministry with. In the summer of 2012 while C.D. was speaking for a 3ABN camp meeting a robust White man from Mississippi grabbed his hand enthusiastically, tears forming at the corners of his eyes.

"Hey, Pastor Brooks," the man said in a thick Down South accent, trying to keep himself together, "I am in the truth today because of listening to your tapes."

***

Church leadership just as vigorously acknowledged Brooks's ministry. As premier elder statesman of Adventism, he has received honor upon honor and was frequently interviewed for television, radio, Web casts, magazines, and books. His face often appeared on the front of church periodicals. Dozens of his articles appeared in print. The younger generations of preachers cited him as a key influence in their lives and ministries.

On November 2-3, 2012, Carlton Byrd, current speaker/director of Breath of Life, arranged a Breath of Life Reunion Weekend at the Oakwood University church, where he now records its programs and has its headquarters. Reunited with Walter Arties, Walter Pearson, and the Breath of Life Quartet, Brooks was thankful to God for the opportunity for them all to be together again to commemorate almost 40 years of ministry. C.D., who preached the opening message on Friday night, was honored for making Breath of Life an established, enduring, international evangelistic ministry.

The Ellen G. White Estate acknowledged C. D. Brooks's lifelong love and dedication to the writings and ministry of Ellen White by electing him a lifetime member of the Ellen G. White Estate board on December 1, 2010, the first Black person to be thus selected. On February 24, 2013, he was appointed chaplain of the North American Division.

***

But Charles's greatest fulfillment in retirement was spending time with the love of his life. Walterene retired from 40 years of teaching the same year as her husband. Instead of the sunset years, their retirement is more like springtime. The two have been reliving their youth, waking up excited about the prospect of spending the day together, outdoing each other in romance, learning new things about each other, and falling asleep in each other's arms.

Walterene's mother, Jessie, outlived her beloved husband by some 23 years. Well-meaning friends often gently urged her to think about getting remarried. But she would have none of it.

"When I get to heaven," she would say, "I don't want there to be any mix-up as to whom I hold hands with. I want to hold hands in heaven with my John."

She repeated that until her dying day.

And the older she got, the more Walterene understood her mother's sentiment. For she wanted nothing more in eternity than to hold her honey's hand in glory.

How It All Began

In 2010 the Hope Channel asked C. D. Brooks to preach for a series it was airing on the world church's new theme: "Revival and Reformation." Ted N. C. Wilson, son of Neal Wilson, had been elected president of the world church that summer and had a burden that the Seventh-day Adventist movement complete its God-given mission so that Jesus could come. Aired just days before the new year of 2011, an 81-year-old C. D. Brooks stood at the pulpit, hair snowy-white, bearing regal, mind as brilliant as ever. He began his message with how it all began:

"Many of you know that my blessed mother received a vision when I was 6 months old and the Lord told her to keep the Sabbath. We had no books, no teachers, no directions, just Mother, her vision, and her Bible. A decade later I walked into the Seventh-day Adventist Church, a bright November morning in 1940. I remember how impressed I was—oh, the building was not impressive. But there was a spirit there. And hanging above the pulpit was the fourth commandment. And something seemed to say to me, 'This is it.' In the 70 years that have followed I have not changed my mind one iota."

INDEX

What Good Leaders Know

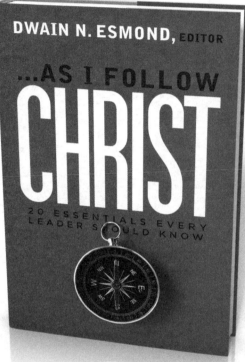

Ted N. C. Wilson
Charles Bradford
Cindy Tutsch
Dan Jackson
Lowell Cooper
Delbert Baker
Prudence LaBeach Pollard
Gordon Bietz
Jim Gilley
Leslie Pollard
Gerry Karst
Derek Morris
Willie and Elaine Oliver
David Smith
Sung Kwon
Ivan Leigh Warden
Ella Simmons
Pardon Mwansa
David S. Penner
Lilya Wagner,
with Halvard Thomsen

DWAIN N. ESMOND, EDITOR

...AS I FOLLOW CHRIST

20 ESSENTIALS EVERY LEADER SHOULD KNOW

As I Follow Christ

Whether you're leading in a ministry, an organization, or a family, God has given you a special mission. *As I Follow Christ* helps you fulfill that mission with excellence. In this book some of the most notable leaders in the Seventh-day Adventist Church share what they've learned about effective leadership from their own experience, the Bible, and the Spirit of Prophecy. They describe:

- What kind of person God calls to lead
- What leaders can learn from failure
- The key elements of a leader's spiritual life
- How to set priorities and family time
- The role of accountability and discipline in the life of a leader

If you want to influence people and inspire positive change, open these pages and discover the principles that are practiced by our most outstanding leaders. Hardcover.
978-0-8280-2724-3

Prices and availability subject to change.
Canadian prices higher.

AdventistBookCenter.com | 800.765.6955

Review & Herald®
Spread the Word